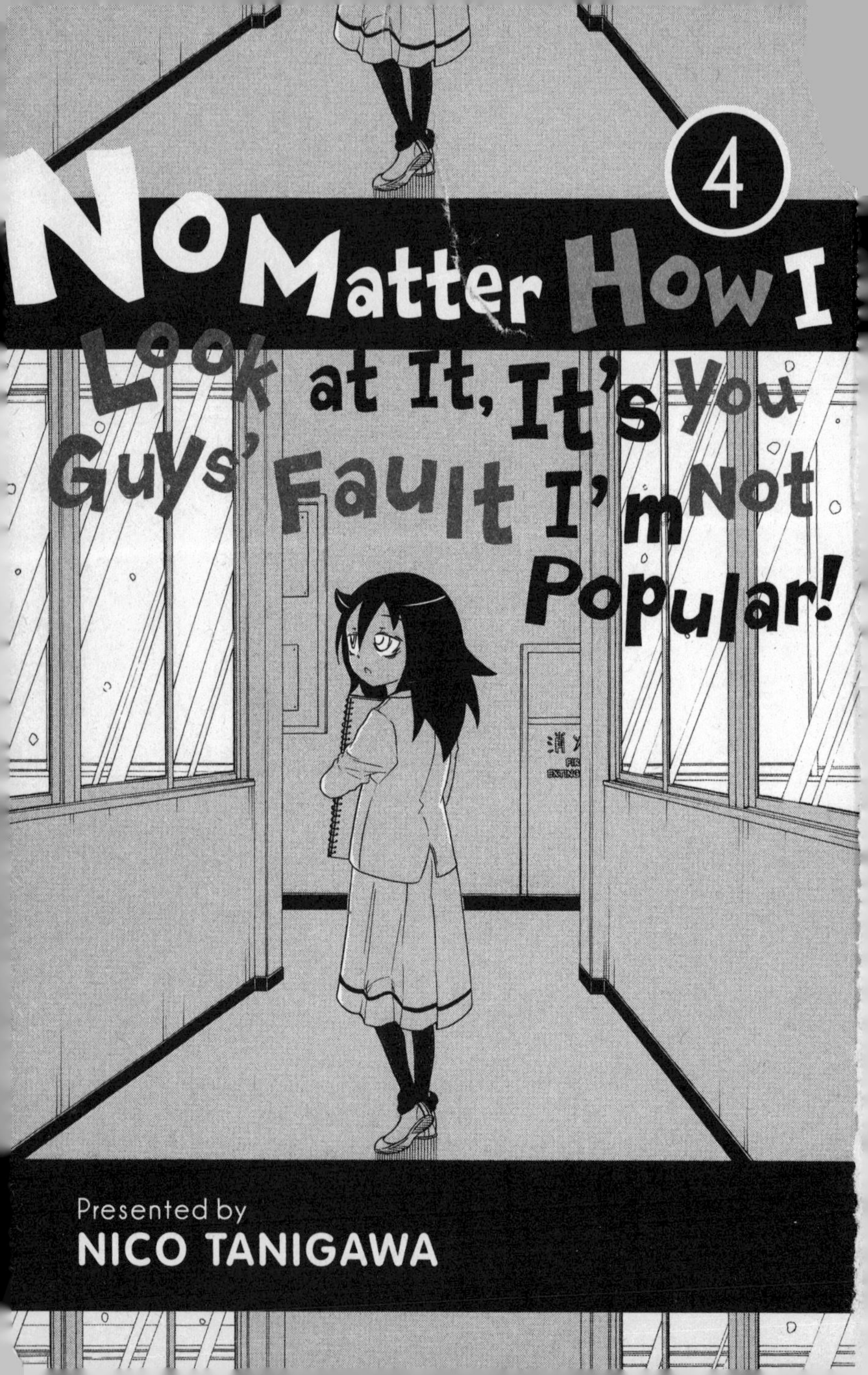

No Matter How I Look at It, It's You Guys' Fault I'm Not Popular!

4

Presented by

NICO TANIGAWA

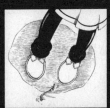

...AWW, IF I'D BEEN A WORM, I WOULD'VE HAD A MAN FROM THE GET-GO AND DEFINITELY HAVE HAD S●X, NOT TO MENTION KIDS...

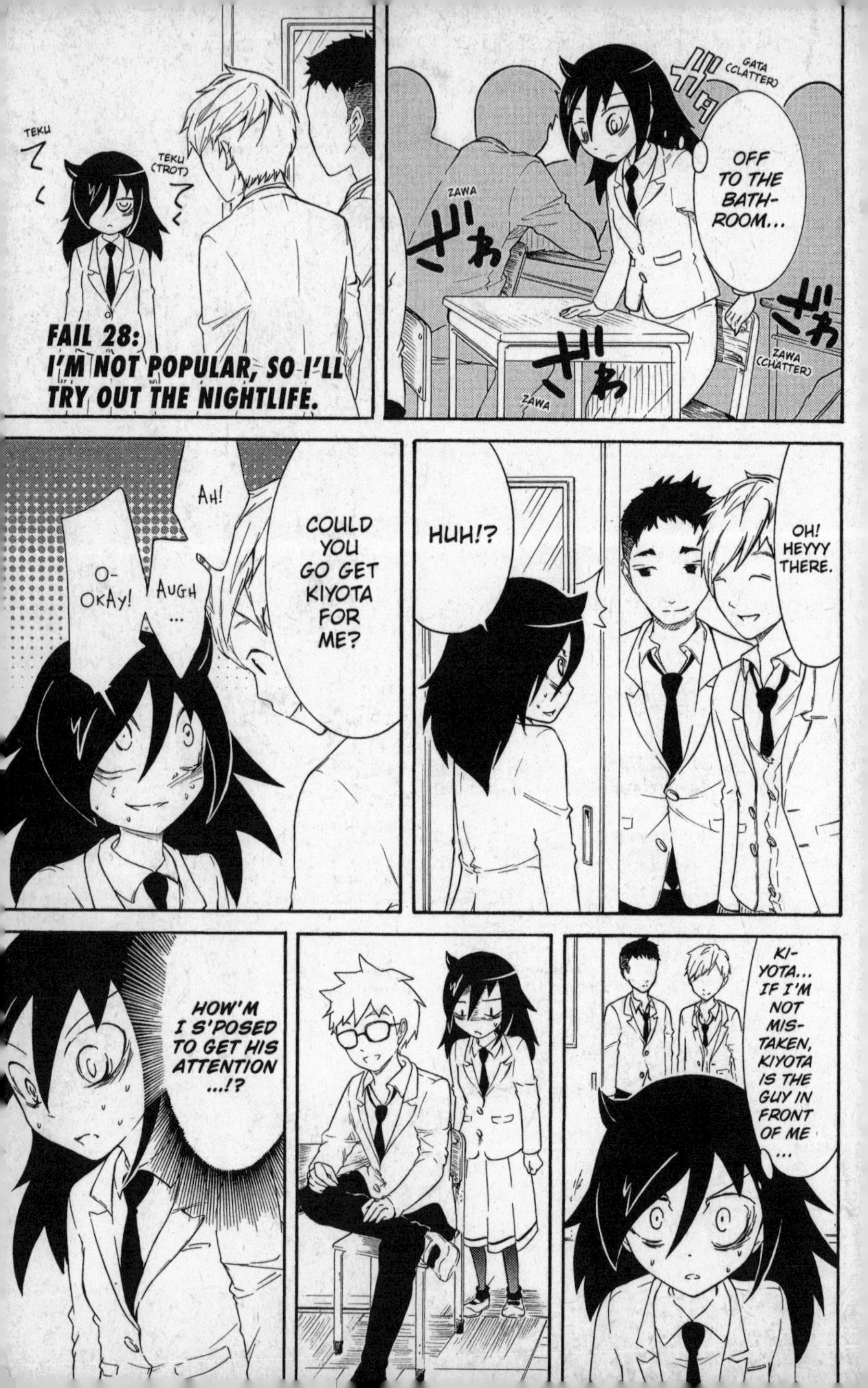
GATA (CLATTER)
OFF TO THE BATH-ROOM...
ZAWA
ZAWA (CHATTER)
ZAWA
TEKU (TROT)
TEKU
FAIL 28: I'M NOT POPULAR, SO I'LL TRY OUT THE NIGHTLIFE.
OH! HEYYY THERE.
HUH!?
COULD YOU GO GET KIYOTA FOR ME?
AH!
AUGH ...
O-OKAY!
KI-YOTA... IF I'M NOT MIS-TAKEN, KIYOTA IS THE GUY IN FRONT OF ME ...
HOW'M I S'POSED TO GET HIS ATTENTION ...!?

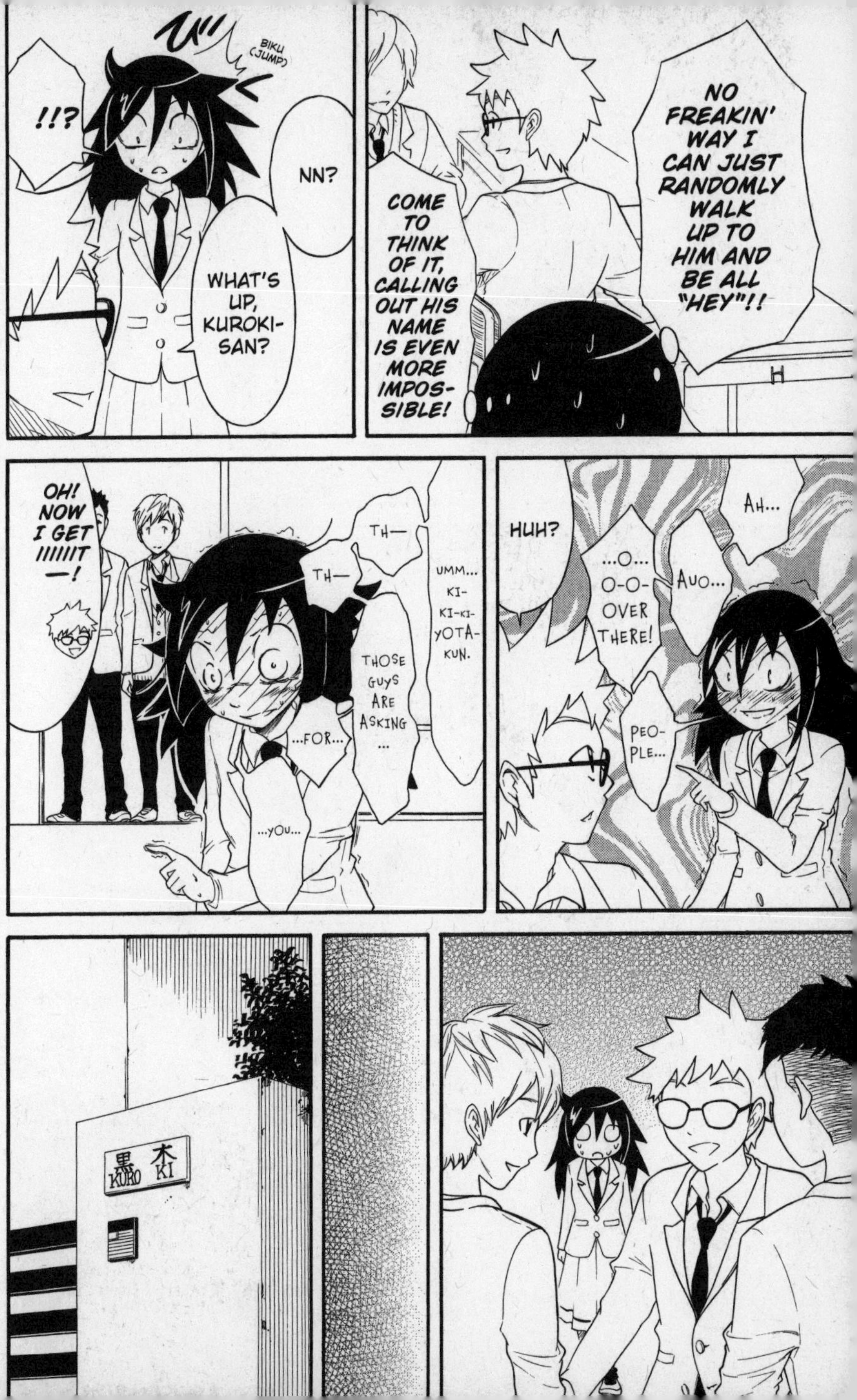
NO FREAKIN' WAY I CAN JUST RANDOMLY WALK UP TO HIM AND BE ALL "HEY"!!
COME TO THINK OF IT, CALLING OUT HIS NAME IS EVEN MORE IMPOSSIBLE!
BIKU (JUMP)
NN?
!!?
WHAT'S UP, KUROKI-SAN?
AH...
HUH?
AUO...
...O... O-O- OVER THERE!
PEO-PLE...
UMM... KI-KI-KI-YOTA-KUN.
TH—
TH—
THOSE GUYS ARE ASKING ...
...FOR...
...YOU...
OH! NOW I GET IIIIIIT—!
黒 木
KURO KI

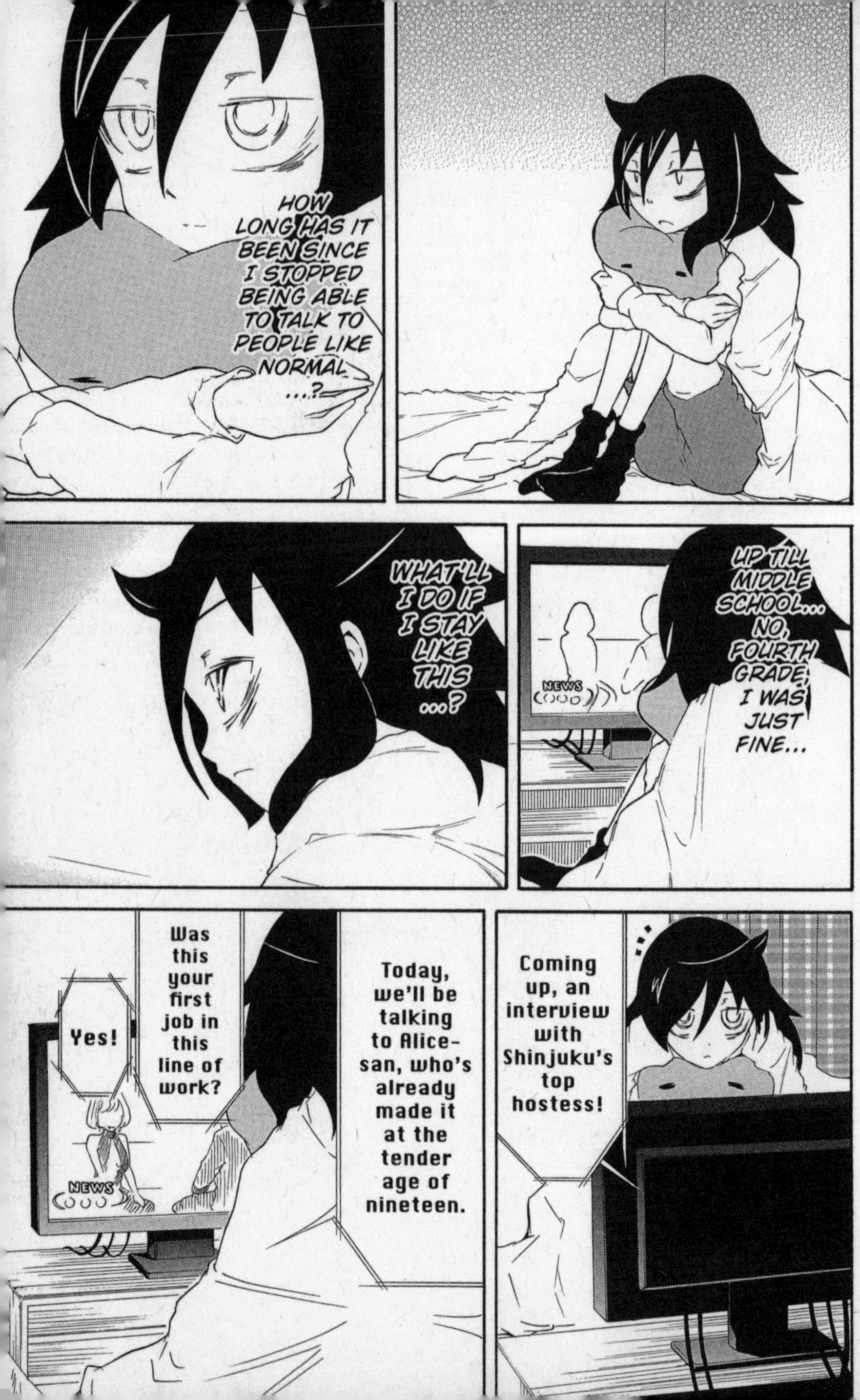
HOW LONG HAS IT BEEN SINCE I STOPPED BEING ABLE TO TALK TO PEOPLE LIKE NORMAL ...?
UP TILL MIDDLE SCHOOL... NO, FOURTH GRADE, I WAS JUST FINE...
NEWS
WHAT'LL I DO IF I STAY LIKE THIS ...?
Coming up, an interview with Shinjuku's top hostess!
Today, we'll be talking to Alice-san, who's already made it at the tender age of nineteen.
Was this your first job in this line of work?
Yes!
NEWS

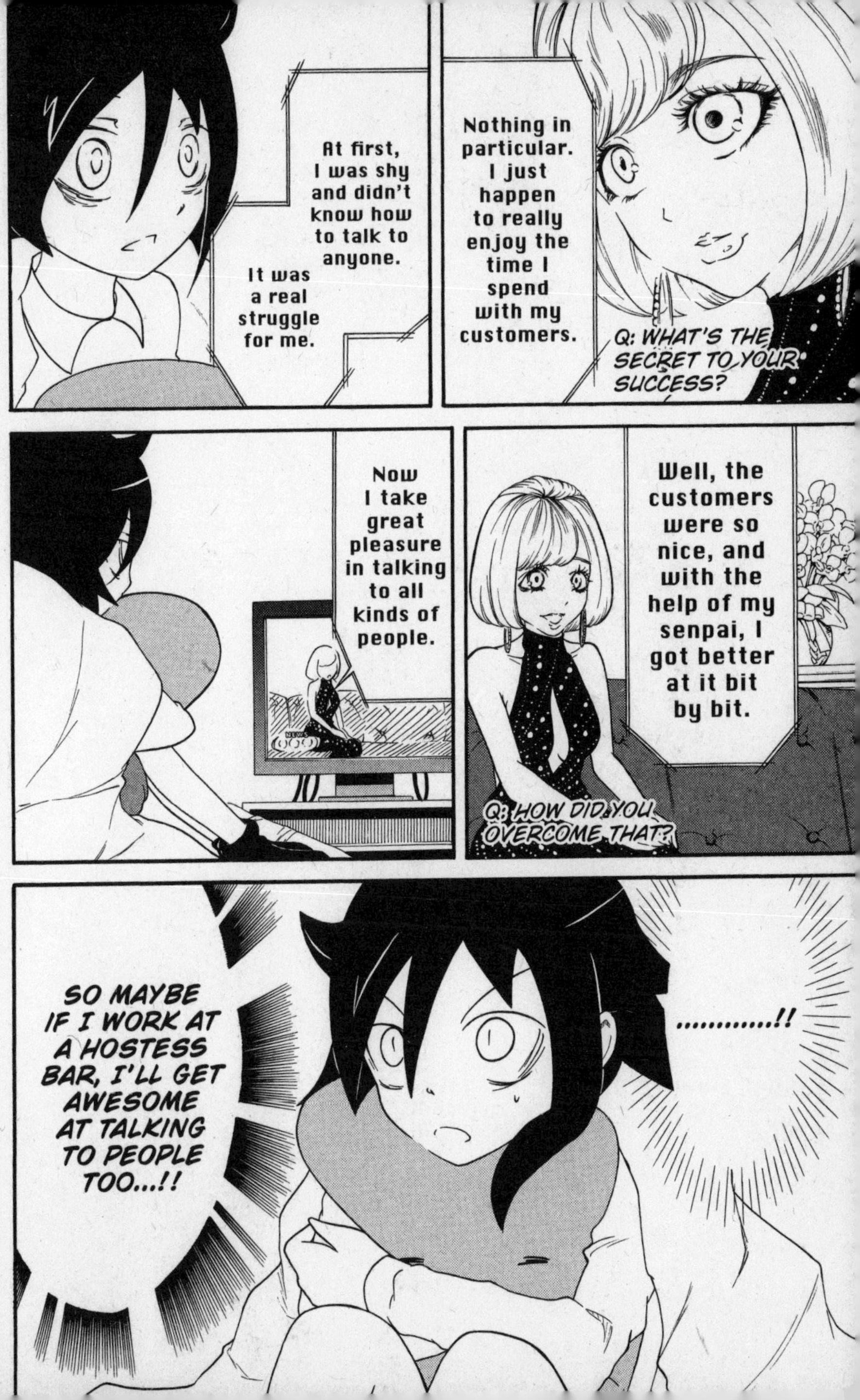
Q: WHAT'S THE SECRET TO YOUR SUCCESS?
Nothing in particular. I just happen to really enjoy the time I spend with my customers.
At first, I was shy and didn't know how to talk to anyone.
It was a real struggle for me.
Q: HOW DID YOU OVERCOME THAT?
Well, the customers were so nice, and with the help of my senpai, I got better at it bit by bit.
Now I take great pleasure in talking to all kinds of people.
............!!
SO MAYBE IF I WORK AT A HOSTESS BAR, I'LL GET AWESOME AT TALKING TO PEOPLE TOO...!!

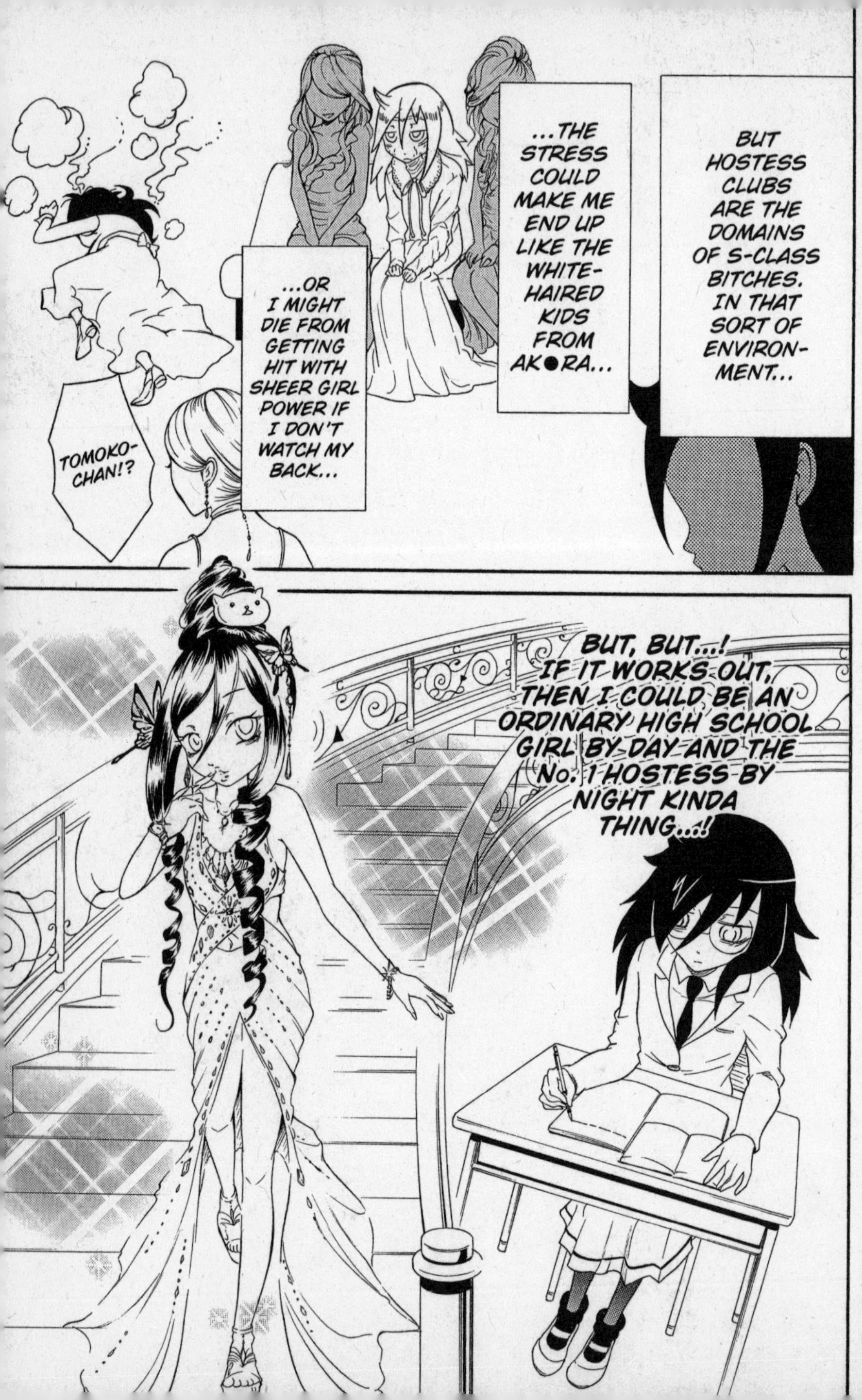
BUT HOSTESS CLUBS ARE THE DOMAINS OF S-CLASS BITCHES. IN THAT SORT OF ENVIRONMENT...
...THE STRESS COULD MAKE ME END UP LIKE THE WHITE-HAIRED KIDS FROM AK●RA...
...OR I MIGHT DIE FROM GETTING HIT WITH SHEER GIRL POWER IF I DON'T WATCH MY BACK...
TOMOKO-CHAN!?
BUT, BUT...! IF IT WORKS OUT, THEN I COULD BE AN ORDINARY HIGH SCHOOL GIRL BY DAY AND THE No. 1 HOSTESS BY NIGHT KINDA THING...!

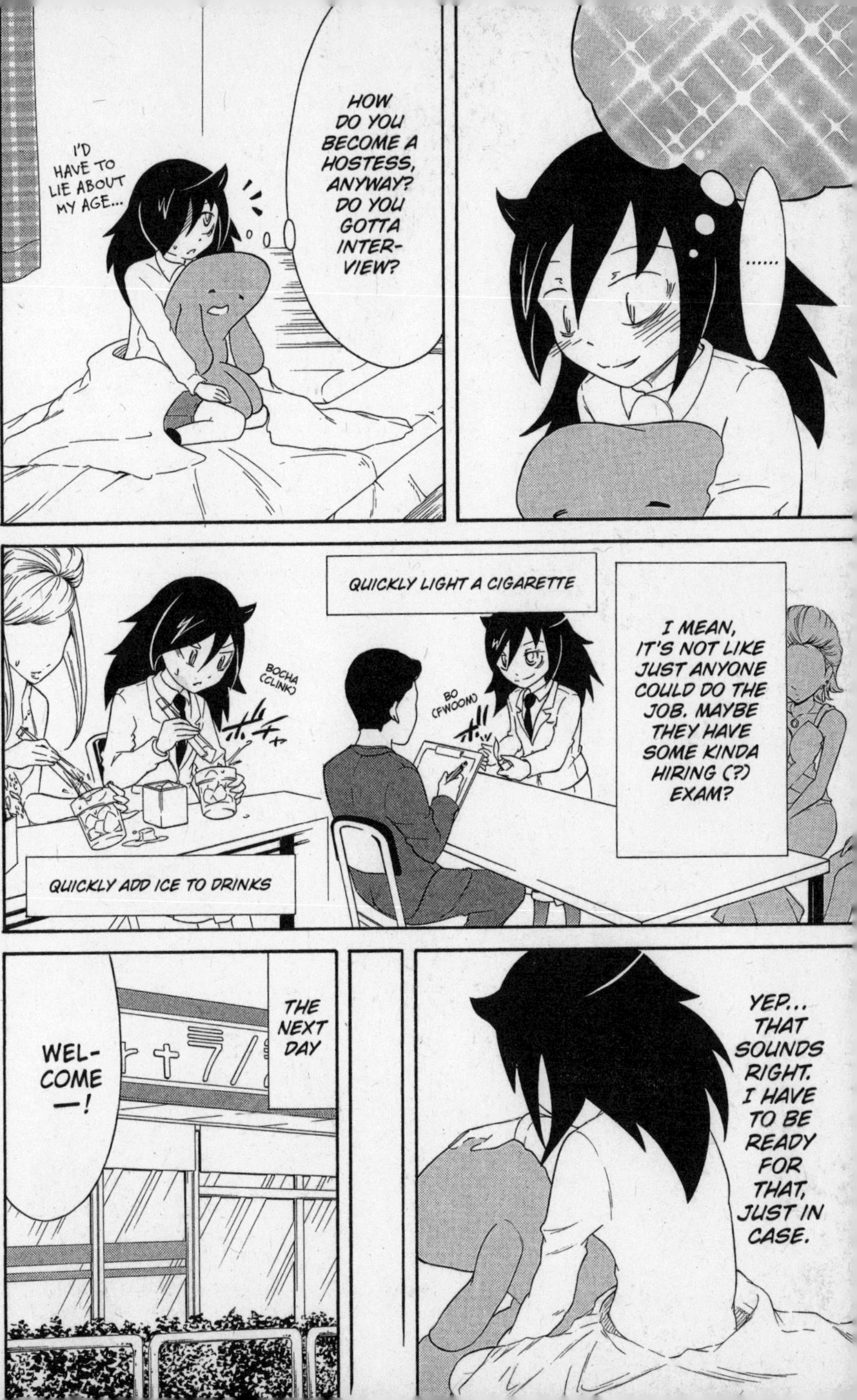
......
HOW DO YOU BECOME A HOSTESS, ANYWAY? DO YOU GOTTA INTERVIEW?
I'D HAVE TO LIE ABOUT MY AGE...
I MEAN, IT'S NOT LIKE JUST ANYONE COULD DO THE JOB. MAYBE THEY HAVE SOME KINDA HIRING (?) EXAM?
QUICKLY LIGHT A CIGARETTE
BO (FWOOM)
BOCHA (CLINK)
QUICKLY ADD ICE TO DRINKS
YEP... THAT SOUNDS RIGHT. I HAVE TO BE READY FOR THAT, JUST IN CASE.
THE NEXT DAY
WEL-COME—!

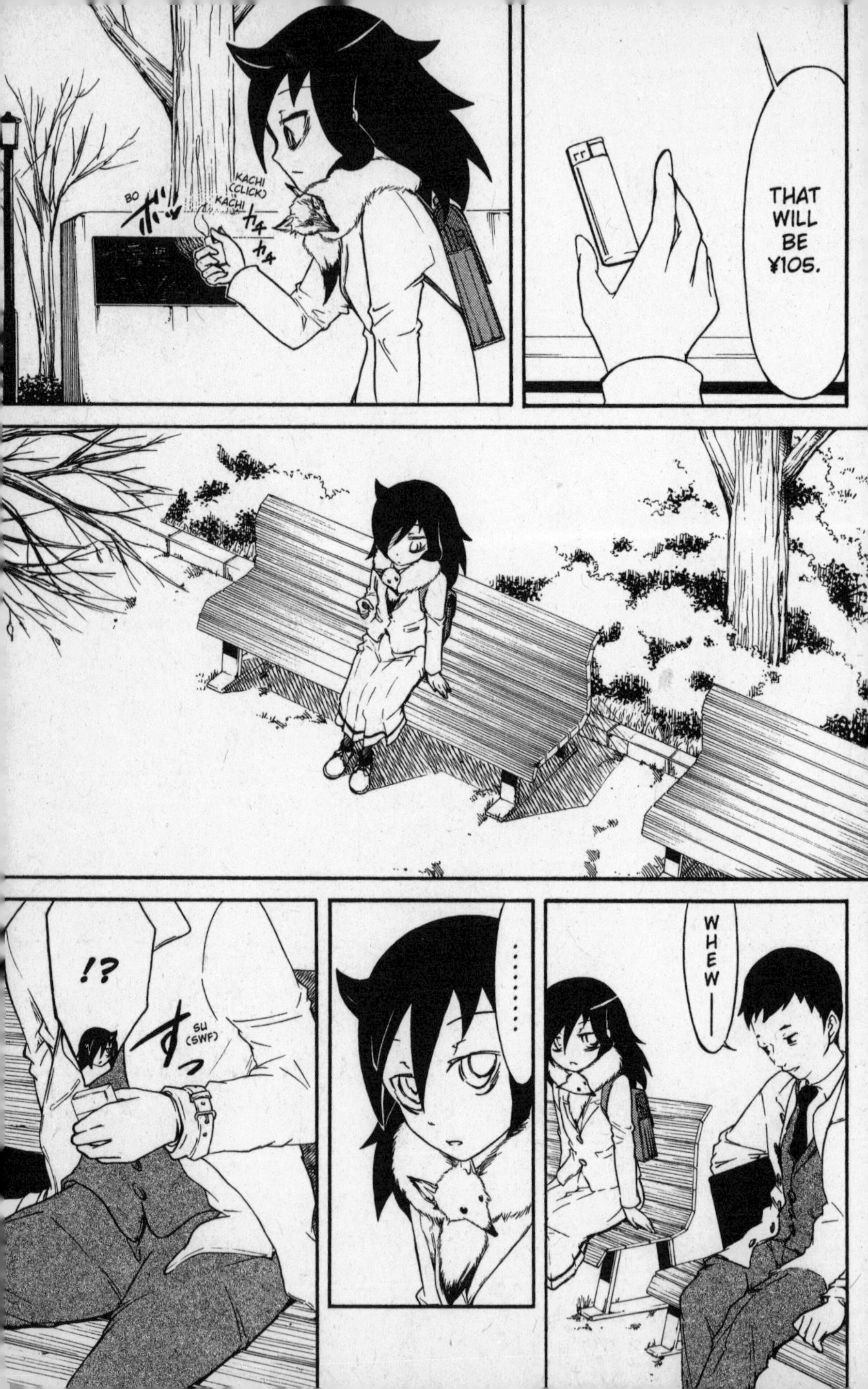

THAT WILL BE ¥105.
KACHI (CLICK) KACHI
カチ カチ
BO
ボッ
WHEW—
....
!?
SU (SWF)
すっ

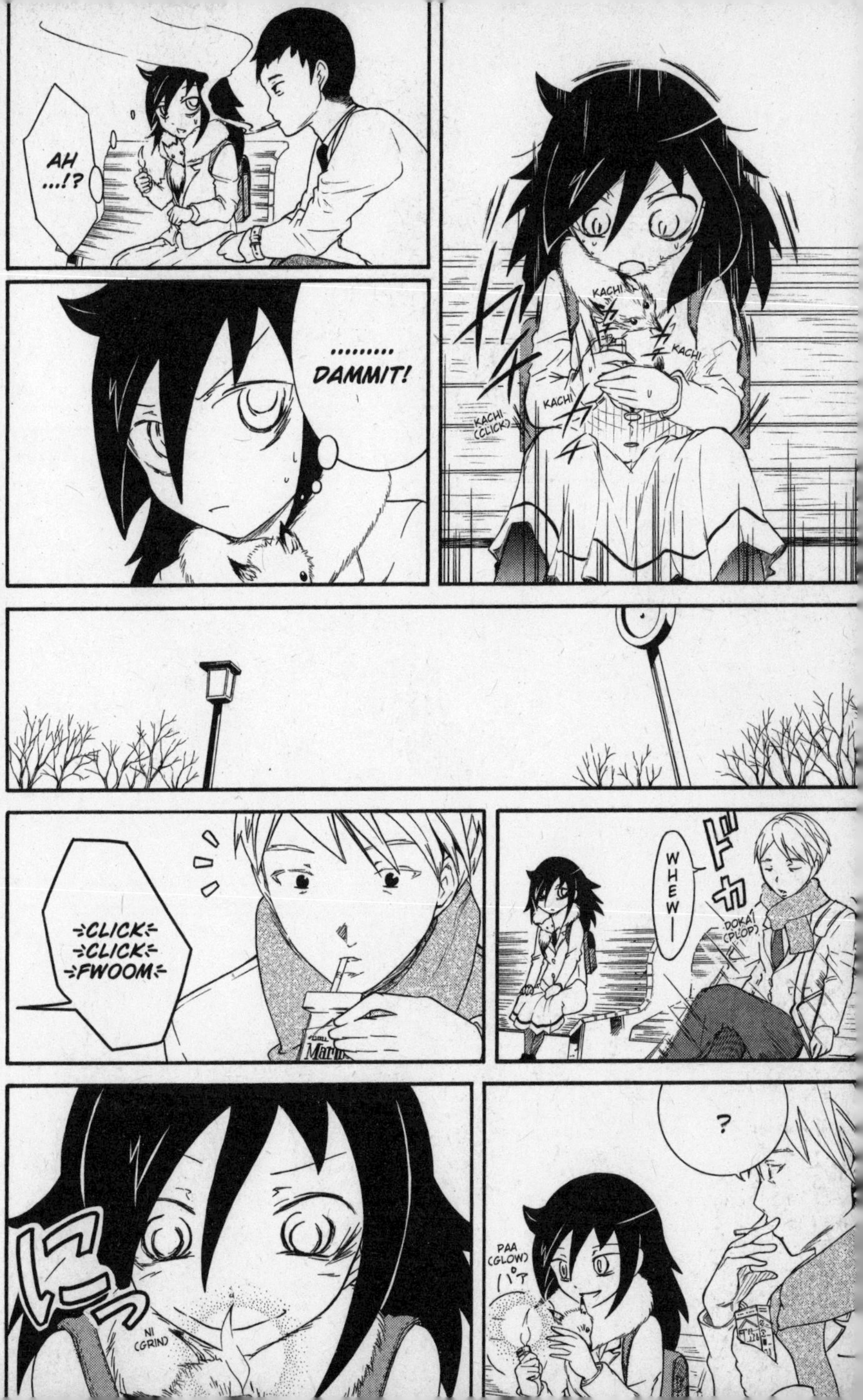
KACHI
KACHI
KACHI
KACHI (CLICK)
AH ...!?
....
DAMMIT!
WHEW—
ドカ
DOKA (PLOP)
CLICK CLICK FWOOM
?
PAA (GLOW)
パア
NI (GRIN)

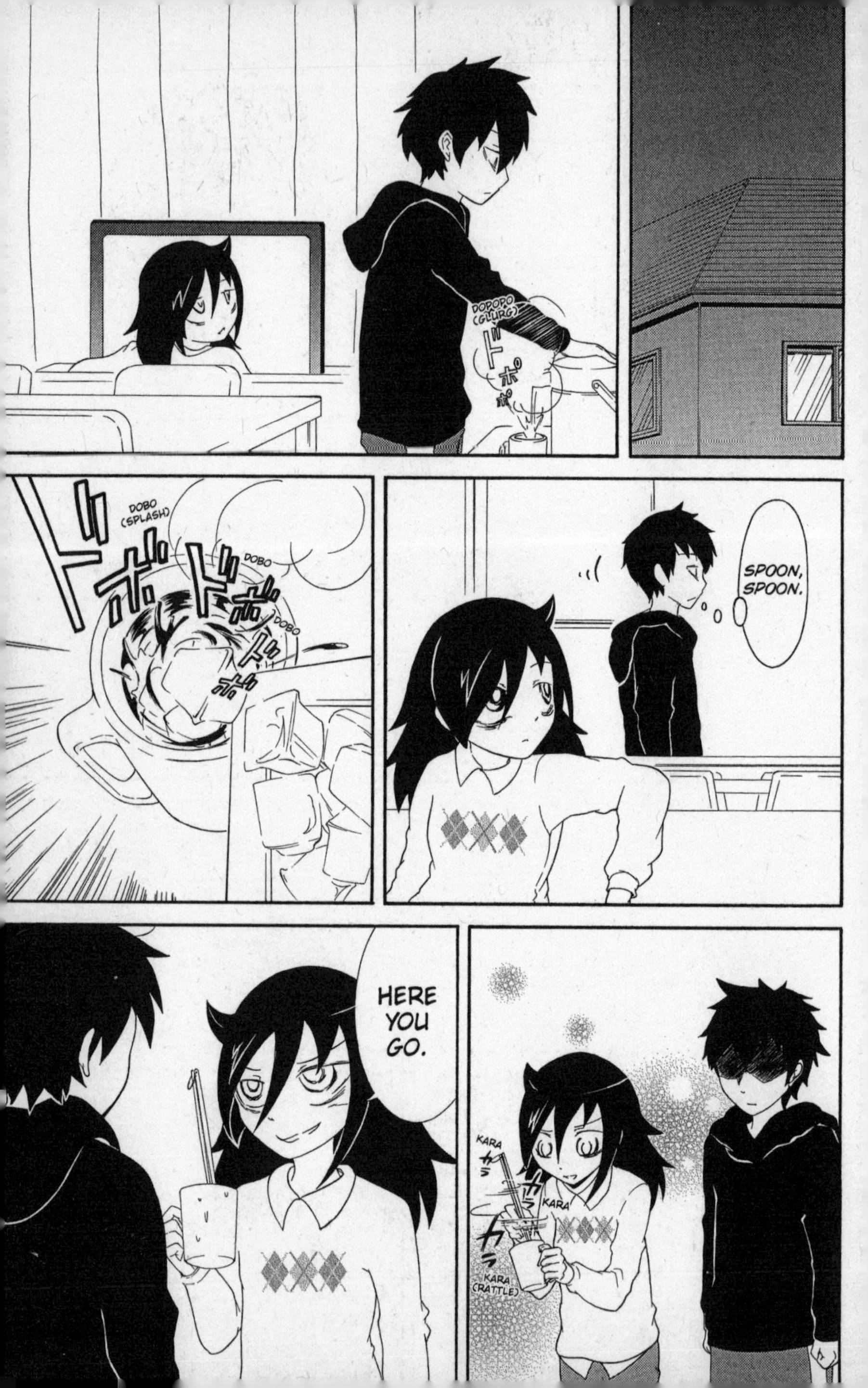
DOPOPO (GLURG)
SPOON, SPOON.
DOBO (SPLASH)
DOBO
DOBO
KARA
KARA
KARA (RATTLE)
HERE YOU GO.

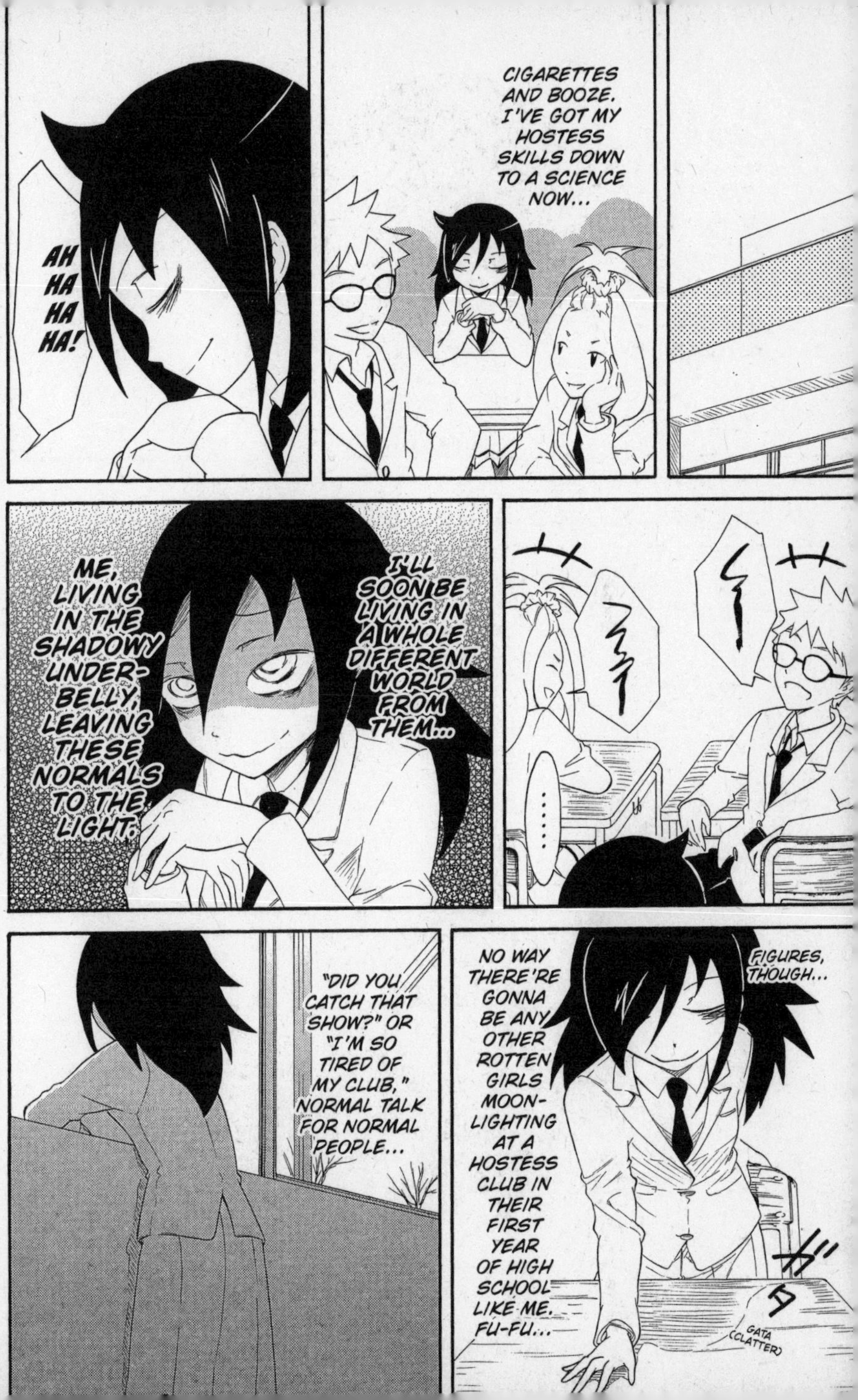
CIGARETTES AND BOOZE. I'VE GOT MY HOSTESS SKILLS DOWN TO A SCIENCE NOW...
AH HA HA HA!
......
I'LL SOON BE LIVING IN A WHOLE DIFFERENT WORLD FROM THEM...
ME, LIVING IN THE SHADOWY UNDER-BELLY, LEAVING THESE NORMALS TO THE LIGHT.
FIGURES, THOUGH...
NO WAY THERE'RE GONNA BE ANY OTHER ROTTEN GIRLS MOON-LIGHTING AT A HOSTESS CLUB IN THEIR FIRST YEAR OF HIGH SCHOOL LIKE ME. FU-FU...
GATA (CLATTER)
"DID YOU CATCH THAT SHOW?" OR "I'M SO TIRED OF MY CLUB," NORMAL TALK FOR NORMAL PEOPLE...

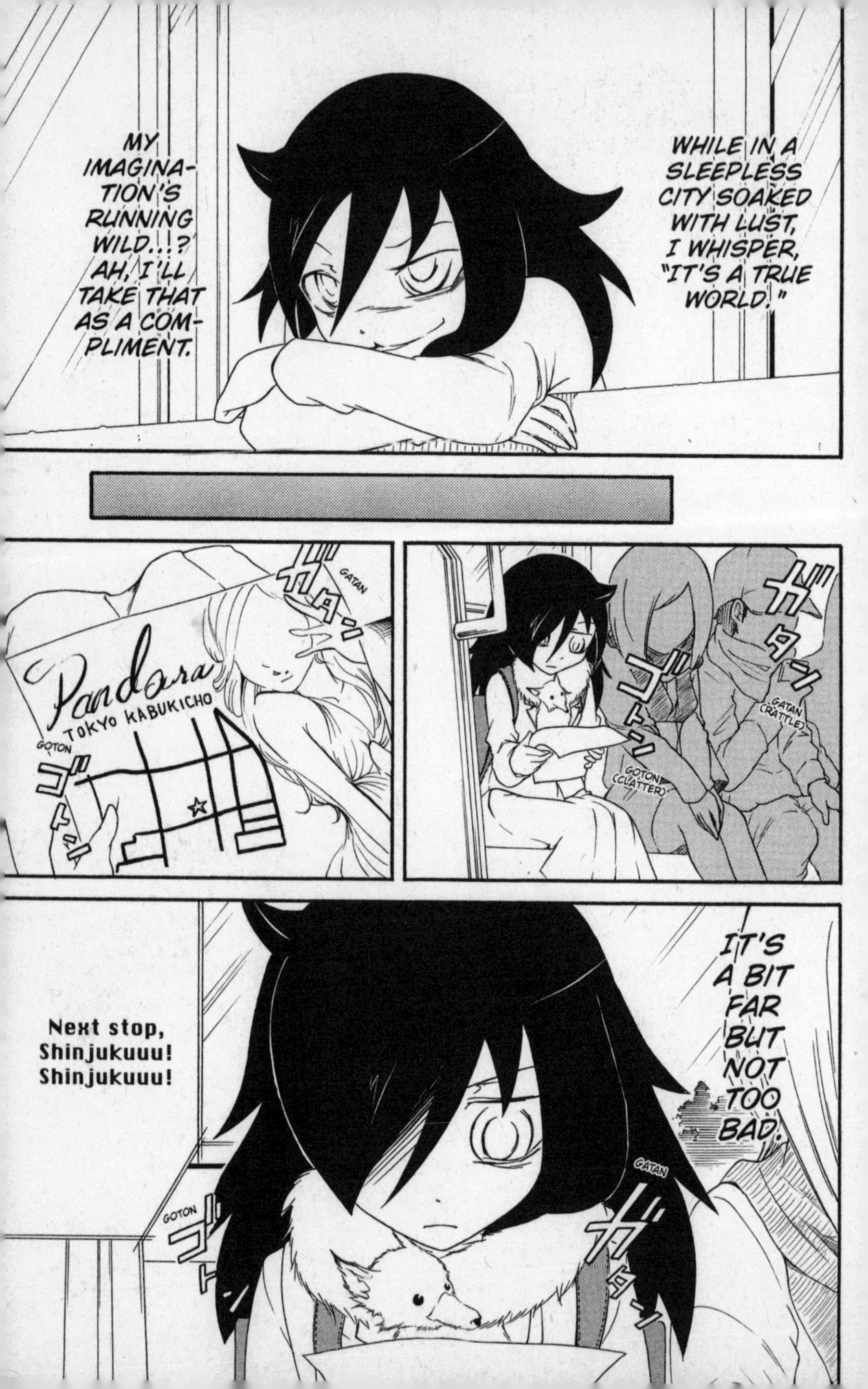
WHILE IN A SLEEPLESS CITY SOAKED WITH LUST, I WHISPER, "IT'S A TRUE WORLD."
MY IMAGINATION'S RUNNING WILD...? AH, I'LL TAKE THAT AS A COMPLIMENT.
GATAN (RATTLE)
GOTON (CLATTER)
GATAN
Pandora
TOKYO KABUKICHO
GOTON
IT'S A BIT FAR BUT NOT TOO BAD.
Next stop, Shinjukuuu! Shinjukuuu!
GATAN
GOTON

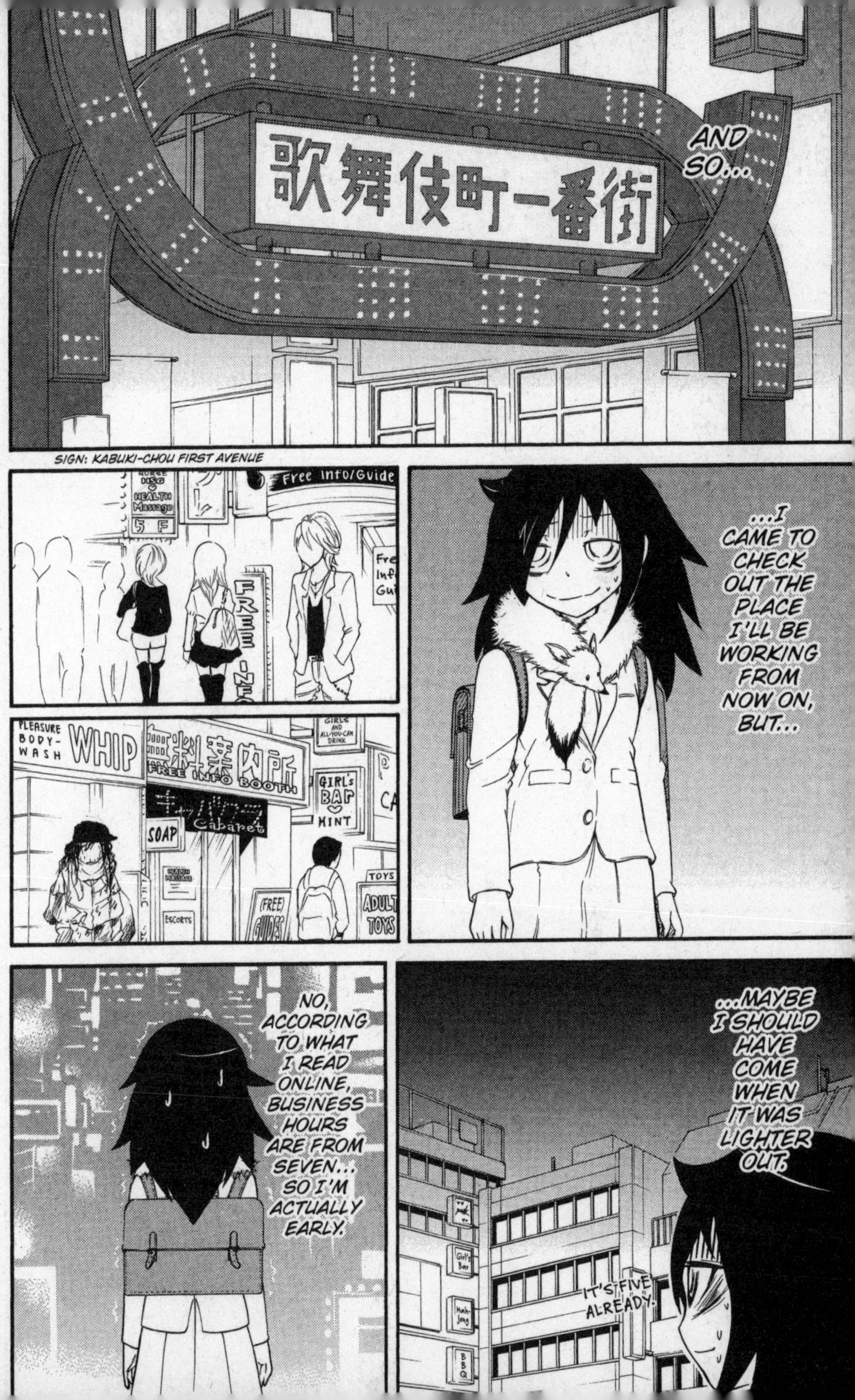
歌舞伎町一番街
AND SO...
SIGN: KABUKI-CHOU FIRST AVENUE
...I CAME TO CHECK OUT THE PLACE I'LL BE WORKING FROM NOW ON, BUT...
Free Info/Guide
NURSE HSG HEALTH Massage
5F
FREE INFO
PLEASURE BODY-WASH
WHIP
無料案内所
FREE INFO BOOTH
GIRLS AND ALL-YOU-CAN DRINK
GIRL's BAR HINT
Cabaret
SOAP
HEALTH MASSAGE
ESCORTS
(FREE) GUIDES
TOYS
ADULT TOYS
...MAYBE I SHOULD HAVE COME WHEN IT WAS LIGHTER OUT.
IT'S FIVE ALREADY.
Girl's Bar
Mah-Jong
BBQ
NO, ACCORDING TO WHAT I READ ONLINE, BUSINESS HOURS ARE FROM SEVEN... SO I'M ACTUALLY EARLY.

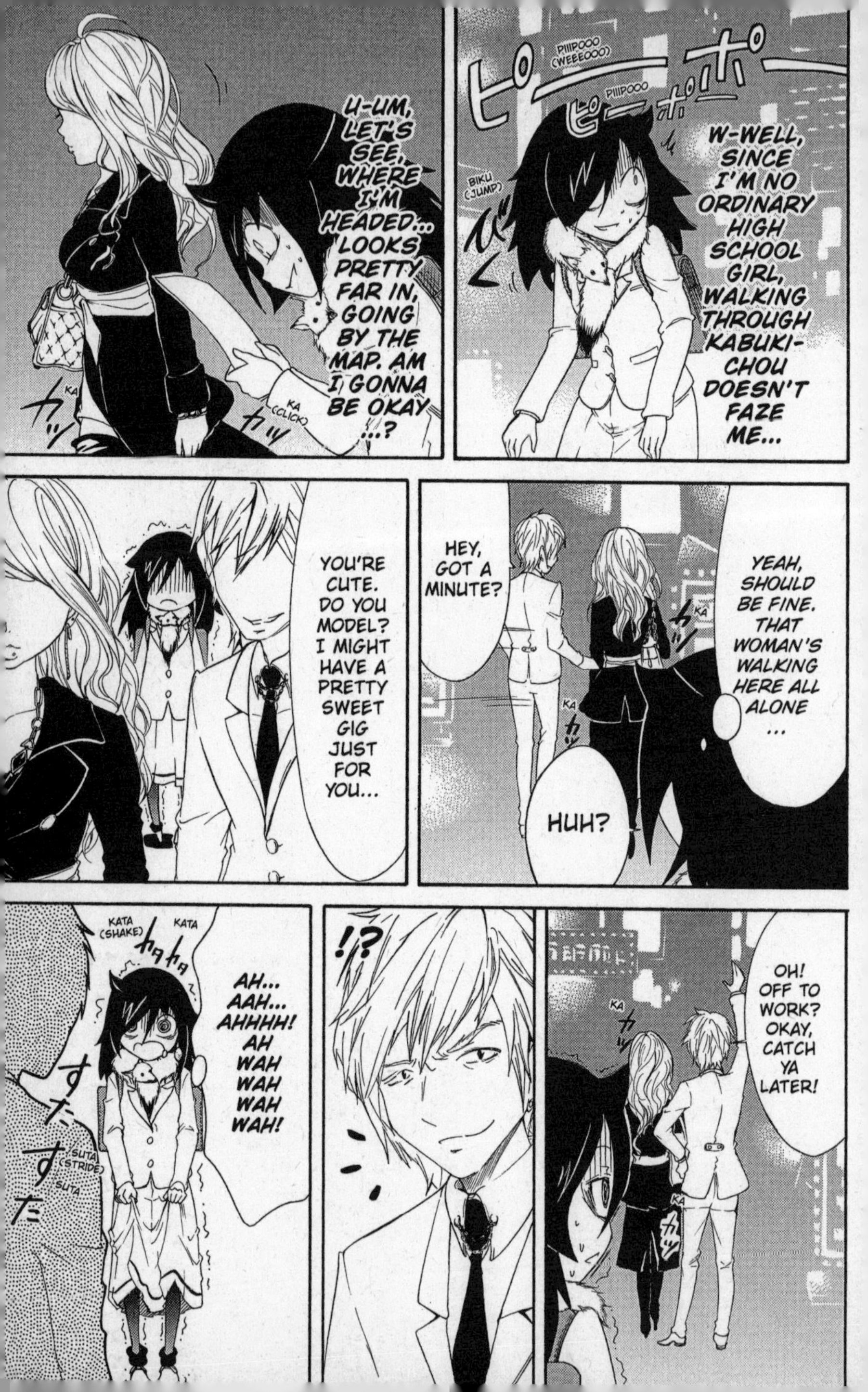
PIIPOOO (WEEEOOO)
ピーポー
PIIPOOO
ピーポー
BIKU (JUMP)
びく
W-WELL, SINCE I'M NO ORDINARY HIGH SCHOOL GIRL, WALKING THROUGH KABUKI-CHOU DOESN'T FAZE ME...
U-UM, LET'S SEE, WHERE I'M HEADED... LOOKS PRETTY FAR IN, GOING BY THE MAP. AM I GONNA BE OKAY...?
KA (CLICK)
カッ
KA
カッ
YEAH, SHOULD BE FINE. THAT WOMAN'S WALKING HERE ALL ALONE...
KA
カッ
KA
カッ
HEY, GOT A MINUTE?
HUH?
YOU'RE CUTE. DO YOU MODEL? I MIGHT HAVE A PRETTY SWEET GIG JUST FOR YOU...
OH! OFF TO WORK? OKAY, CATCH YA LATER!
KA
カッ
KA
カッ
!?
KATA (SHAKE)
KATA
カタカタ
AH... AAH... AHHHH! AH WAH WAH WAH WAH!
SUTA (STRIDE)
すた
SUTA
すた

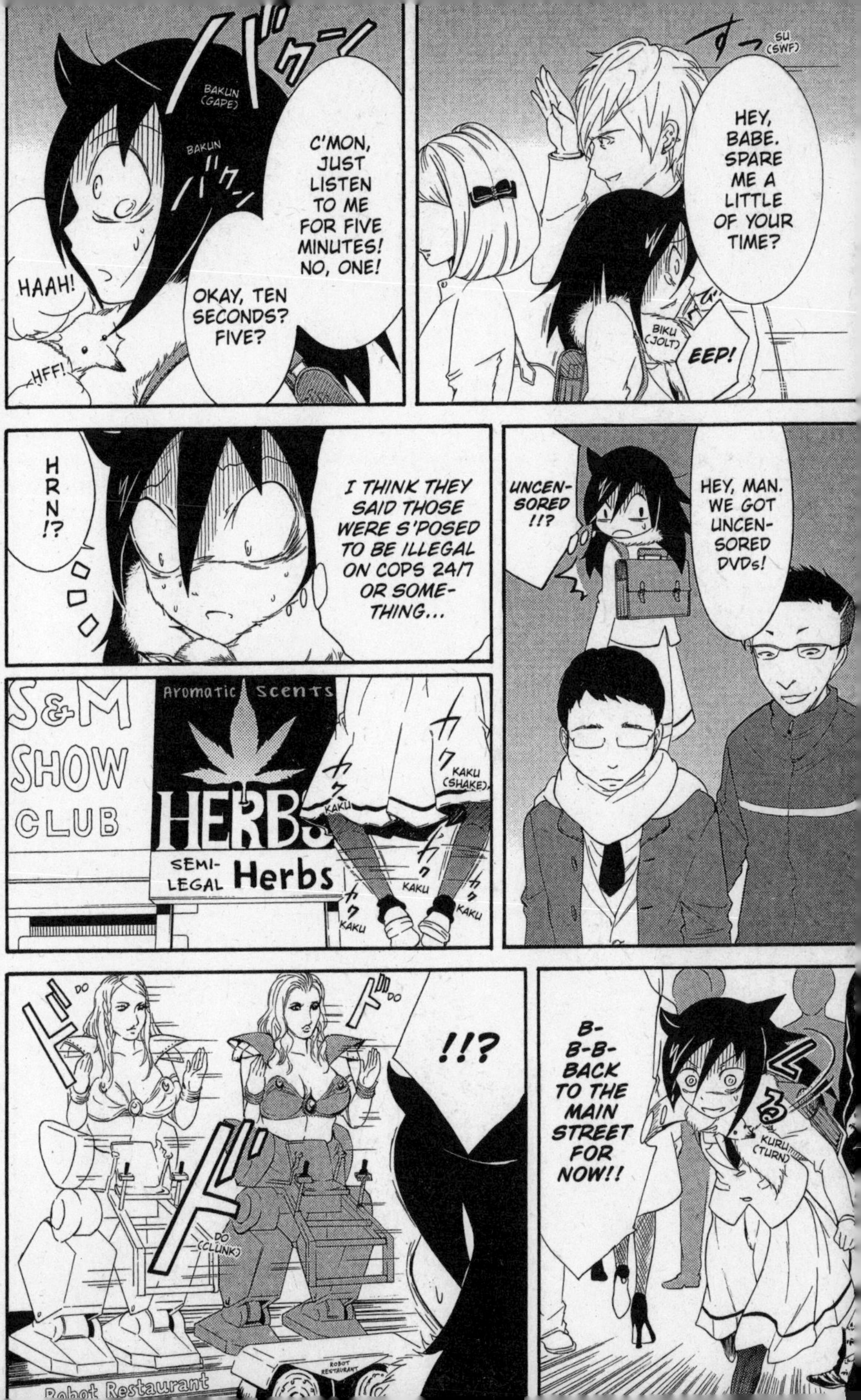
SU (SWF)
HEY, BABE. SPARE ME A LITTLE OF YOUR TIME?
BIKU (JOLT)
EEP!
C'MON, JUST LISTEN TO ME FOR FIVE MINUTES! NO, ONE!
BAKUN (GAPE)
BAKUN
OKAY, TEN SECONDS? FIVE?
HAAH!
HFF!
HEY, MAN. WE GOT UNCENSORED DVDs!
UNCENSORED!!?
I THINK THEY SAID THOSE WERE S'POSED TO BE ILLEGAL ON COPS 24/7 OR SOMETHING...
HRN!?
KAKU (SHAKE)
KAKU
KAKU
KAKU
KAKU
Aromatic Scents
HERBS
SEMI-LEGAL Herbs
S&M SHOW CLUB
B-B-B-BACK TO THE MAIN STREET FOR NOW!!
KURU (TURN)
!!?
DO
DO
DO (CLUNK)
ROBOT RESTAURANT
Robot Restaurant

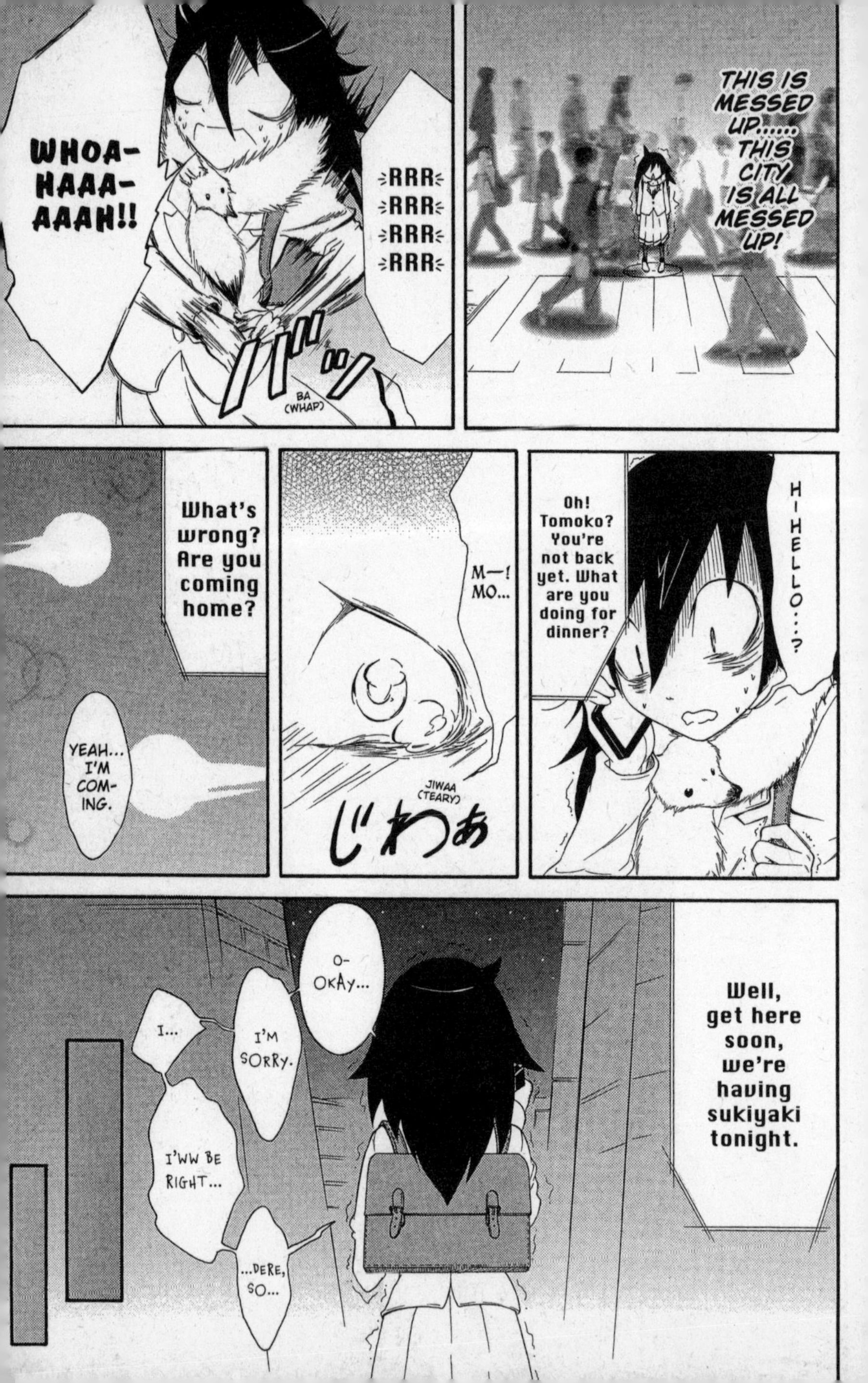
THIS IS MESSED UP...... THIS CITY IS ALL MESSED UP!
RRR RRR RRR RRR
WHOA-HAAAA-AAAH!!
BA (WHAP)
HI HELLO...?
Oh! Tomoko? You're not back yet. What are you doing for dinner?
M—! MO...
JIWAA (TEARY)
じわあ
What's wrong? Are you coming home?
YEAH... I'M COMING.
Well, get here soon, we're having sukiyaki tonight.
O-OKAY...
I'M SORRY.
I...
I'WW BE RIGHT...
...DERE, SO...

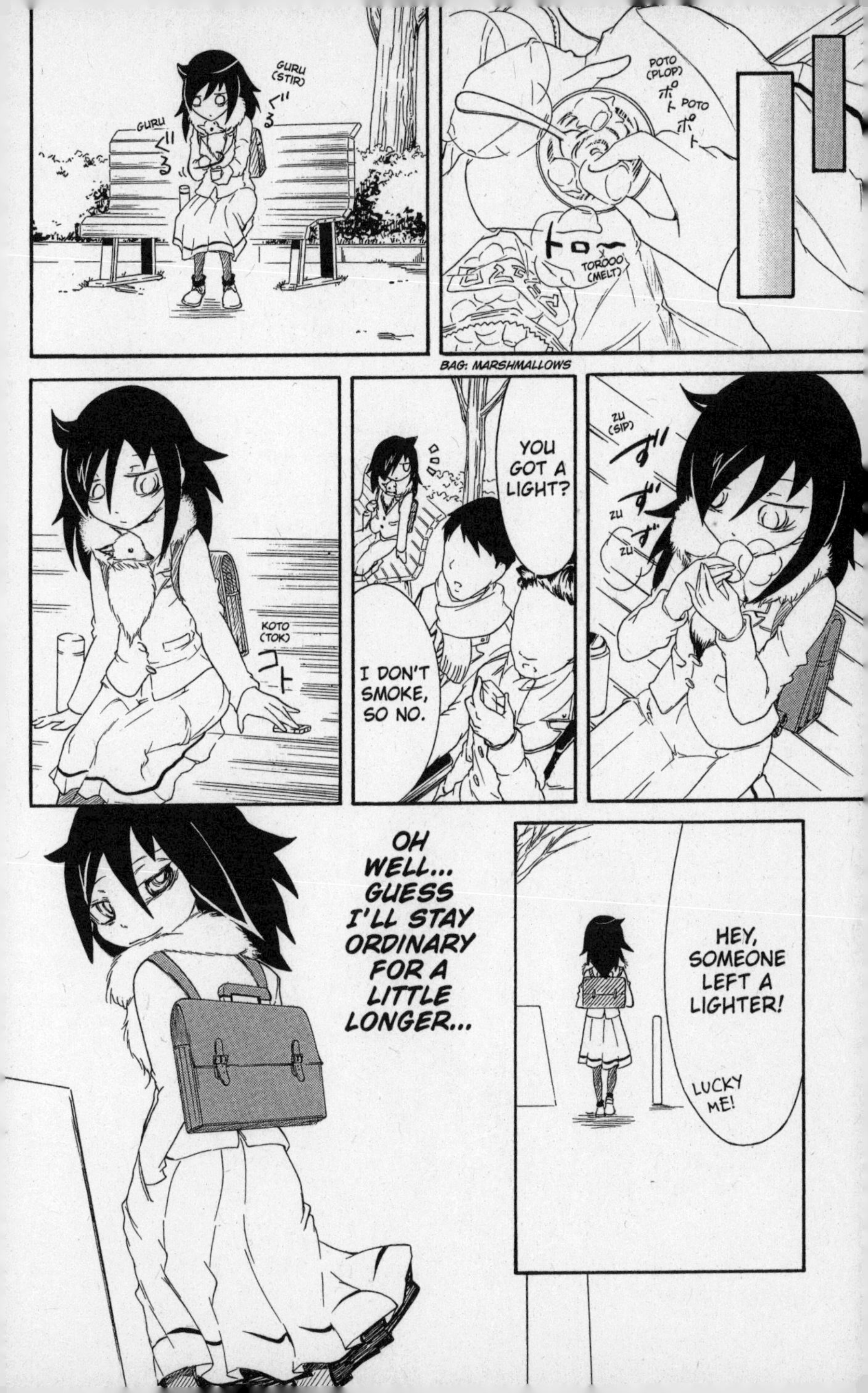
POTO (PLOP)
POTO
TOROOO (MELT)
BAG: MARSHMALLOWS
GURU (STIR)
GURU
ZU (SIP)
ZU
ZU
YOU GOT A LIGHT?
I DON'T SMOKE, SO NO.
KOTO (TOK)
HEY, SOMEONE LEFT A LIGHTER!
LUCKY ME!
OH WELL... GUESS I'LL STAY ORDINARY FOR A LITTLE LONGER...

No Matter How I Look at It, It's You Guys' Fault I'm Not Popular!

FAIL 29: I'M NOT POPULAR, SO I'LL MAKE A CAKE.

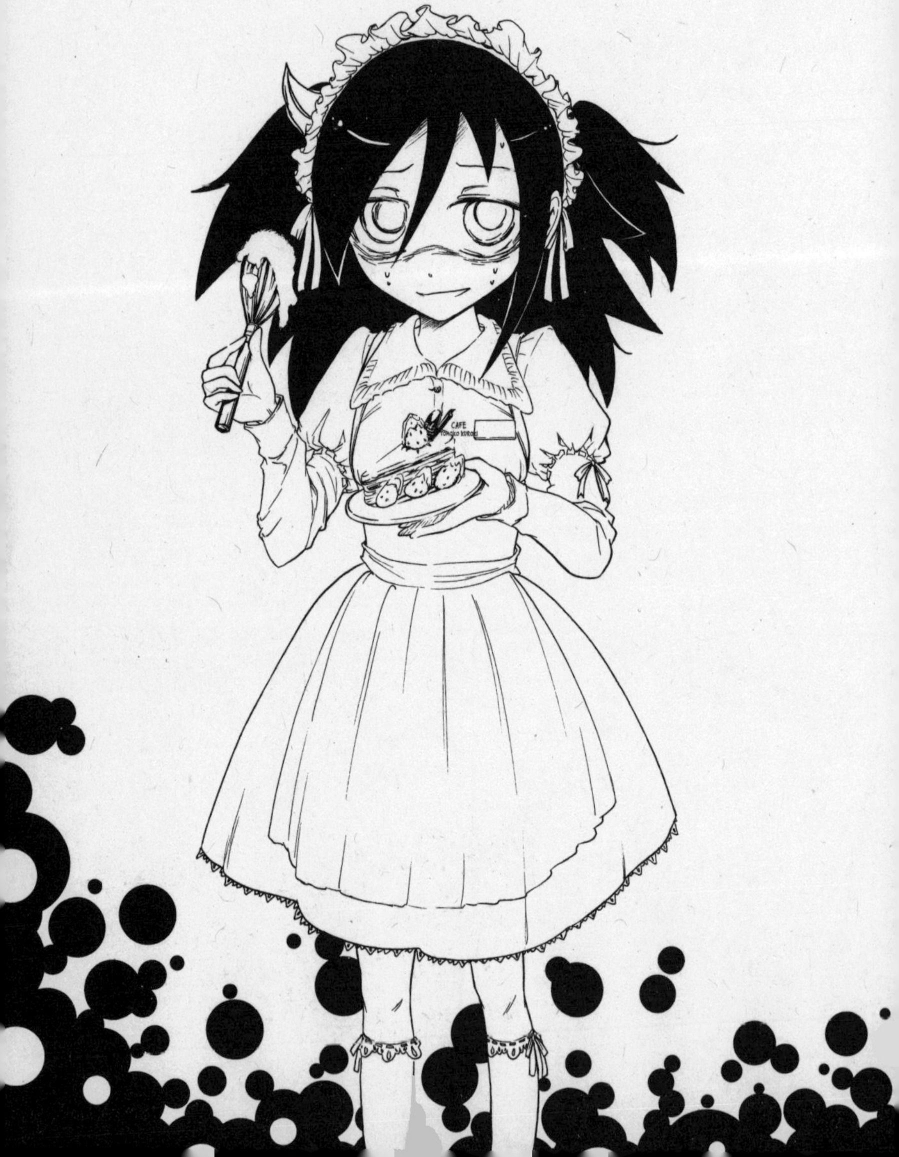
CAFE

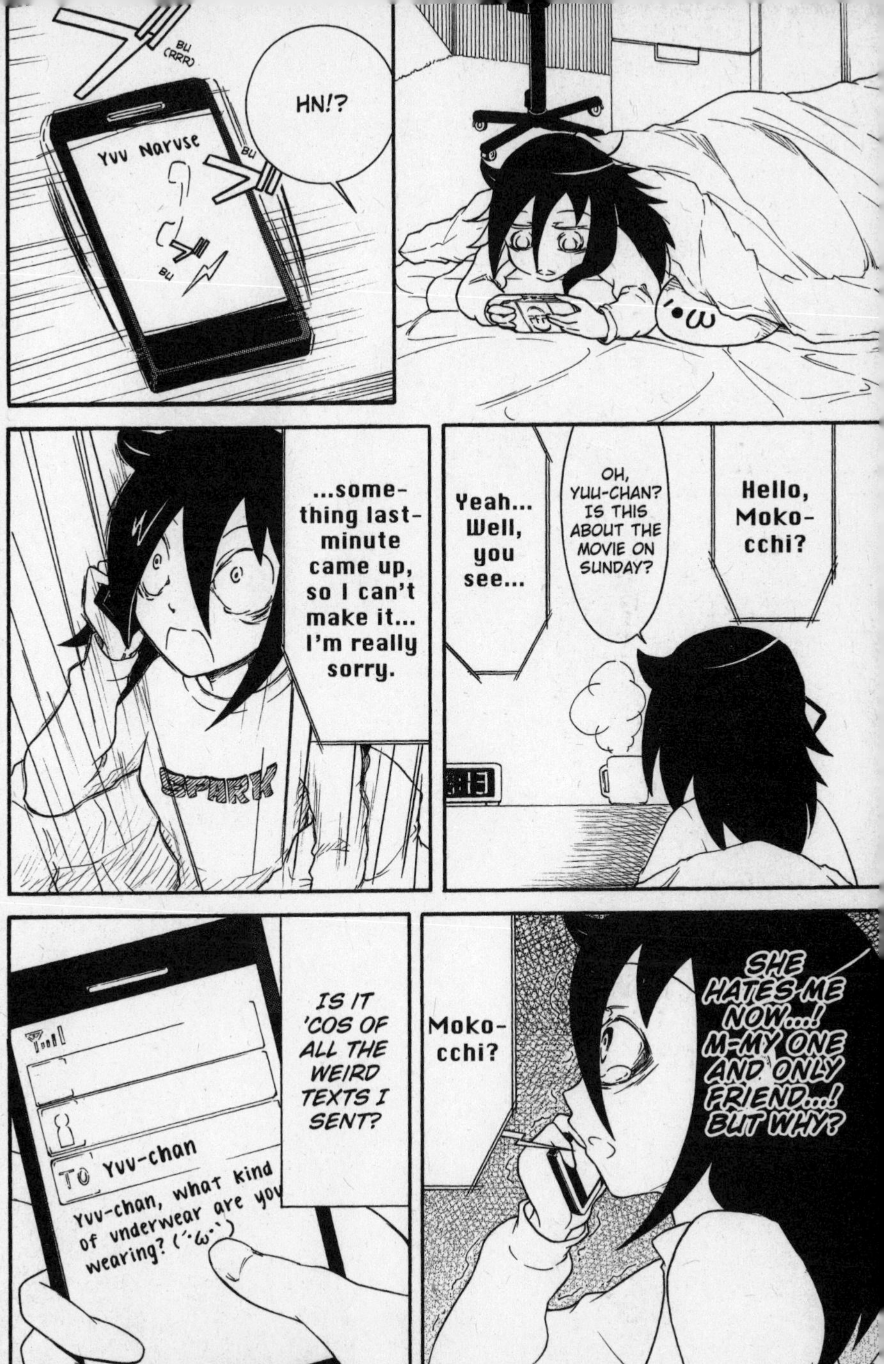
BU (RRR)
HN!?
Yuu Naruse
BU
BU
Hello, Moko-cchi?
OH, YUU-CHAN? IS THIS ABOUT THE MOVIE ON SUNDAY?
Yeah... Well, you see...
...some-thing last-minute came up, so I can't make it... I'm really sorry.
SHE HATES ME NOW...! M-MY ONE AND ONLY FRIEND...! BUT WHY?
Moko-cchi?
IS IT 'COS OF ALL THE WEIRD TEXTS I SENT?
TO Yuu-chan
Yuu-chan, what kind of underwear are you wearing? (´・ω・`)

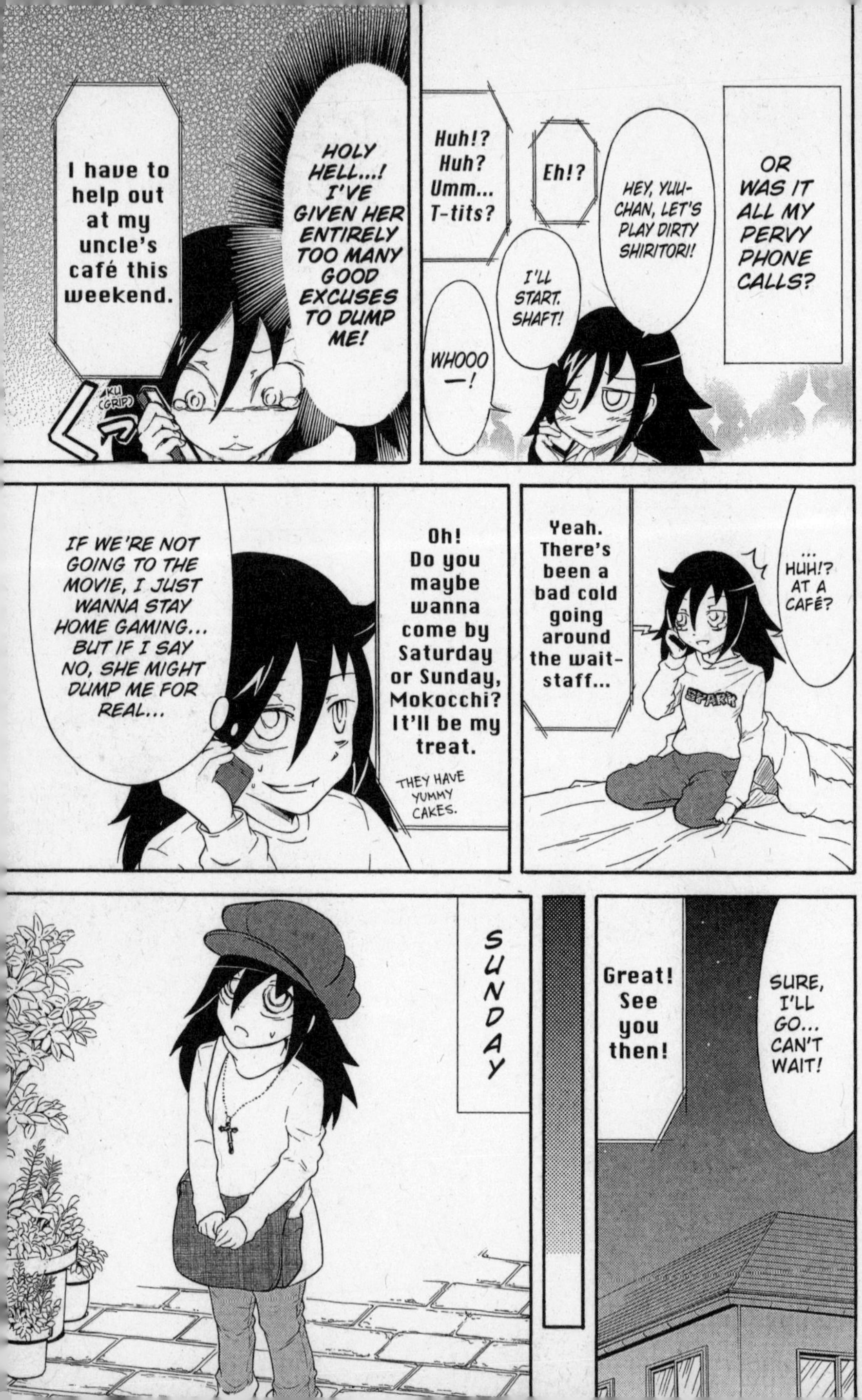
OR WAS IT ALL MY PERVY PHONE CALLS?
HEY, YUU-CHAN, LET'S PLAY DIRTY SHIRITORI!
Eh!?
I'LL START. SHAFT!
Huh!? Huh? Umm... T-tits?
WHOOO—!
HOLY HELL...! I'VE GIVEN HER ENTIRELY TOO MANY GOOD EXCUSES TO DUMP ME!
I have to help out at my uncle's café this weekend.
KU (GRIP)
... HUH!? AT A CAFÉ?
SPARK
Yeah. There's been a bad cold going around the wait-staff...
Oh! Do you maybe wanna come by Saturday or Sunday, Mokocchi? It'll be my treat.
THEY HAVE YUMMY CAKES.
IF WE'RE NOT GOING TO THE MOVIE, I JUST WANNA STAY HOME GAMING... BUT IF I SAY NO, SHE MIGHT DUMP ME FOR REAL...
SURE, I'LL GO... CAN'T WAIT!
Great! See you then!
SUNDAY

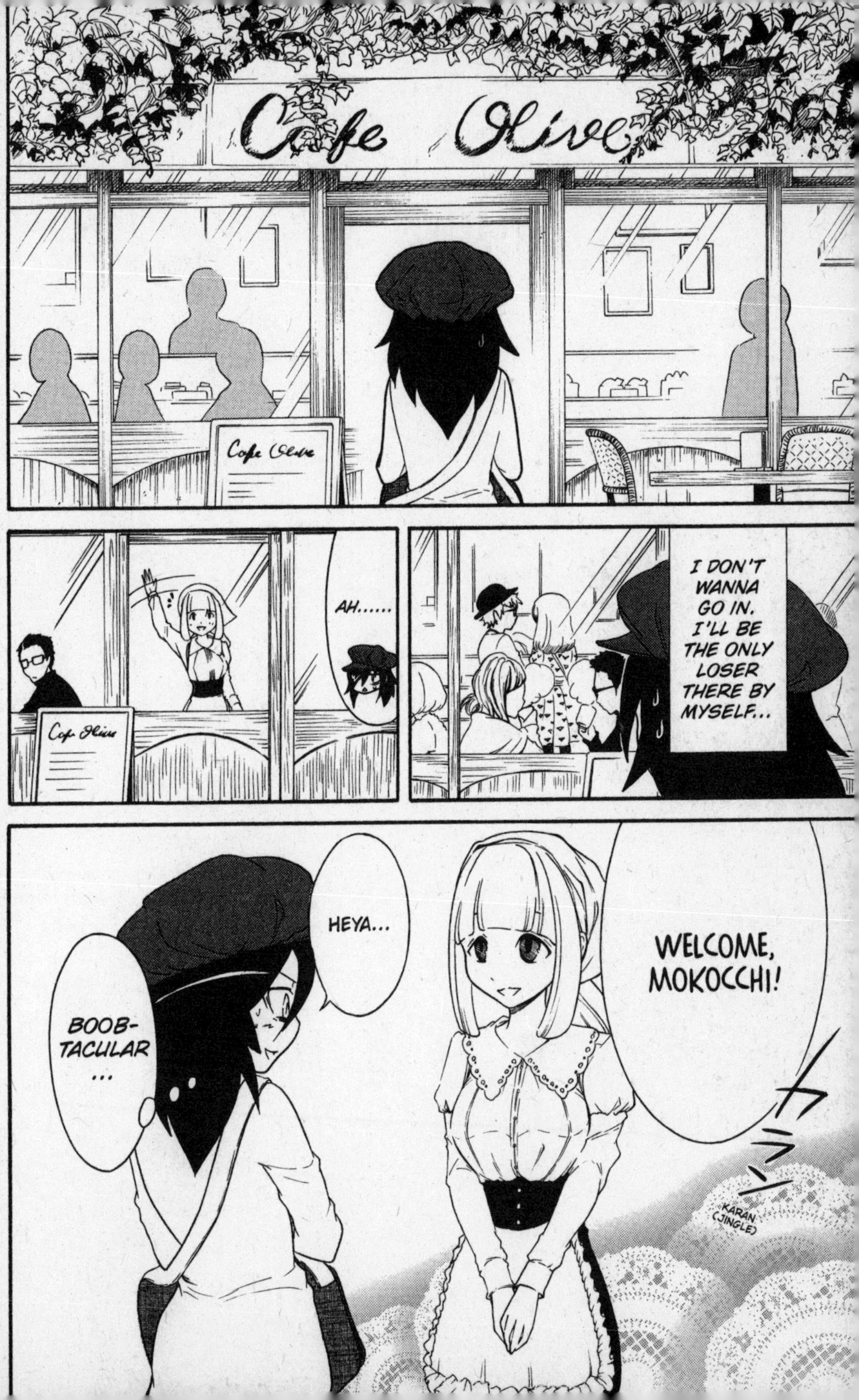
Cafe Olive
Cafe Olive
I DON'T WANNA GO IN. I'LL BE THE ONLY LOSER THERE BY MYSELF...
AH......
Cafe Olive
WELCOME, MOKOCCHI!
KARAN (JINGLE)
HEYA...
BOOB-TACULAR ...

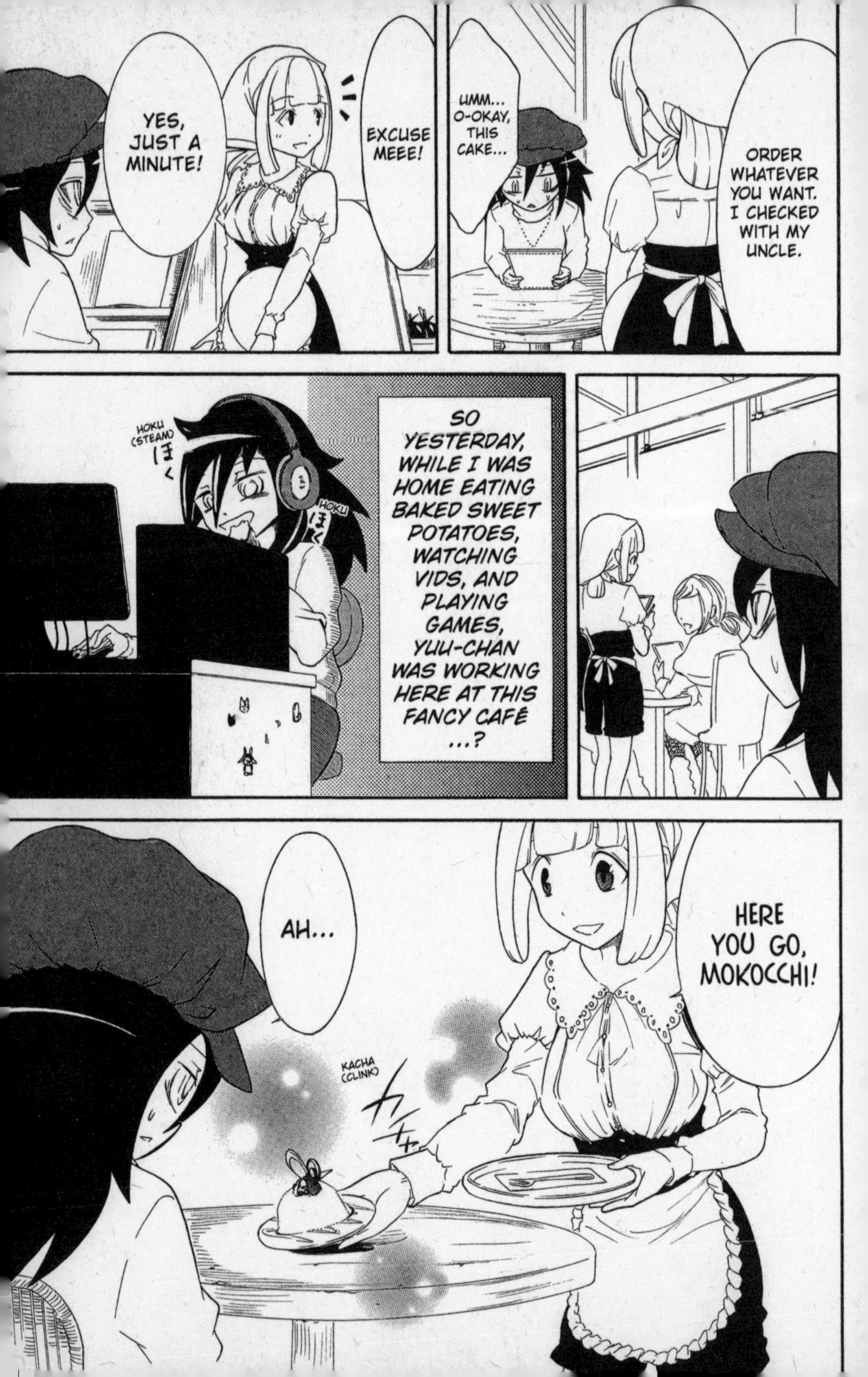
ORDER WHATEVER YOU WANT. I CHECKED WITH MY UNCLE.
UMM... O-OKAY, THIS CAKE...
EXCUSE MEEE!
YES, JUST A MINUTE!
SO YESTERDAY, WHILE I WAS HOME EATING BAKED SWEET POTATOES, WATCHING VIDS, AND PLAYING GAMES, YUU-CHAN WAS WORKING HERE AT THIS FANCY CAFÉ ...?
HOKU ほく
HOKU (STEAM) ほく
HERE YOU GO, MOKOCCHI!
AH...
KACHA (CLINK)

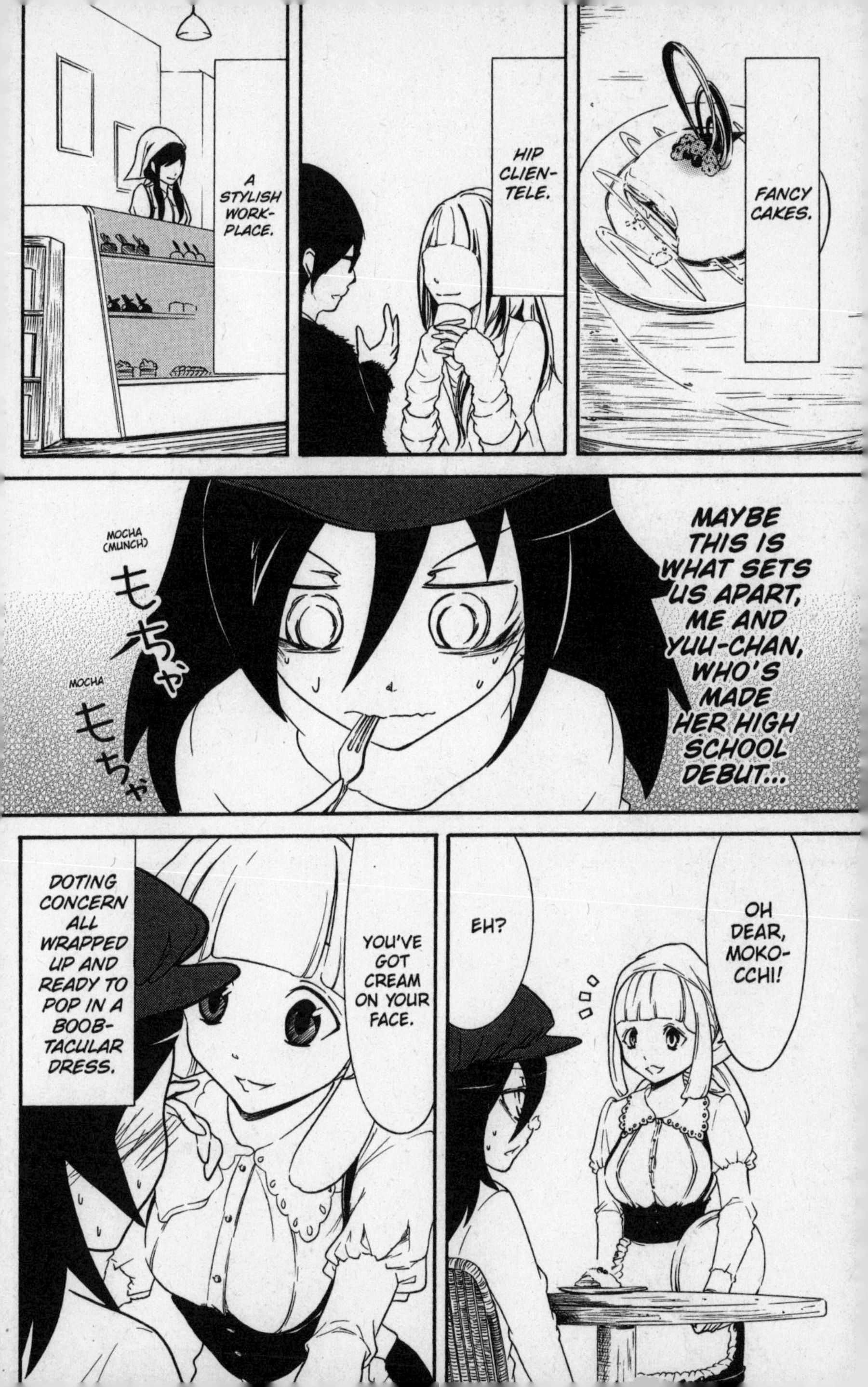
FANCY CAKES.
HIP CLIENTELE.
A STYLISH WORKPLACE.
MAYBE THIS IS WHAT SETS US APART, ME AND YUU-CHAN, WHO'S MADE HER HIGH SCHOOL DEBUT...
MOCHA (MUNCH)
もちゃ
MOCHA
もちゃ
OH DEAR, MOKOCCHI!
EH?
YOU'VE GOT CREAM ON YOUR FACE.
DOTING CONCERN ALL WRAPPED UP AND READY TO POP IN A BOOB-TACULAR DRESS.

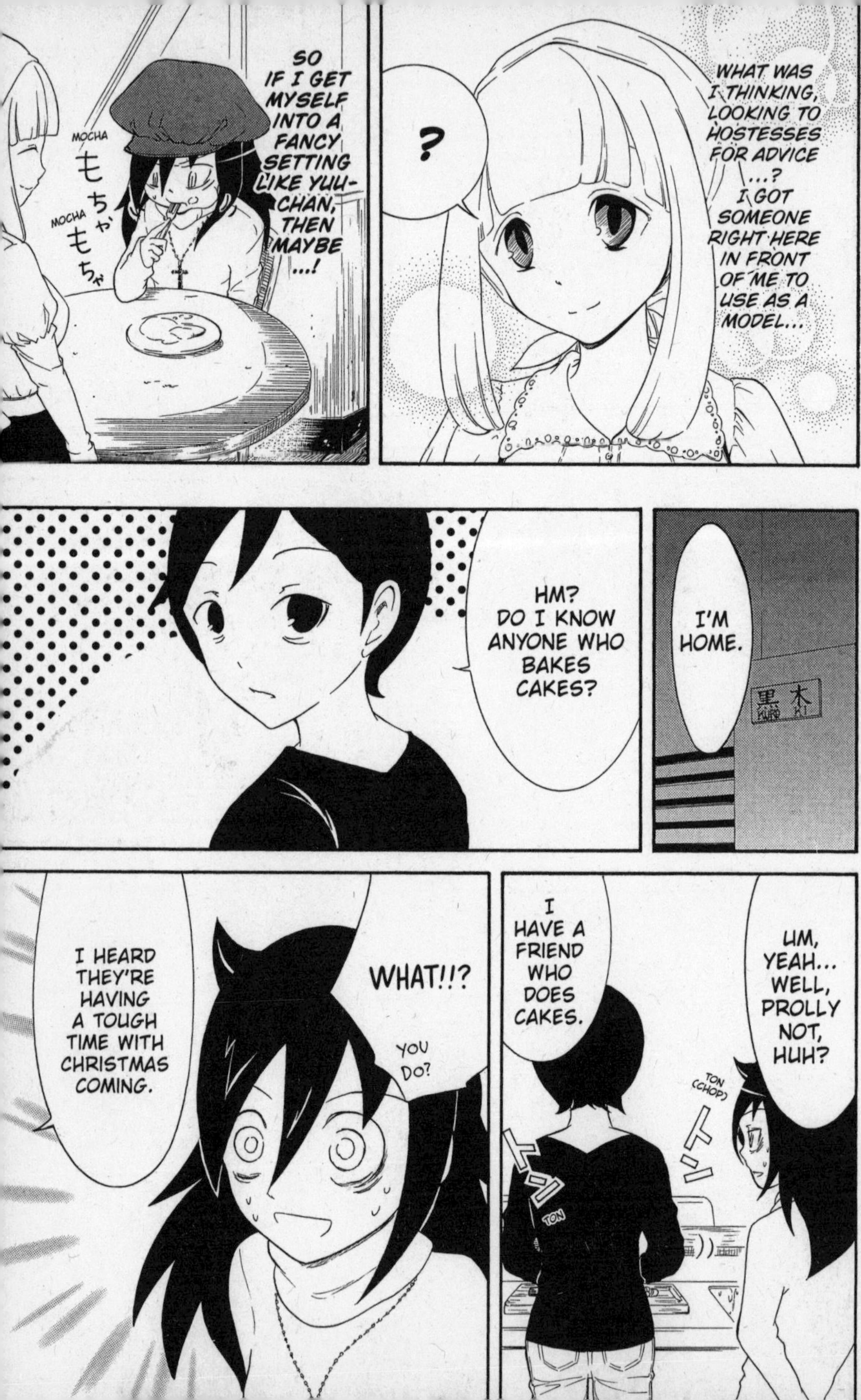
?
WHAT WAS I THINKING, LOOKING TO HOSTESSES FOR ADVICE...? I GOT SOMEONE RIGHT HERE IN FRONT OF ME TO USE AS A MODEL...
SO IF I GET MYSELF INTO A FANCY SETTING LIKE YUU-CHAN, THEN MAYBE...!
もちゃ MOCHA
もちゃ MOCHA
I'M HOME.
黒木 KURO KI
HM? DO I KNOW ANYONE WHO BAKES CAKES?
UM, YEAH... WELL, PROLLY NOT, HUH?
I HAVE A FRIEND WHO DOES CAKES.
トン TON (CHOP)
トン TON
WHAT!!?
YOU DO?
I HEARD THEY'RE HAVING A TOUGH TIME WITH CHRISTMAS COMING.

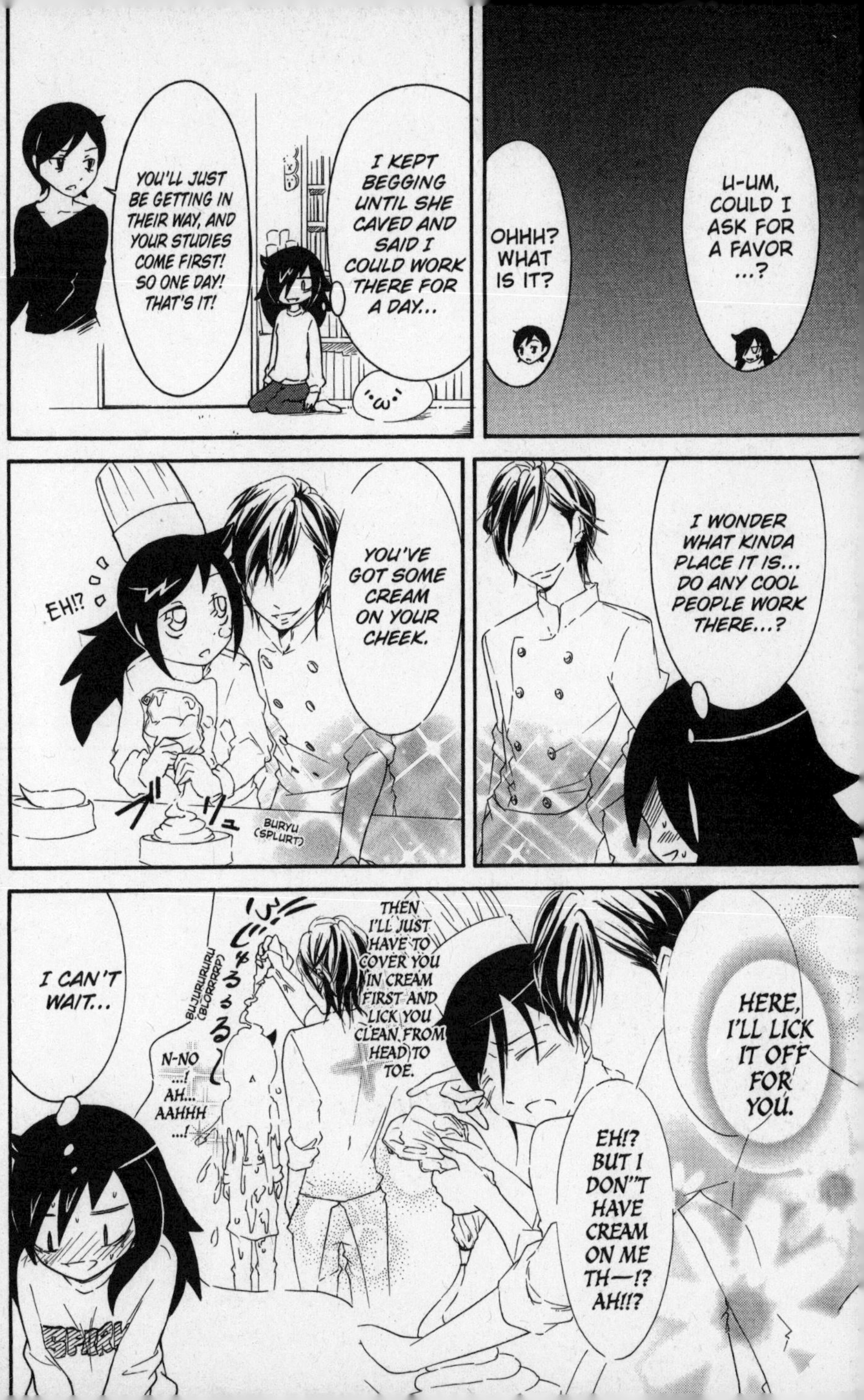
U-UM, COULD I ASK FOR A FAVOR ...?
OHHH? WHAT IS IT?
I KEPT BEGGING UNTIL SHE CAVED AND SAID I COULD WORK THERE FOR A DAY...
YOU'LL JUST BE GETTING IN THEIR WAY, AND YOUR STUDIES COME FIRST! SO ONE DAY! THAT'S IT!
I WONDER WHAT KINDA PLACE IT IS... DO ANY COOL PEOPLE WORK THERE...?
YOU'VE GOT SOME CREAM ON YOUR CHEEK.
EH!?
BURYU (SPLURT)
HERE, I'LL LICK IT OFF FOR YOU.
EH!? BUT I DON"T HAVE CREAM ON ME TH—!? AH!!?
THEN I'LL JUST HAVE TO COVER YOU IN CREAM FIRST AND LICK YOU CLEAN FROM HEAD TO TOE.
BUJURURURU (BLORRRRP)
N-NO ...! AH... AAHHH ...!
I CAN'T WAIT...

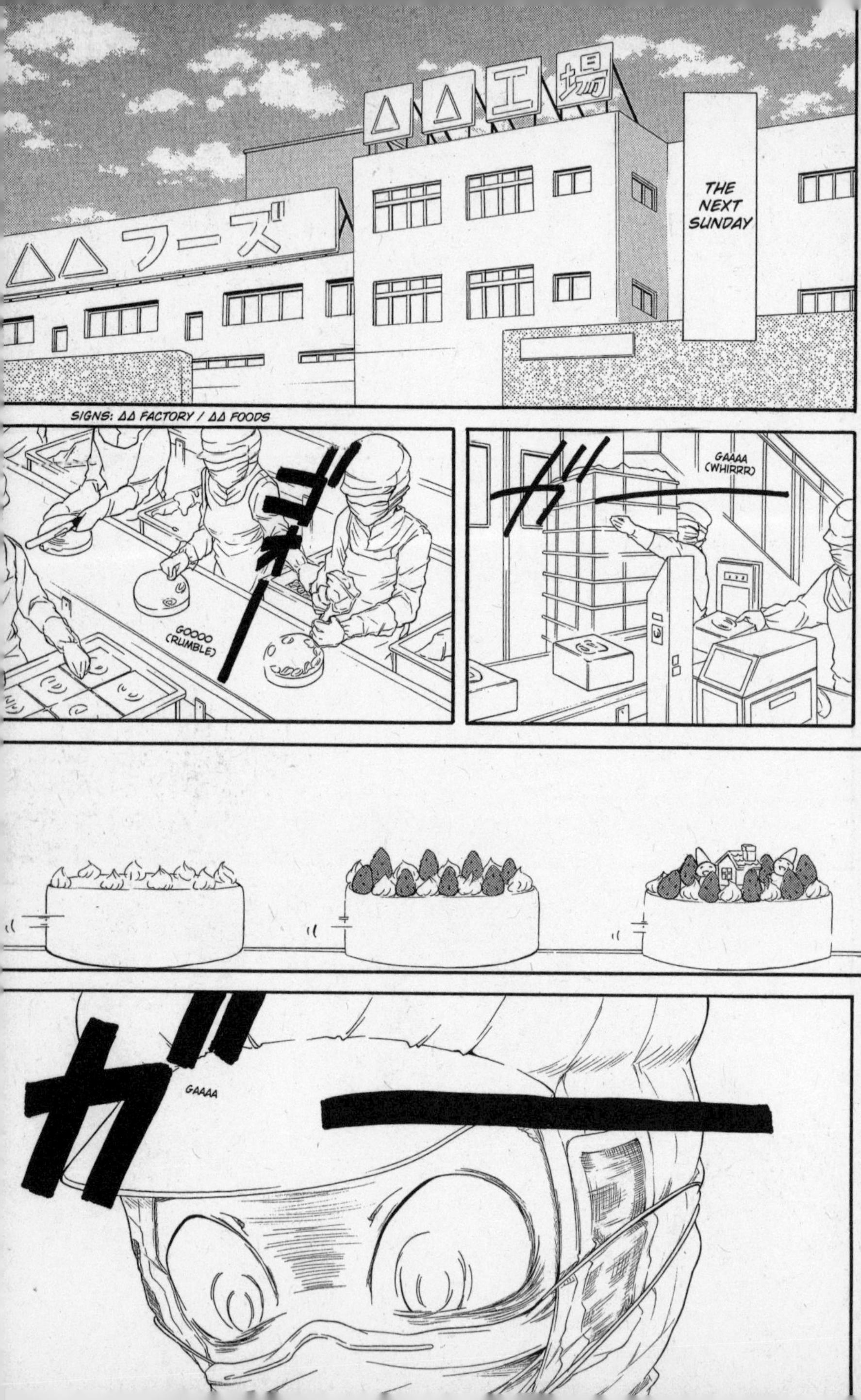
△△工場
△△フーズ
THE NEXT SUNDAY
SIGNS: ΔΔ FACTORY / ΔΔ FOODS
GAAAA (WHIRRR)
GOOOO (RUMBLE)
GAAAA

Break time, every-one.

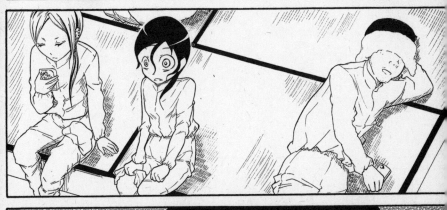

WELL... WE ARE MAKING CAKES, BUT...

No Matter How I Look at It, It's You Guys' Fault I'm Not Popular!

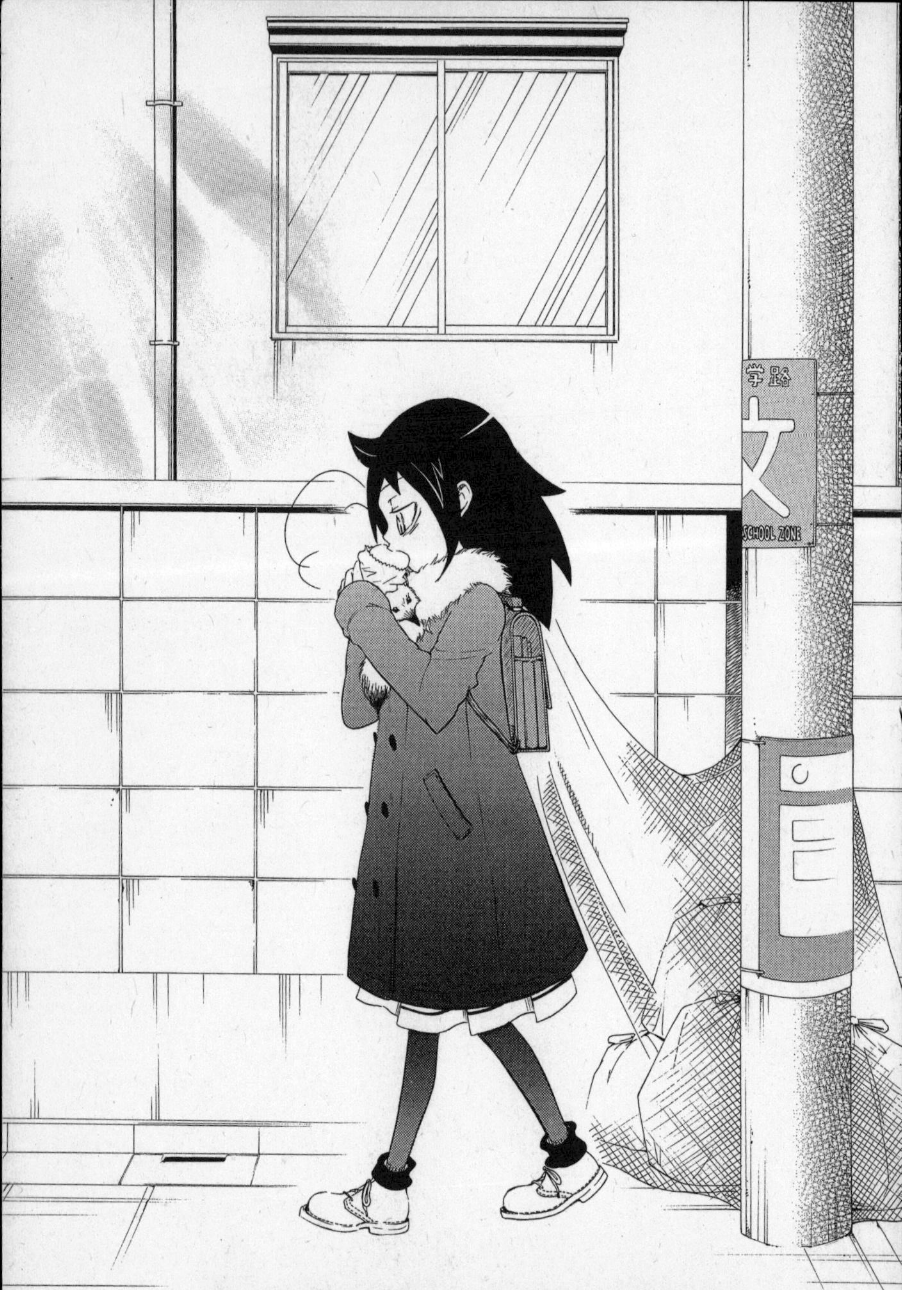

学路
文
SCHOOL ZONE

FAIL 30: I'M NOT POPULAR, SO I'LL RUN.

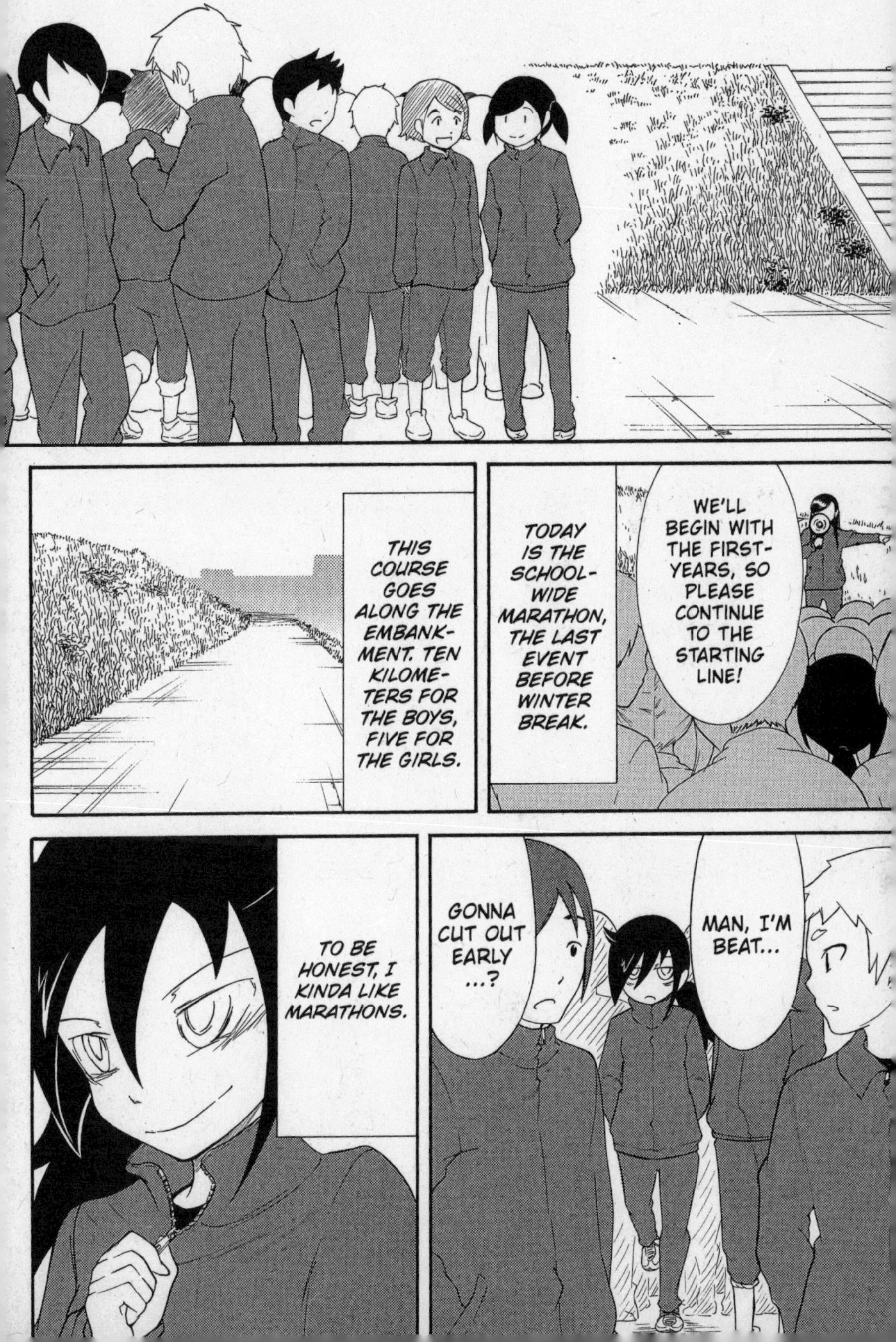
WE'LL BEGIN WITH THE FIRST-YEARS, SO PLEASE CONTINUE TO THE STARTING LINE!
TODAY IS THE SCHOOL-WIDE MARATHON, THE LAST EVENT BEFORE WINTER BREAK.
THIS COURSE GOES ALONG THE EMBANKMENT. TEN KILOMETERS FOR THE BOYS, FIVE FOR THE GIRLS.
MAN, I'M BEAT...
GONNA CUT OUT EARLY ...?
TO BE HONEST, I KINDA LIKE MARATHONS.

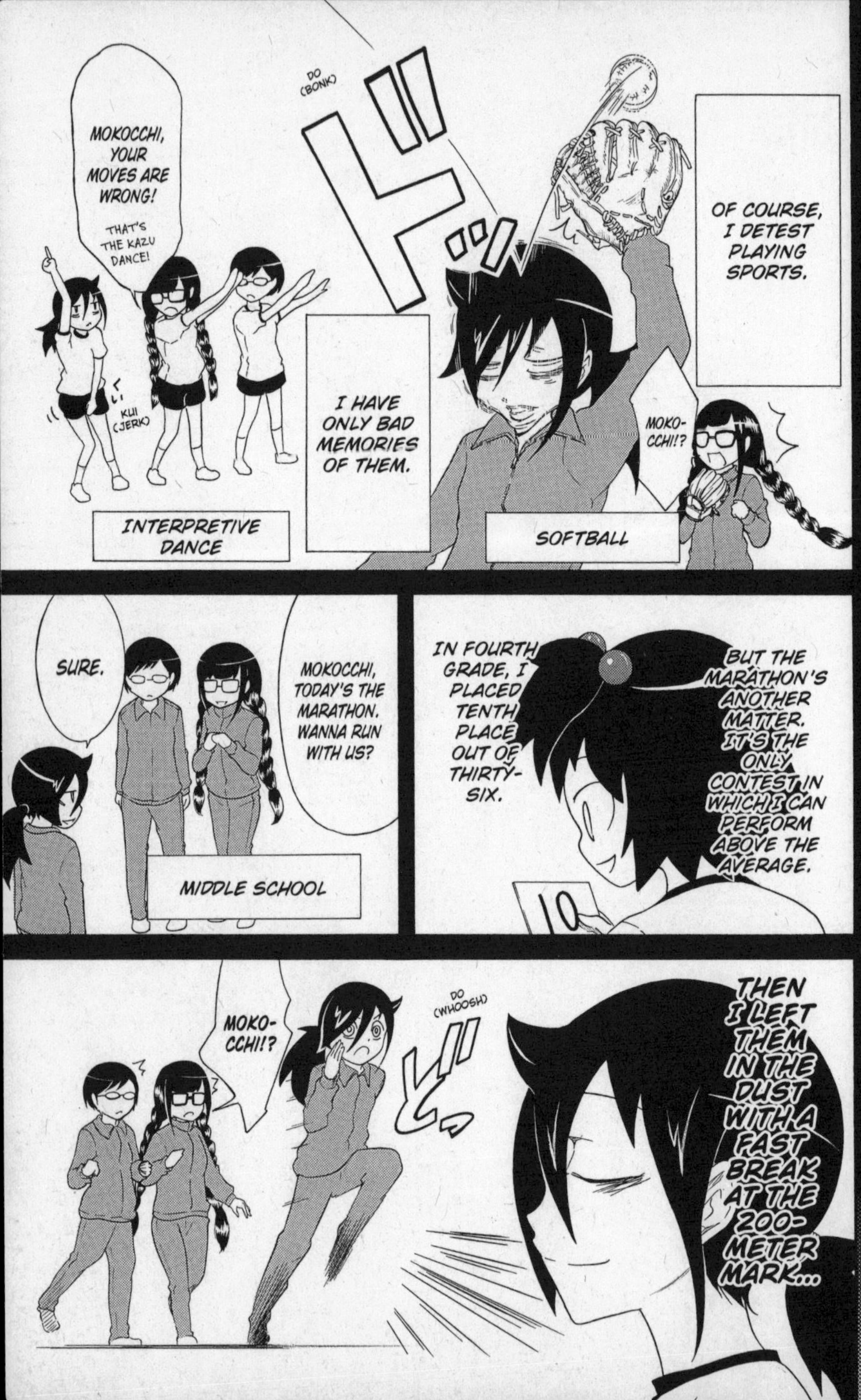
OF COURSE, I DETEST PLAYING SPORTS.
SOFTBALL
MOKO-CCHI!?
DO (BONK)
I HAVE ONLY BAD MEMORIES OF THEM.
INTERPRETIVE DANCE
MOKOCCHI, YOUR MOVES ARE WRONG!
THAT'S THE KAZU DANCE!
KUI (JERK)
BUT THE MARATHON'S ANOTHER MATTER. IT'S THE ONLY CONTEST IN WHICH I CAN PERFORM ABOVE THE AVERAGE.
IN FOURTH GRADE, I PLACED TENTH PLACE OUT OF THIRTY-SIX.
10
MIDDLE SCHOOL
MOKOCCHI, TODAY'S THE MARATHON. WANNA RUN WITH US?
SURE.
THEN I LEFT THEM IN THE DUST WITH A FAST BREAK AT THE 200-METER MARK...
DO (WHOOSH)
MOKO-CCHI!?

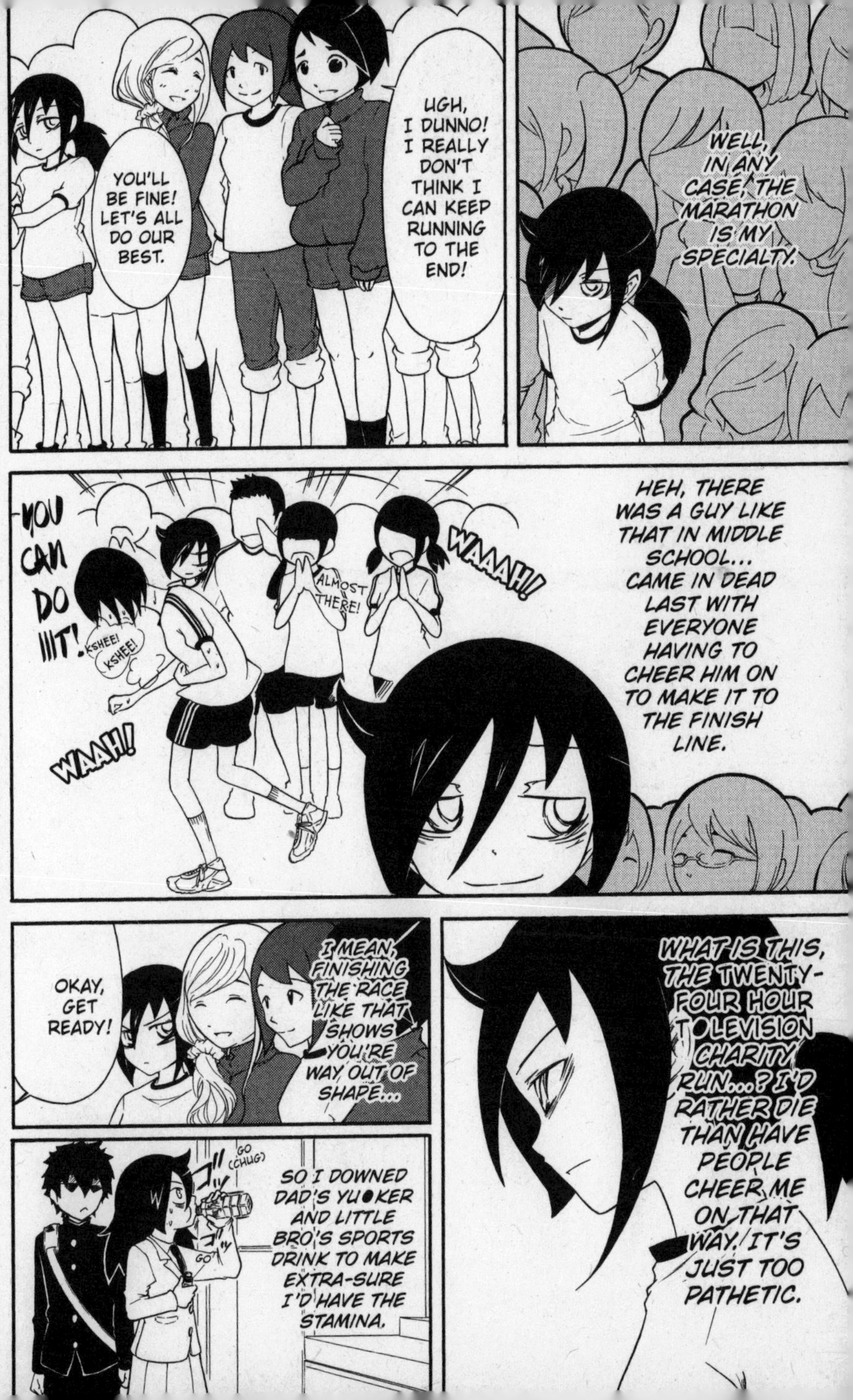
WELL, IN ANY CASE, THE MARATHON IS MY SPECIALTY.
UGH, I DUNNO! I REALLY DON'T THINK I CAN KEEP RUNNING TO THE END!
YOU'LL BE FINE! LET'S ALL DO OUR BEST.
HEH, THERE WAS A GUY LIKE THAT IN MIDDLE SCHOOL... CAME IN DEAD LAST WITH EVERYONE HAVING TO CHEER HIM ON TO MAKE IT TO THE FINISH LINE.
WAAAH!!
ALMOST THERE!
YOU CAN DO IIIT!
KSHEE! KSHEE!
WAAH!
WHAT IS THIS, THE TWENTY-FOUR HOUR TELEVISION CHARITY RUN...? I'D RATHER DIE THAN HAVE PEOPLE CHEER ME ON THAT WAY. IT'S JUST TOO PATHETIC.
I MEAN, FINISHING THE RACE LIKE THAT SHOWS YOU'RE WAY OUT OF SHAPE...
OKAY, GET READY!
SO I DOWNED DAD'S YU●KER AND LITTLE BRO'S SPORTS DRINK TO MAKE EXTRA-SURE I'D HAVE THE STAMINA.
GO (CHUG)
GO

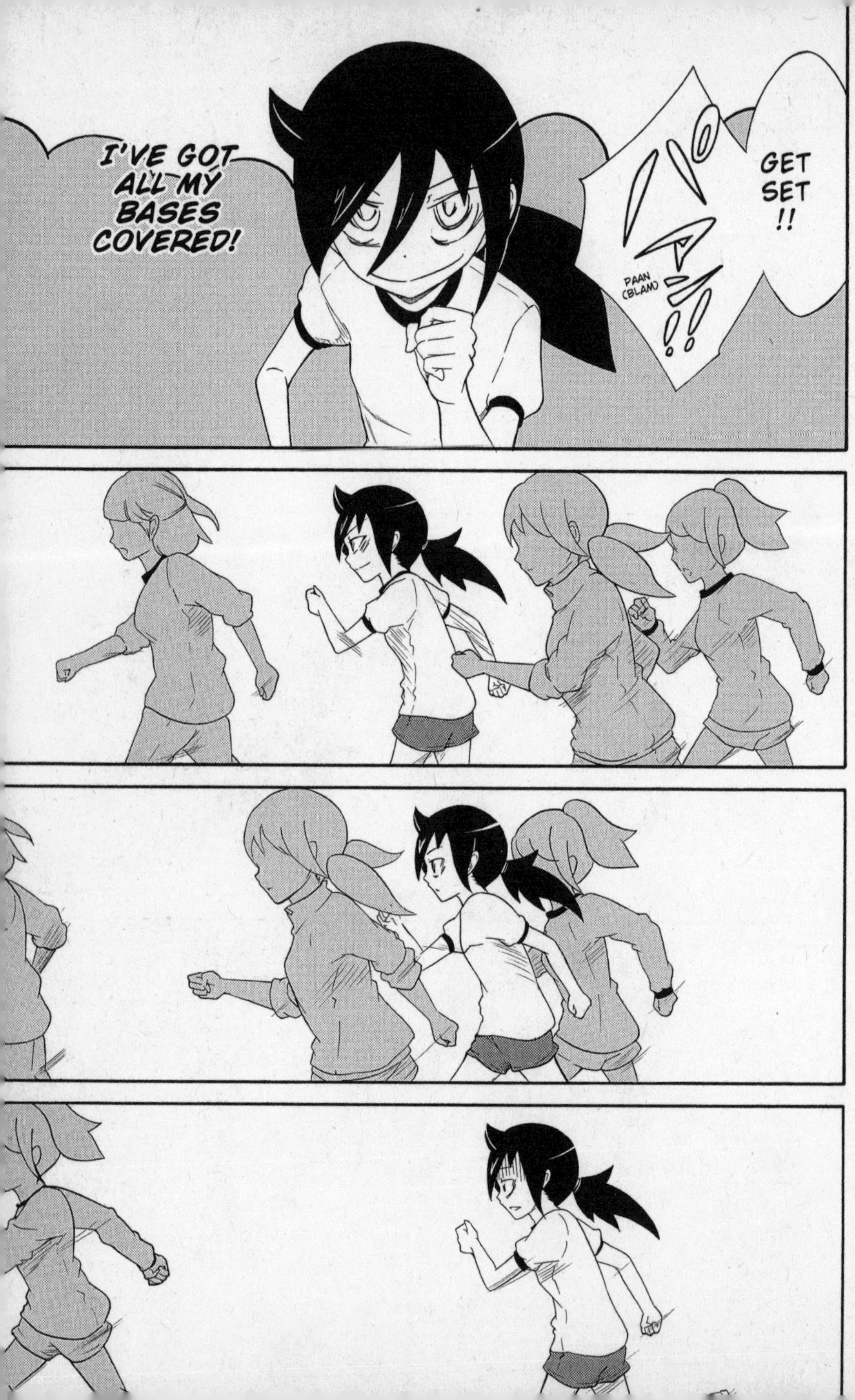
GET SET !!
PAAN (BLAM)
I'VE GOT ALL MY BASES COVERED!

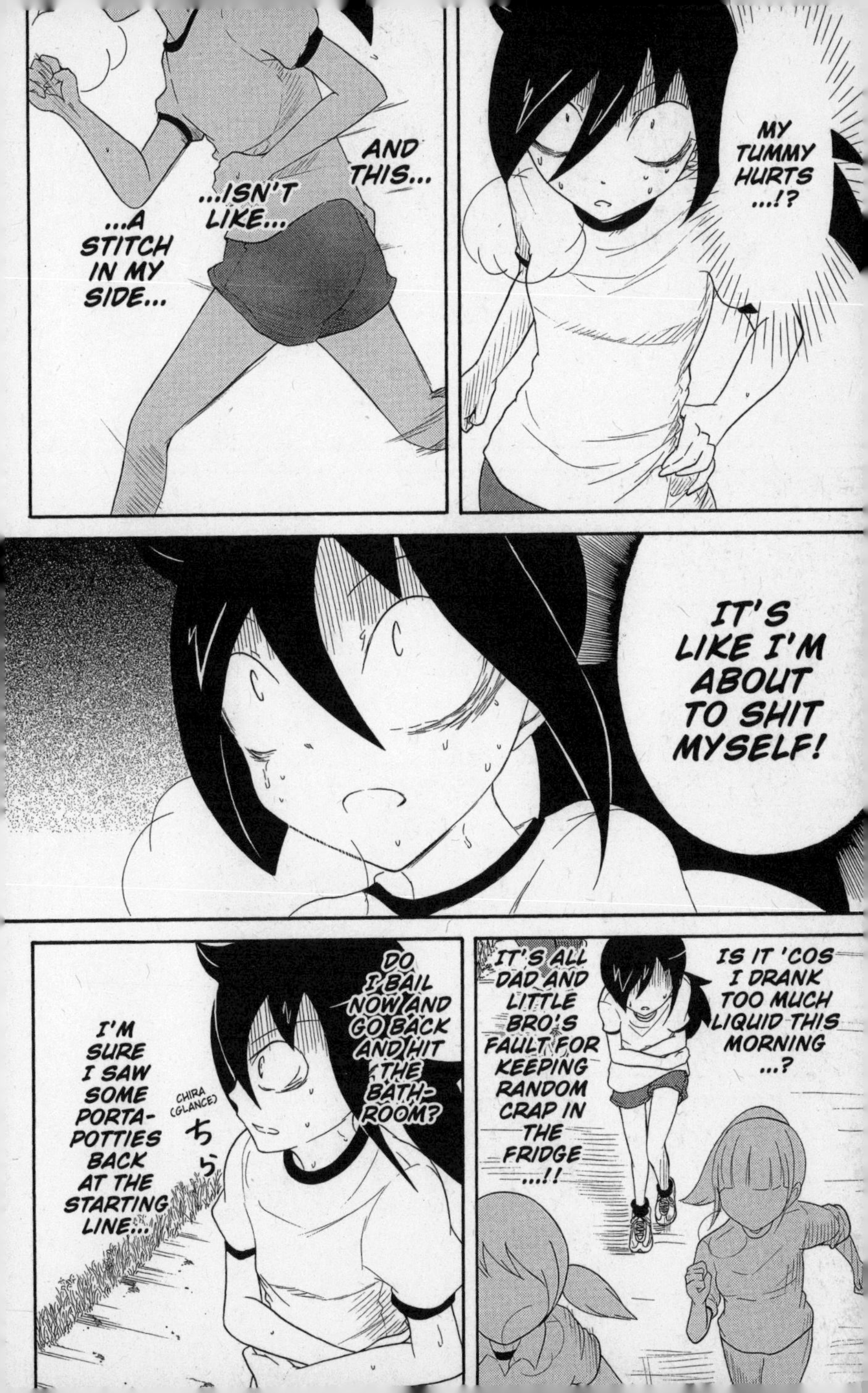
MY TUMMY HURTS ...!?
AND THIS...
...ISN'T LIKE...
...A STITCH IN MY SIDE...
IT'S LIKE I'M ABOUT TO SHIT MYSELF!
IS IT 'COS I DRANK TOO MUCH LIQUID THIS MORNING ...?
IT'S ALL DAD AND LITTLE BRO'S FAULT FOR KEEPING RANDOM CRAP IN THE FRIDGE ...!!
DO I BAIL NOW AND GO BACK AND HIT THE BATHROOM?
CHIRA (GLANCE)
ちら
I'M SURE I SAW SOME PORTA-POTTIES BACK AT THE STARTING LINE...

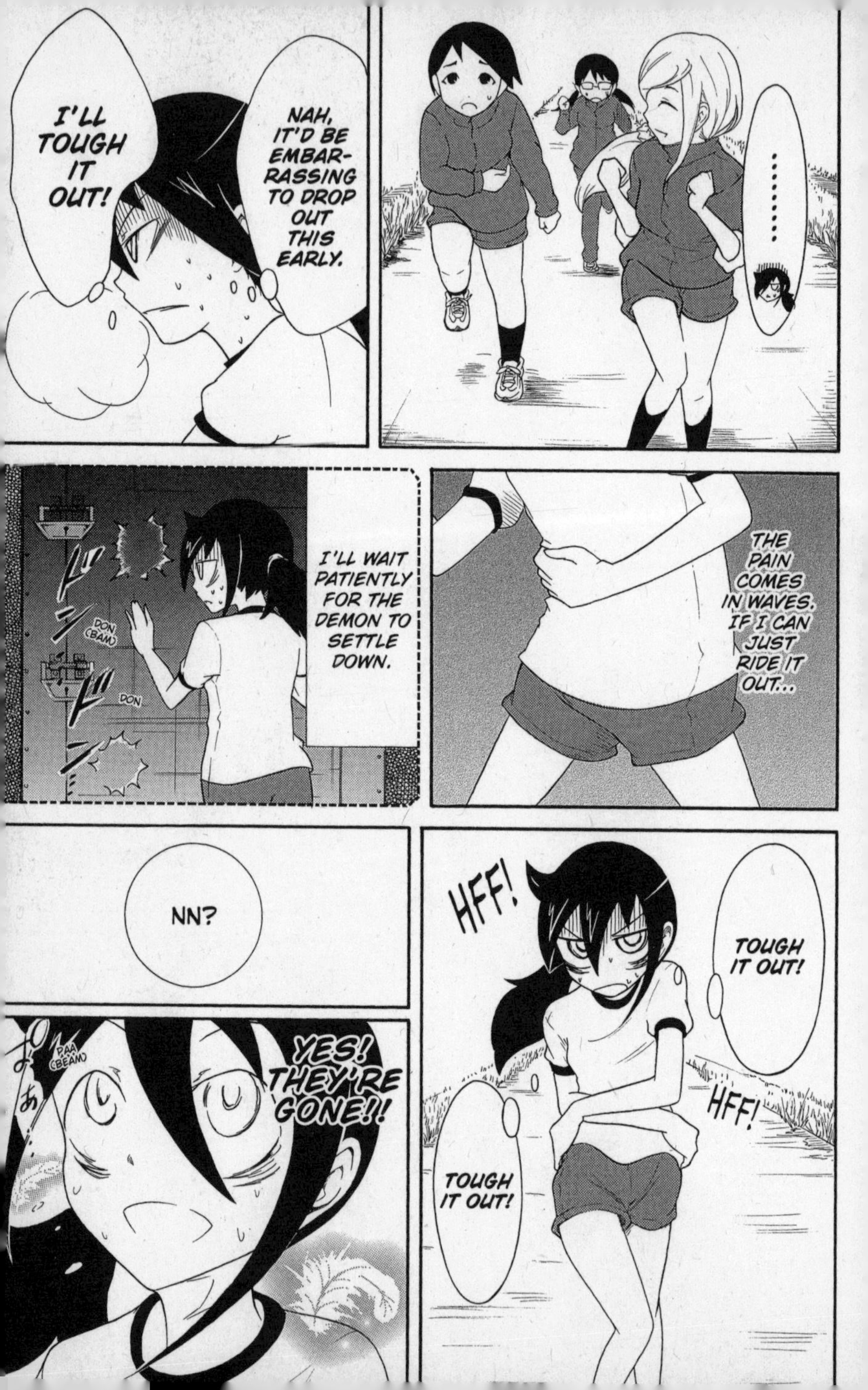
......
NAH, IT'D BE EMBAR-RASSING TO DROP OUT THIS EARLY.
I'LL TOUGH IT OUT!
THE PAIN COMES IN WAVES. IF I CAN JUST RIDE IT OUT...
I'LL WAIT PATIENTLY FOR THE DEMON TO SETTLE DOWN.
DON (BAM)
DON
HFF!
TOUGH IT OUT!
HFF!
TOUGH IT OUT!
NN?
YES! THEY'RE GONE!!
PAA (BEAM)

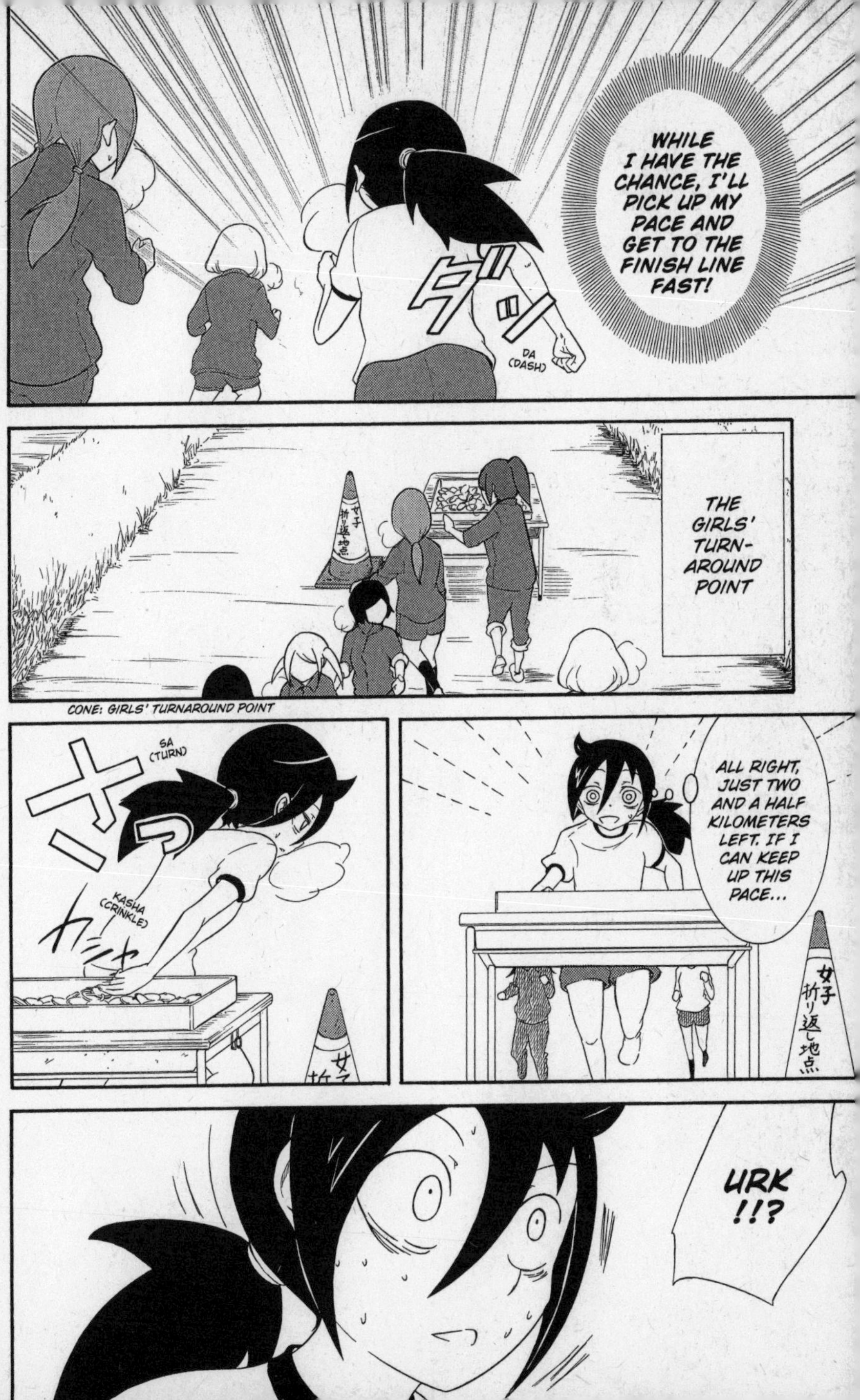
WHILE I HAVE THE CHANCE, I'LL PICK UP MY PACE AND GET TO THE FINISH LINE FAST!
DA (DASH)
THE GIRLS' TURN-AROUND POINT
女子折り返し地点
CONE: GIRLS' TURNAROUND POINT
ALL RIGHT, JUST TWO AND A HALF KILOMETERS LEFT. IF I CAN KEEP UP THIS PACE...
女子折り返し地点
SA (TURN)
KASHA (CRINKLE)
URK !!?

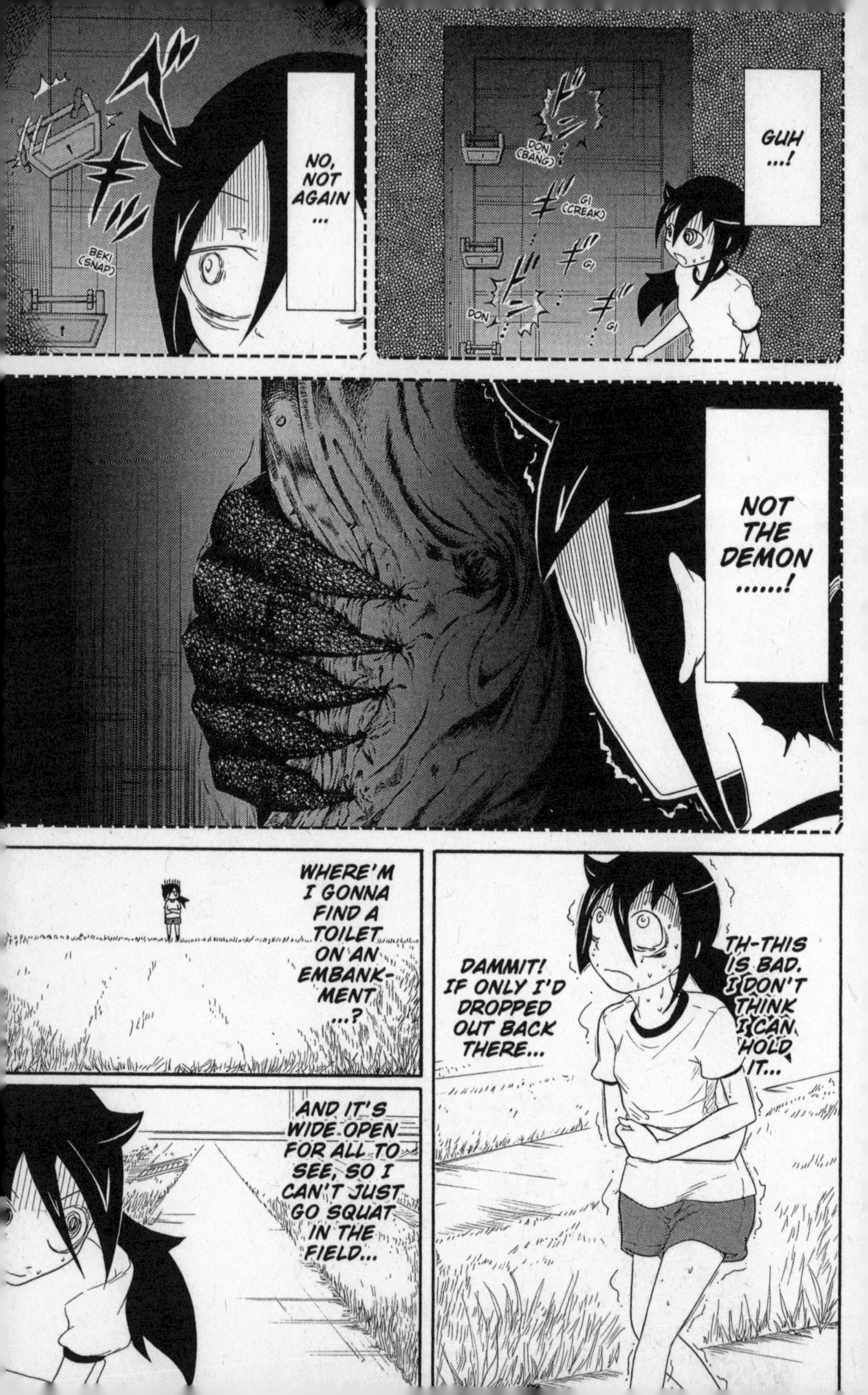
GUH ...!
DON (BANG)
GI (CREAK)
GI
DON
GI
NO, NOT AGAIN ...
BEKI (SNAP)
NOT THE DEMON ......!
TH-THIS IS BAD. I DON'T THINK I CAN HOLD IT...
DAMMIT! IF ONLY I'D DROPPED OUT BACK THERE...
WHERE'M I GONNA FIND A TOILET ON AN EMBANKMENT ...?
AND IT'S WIDE OPEN FOR ALL TO SEE, SO I CAN'T JUST GO SQUAT IN THE FIELD...

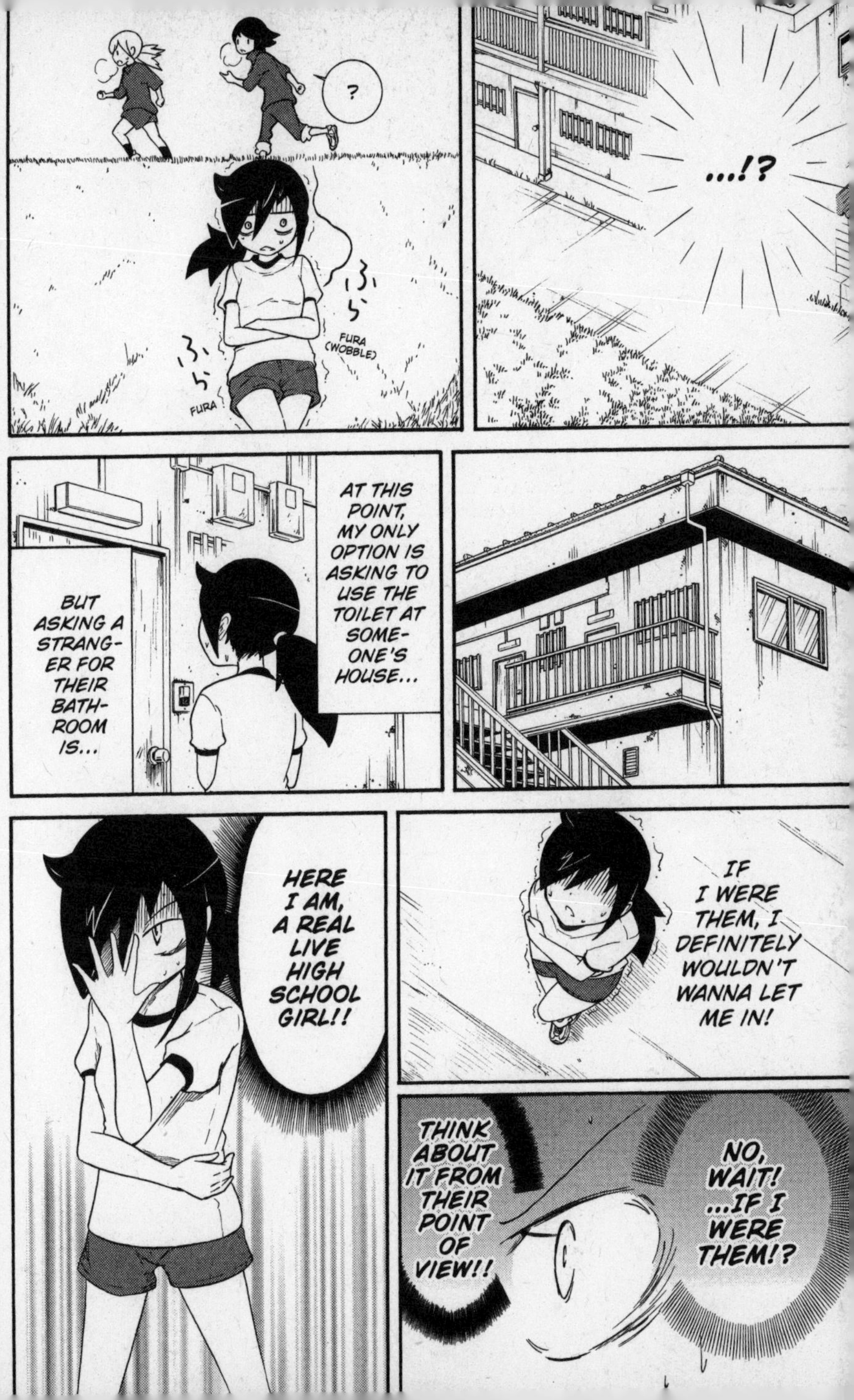
...!?
?
ふら
FURA (WOBBLE)
ふら
FURA
AT THIS POINT, MY ONLY OPTION IS ASKING TO USE THE TOILET AT SOME-ONE'S HOUSE...
BUT ASKING A STRANGER FOR THEIR BATHROOM IS...
IF I WERE THEM, I DEFINITELY WOULDN'T WANNA LET ME IN!
NO, WAIT! ...IF I WERE THEM!?
THINK ABOUT IT FROM THEIR POINT OF VIEW!!
HERE I AM, A REAL LIVE HIGH SCHOOL GIRL!!

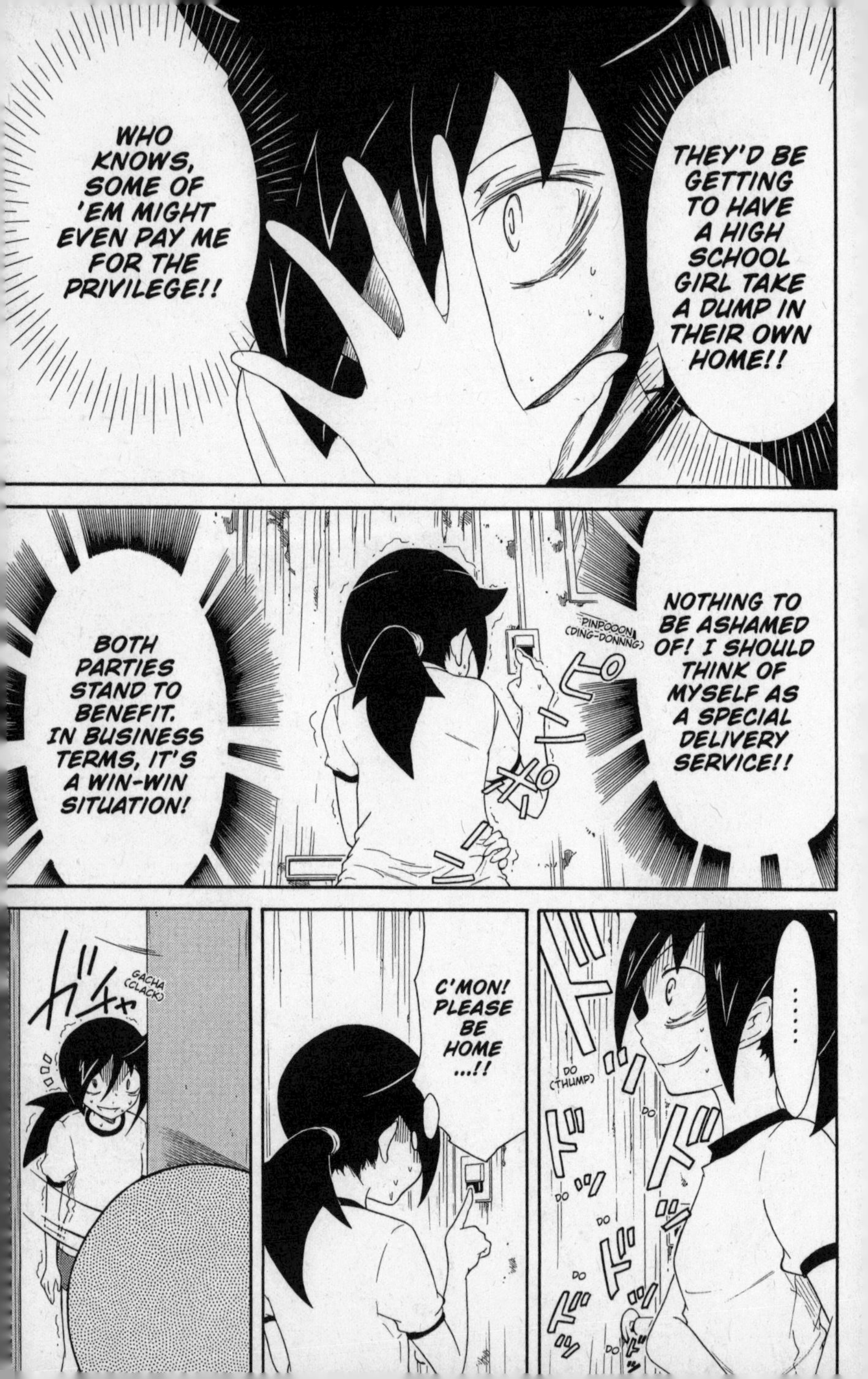
THEY'D BE GETTING TO HAVE A HIGH SCHOOL GIRL TAKE A DUMP IN THEIR OWN HOME!!
WHO KNOWS, SOME OF 'EM MIGHT EVEN PAY ME FOR THE PRIVILEGE!!
NOTHING TO BE ASHAMED OF! I SHOULD THINK OF MYSELF AS A SPECIAL DELIVERY SERVICE!!
PINPOOON (DING-DONNNG)
BOTH PARTIES STAND TO BENEFIT. IN BUSINESS TERMS, IT'S A WIN-WIN SITUATION!
......
DO (THUMP)
DO
DO
DO
DO
C'MON! PLEASE BE HOME ...!!
GACHA (CLACK)

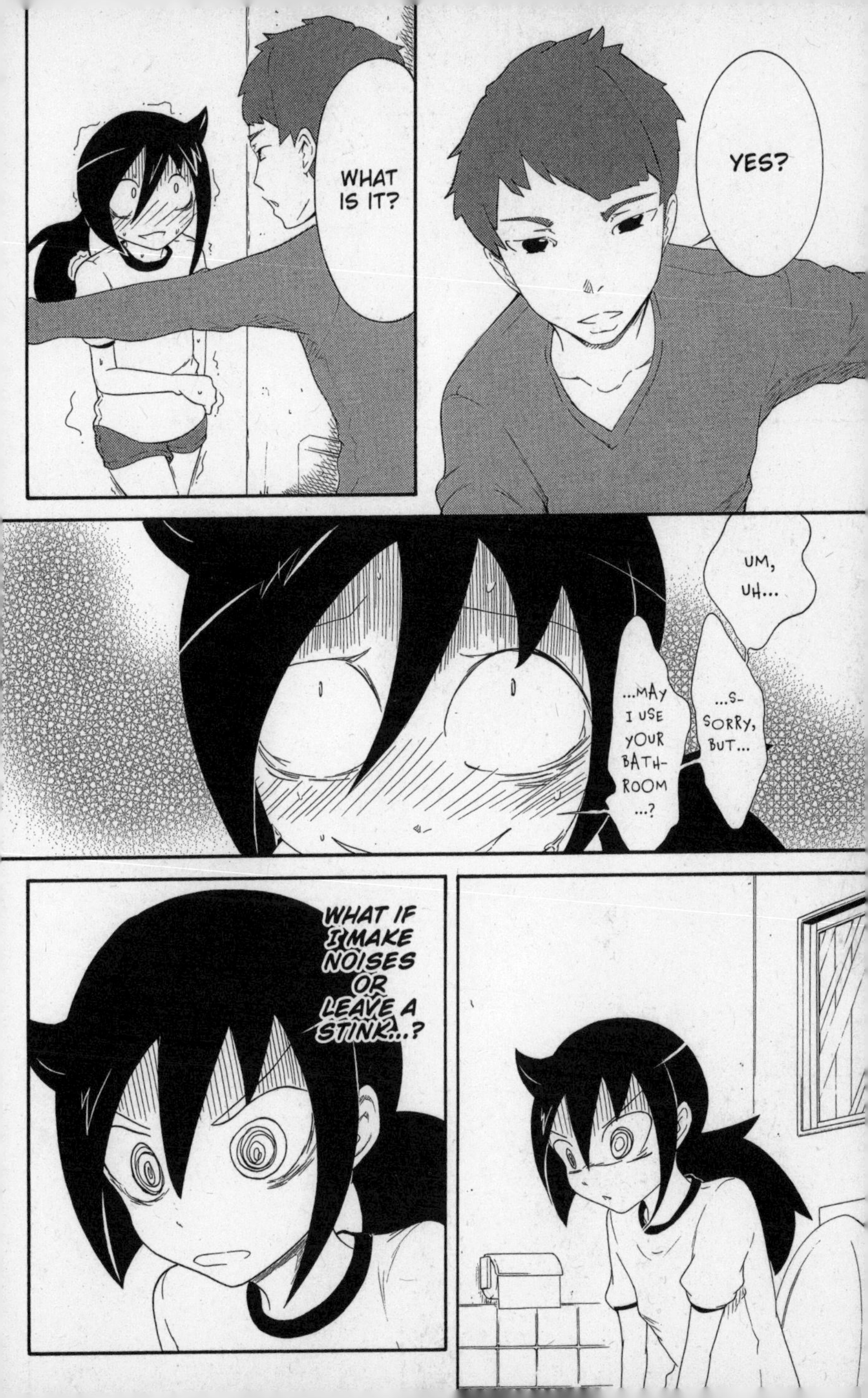
YES?
WHAT IS IT?
UM, UH...
...S-SORRY, BUT...
...MAY I USE YOUR BATHROOM...?
WHAT IF I MAKE NOISES OR LEAVE A STINK...?

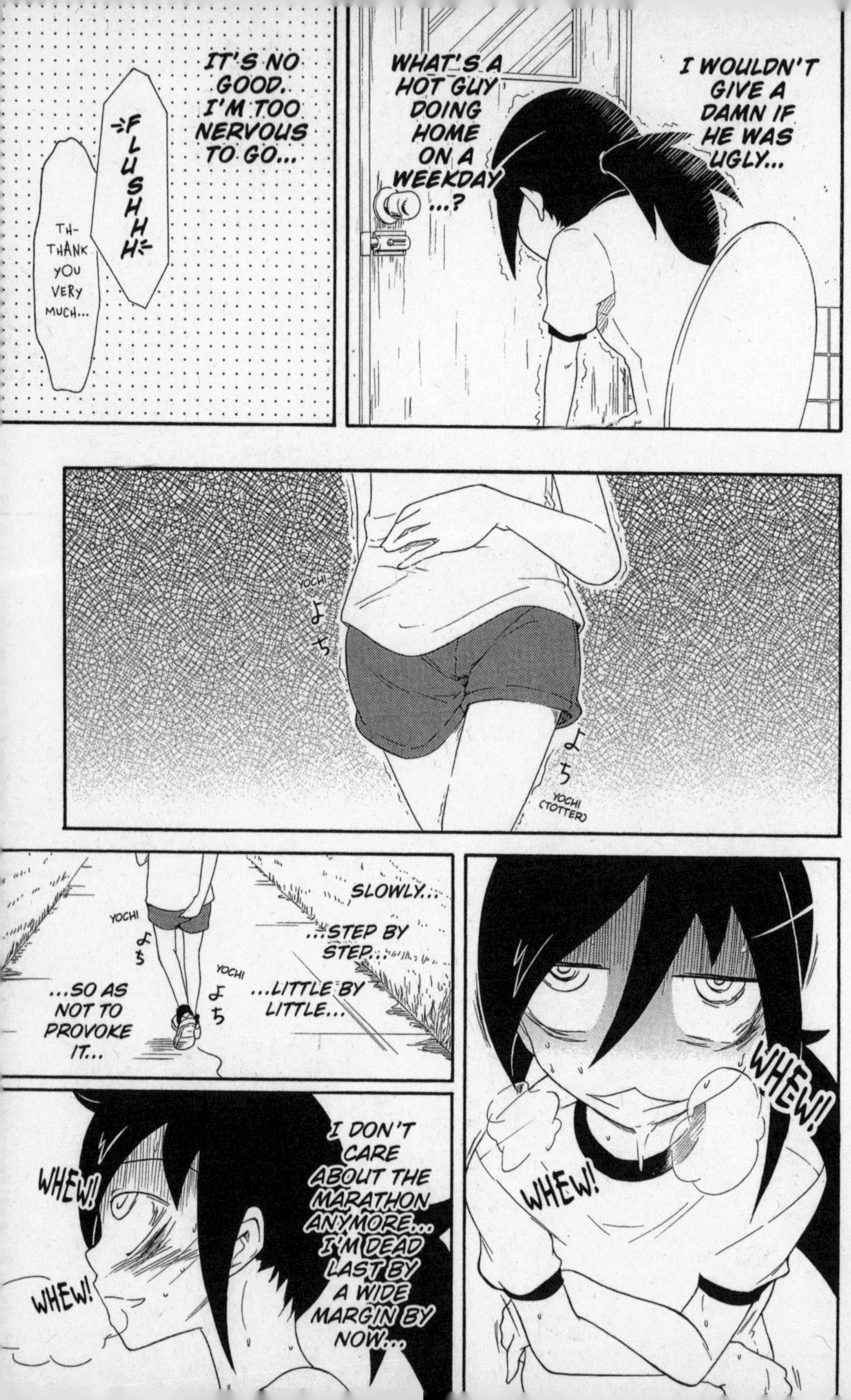
I WOULDN'T GIVE A DAMN IF HE WAS UGLY...
WHAT'S A HOT GUY DOING HOME ON A WEEKDAY ...?
IT'S NO GOOD. I'M TOO NERVOUS TO GO...
FLUSHHH
TH-THANK YOU VERY MUCH...
YOCHI
よち
よち
YOCHI (TOTTER)
WHEW!
WHEW!
SLOWLY...
...STEP BY STEP...
...LITTLE BY LITTLE...
...SO AS NOT TO PROVOKE IT...
YOCHI
よち
YOCHI
よち
I DON'T CARE ABOUT THE MARATHON ANYMORE... I'M DEAD LAST BY A WIDE MARGIN BY NOW...
WHEW!
WHEW!

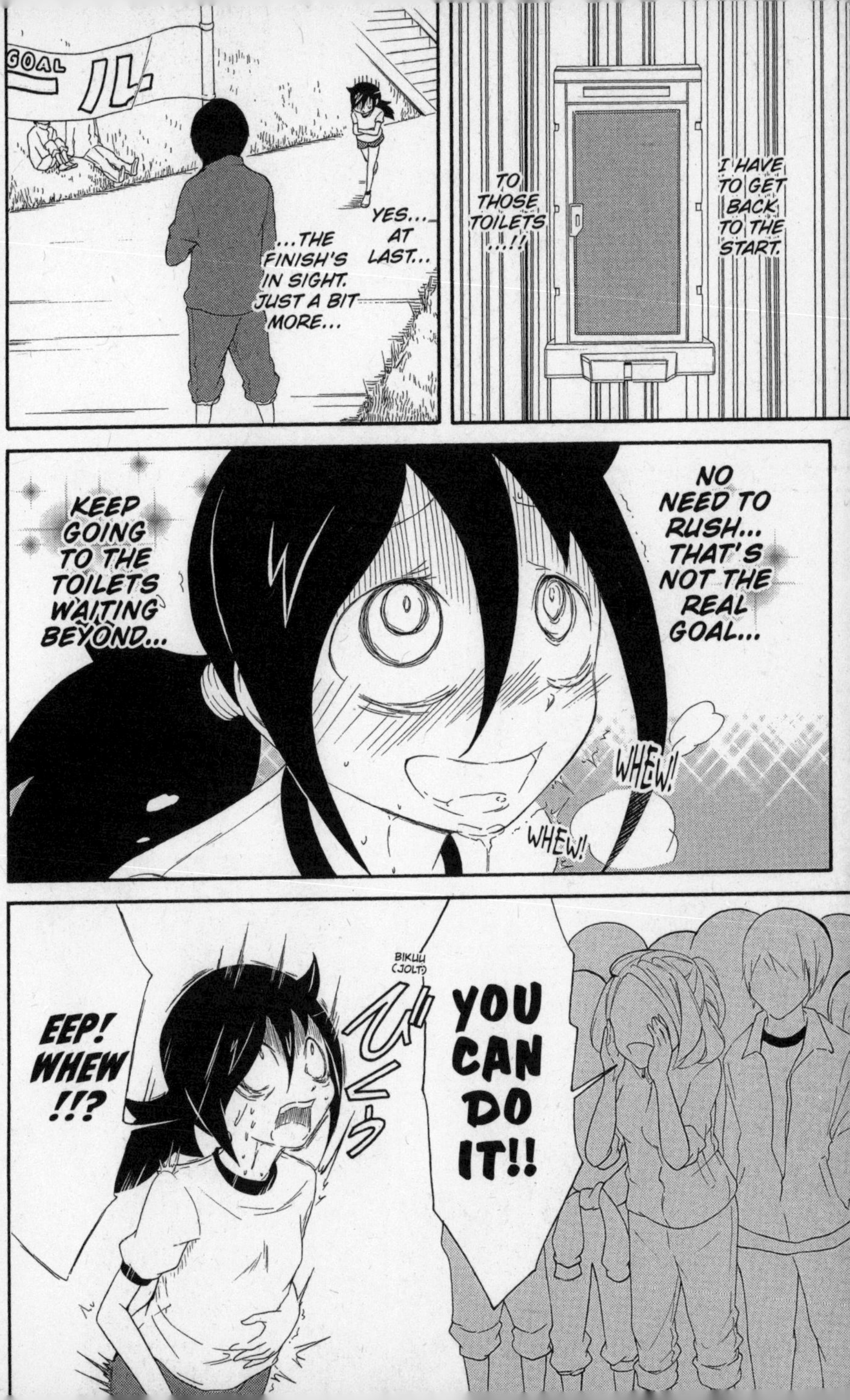
I HAVE TO GET BACK TO THE START.
TO THOSE TOILETS ...!!
YES... AT LAST...
...THE FINISH'S IN SIGHT. JUST A BIT MORE...
GOAL
NO NEED TO RUSH... THAT'S NOT THE REAL GOAL...
KEEP GOING TO THE TOILETS WAITING BEYOND...
WHEW!
WHEW!
YOU CAN DO IT!!
BIKUU (JOLT)
EEP! WHEW !!?

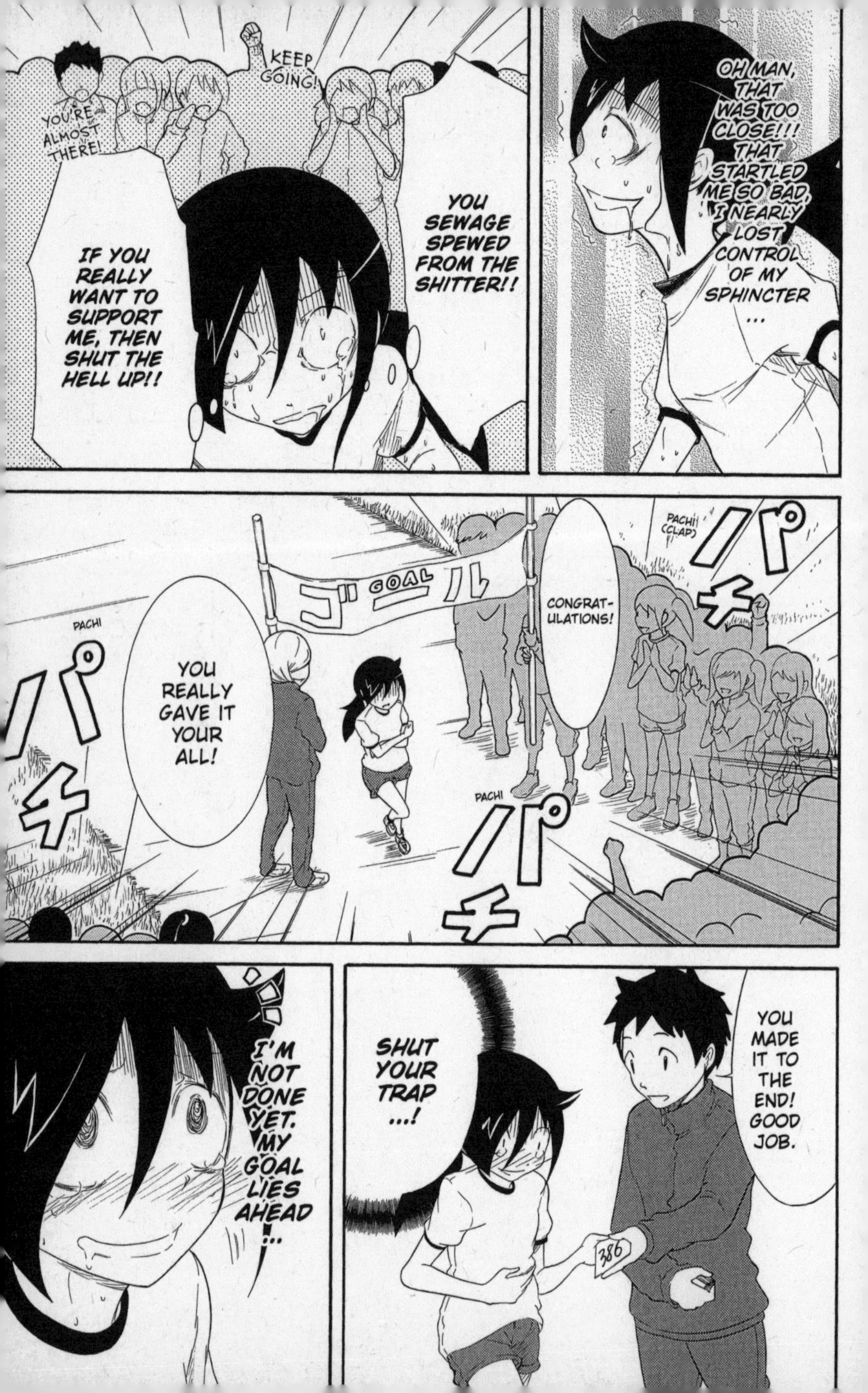
OH MAN, THAT WAS TOO CLOSE!!! THAT STARTLED ME SO BAD, I NEARLY LOST CONTROL OF MY SPHINCTER ...
KEEP GOING!
YOU'RE ALMOST THERE!
YOU SEWAGE SPEWED FROM THE SHITTER!!
IF YOU REALLY WANT TO SUPPORT ME, THEN SHUT THE HELL UP!!
PACHI (CLAP)
CONGRAT-ULATIONS!
GOAL
PACHI
YOU REALLY GAVE IT YOUR ALL!
PACHI
YOU MADE IT TO THE END! GOOD JOB.
386
SHUT YOUR TRAP ...!
I'M NOT DONE YET. MY GOAL LIES AHEAD ...

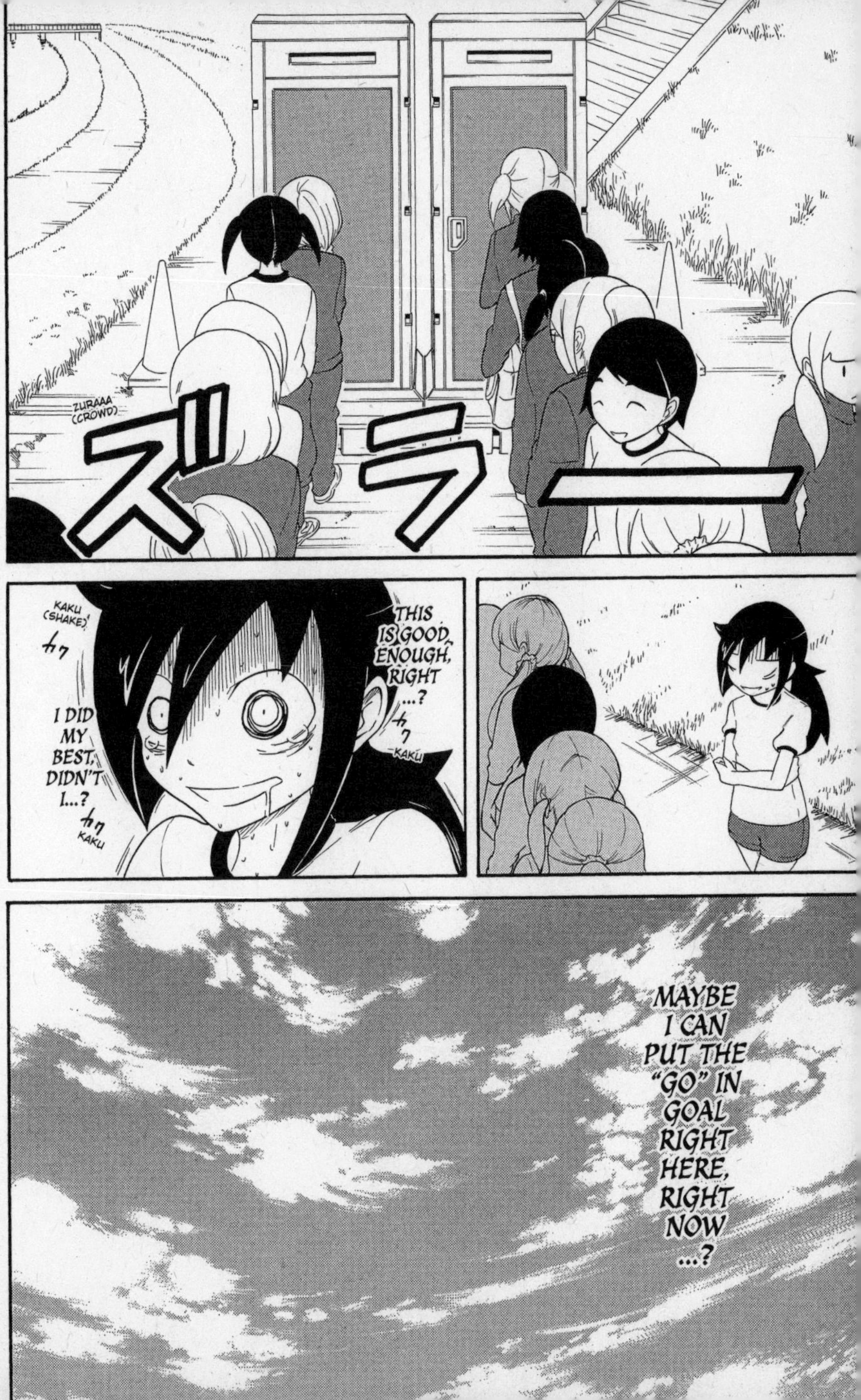
ZURAAA (CROWD)
ズラー
THIS IS GOOD ENOUGH, RIGHT ...?
カク
KAKU
KAKU (SHAKE)
カク
I DID MY BEST, DIDN'T I...?
カク
KAKU
MAYBE I CAN PUT THE "GO" IN GOAL RIGHT HERE, RIGHT NOW ...?

No Matter How I Look at It, It's You Guys' Fault I'm Not Popular!

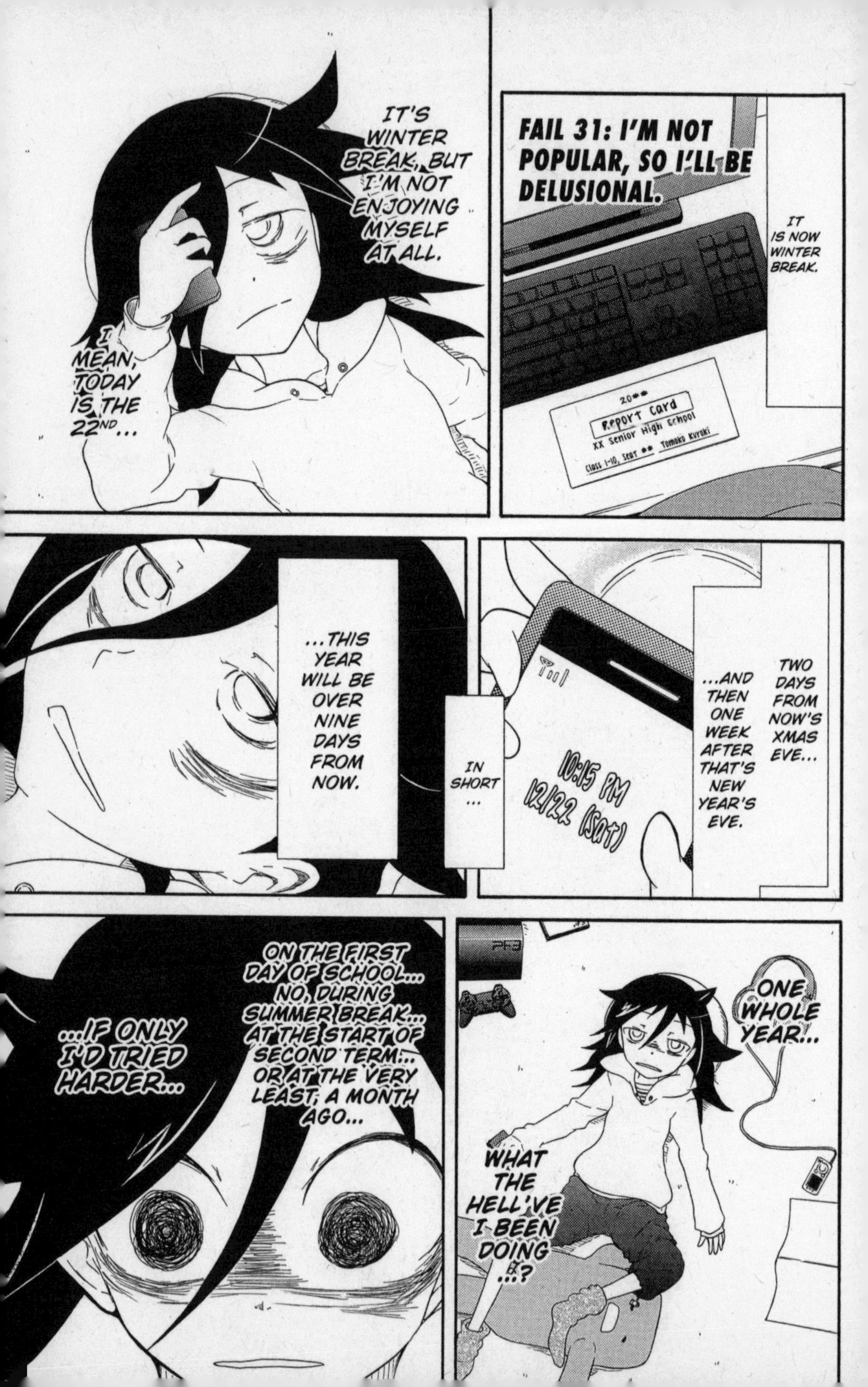
FAIL 31: I'M NOT POPULAR, SO I'LL BE DELUSIONAL.
IT IS NOW WINTER BREAK.
20**
Report Card
XX Senior High School
Class 1-10, Seat ** Tomoko Kuroki
IT'S WINTER BREAK, BUT I'M NOT ENJOYING MYSELF AT ALL.
I MEAN, TODAY IS THE 22ND...
TWO DAYS FROM NOW'S XMAS EVE...
...AND THEN ONE WEEK AFTER THAT'S NEW YEAR'S EVE.
10:15 PM
12/22 (SAT)
IN SHORT...
...THIS YEAR WILL BE OVER NINE DAYS FROM NOW.
ONE WHOLE YEAR...
WHAT THE HELL'VE I BEEN DOING...?
ON THE FIRST DAY OF SCHOOL... NO, DURING SUMMER BREAK... AT THE START OF SECOND TERM... OR AT THE VERY LEAST, A MONTH AGO...
...IF ONLY I'D TRIED HARDER...

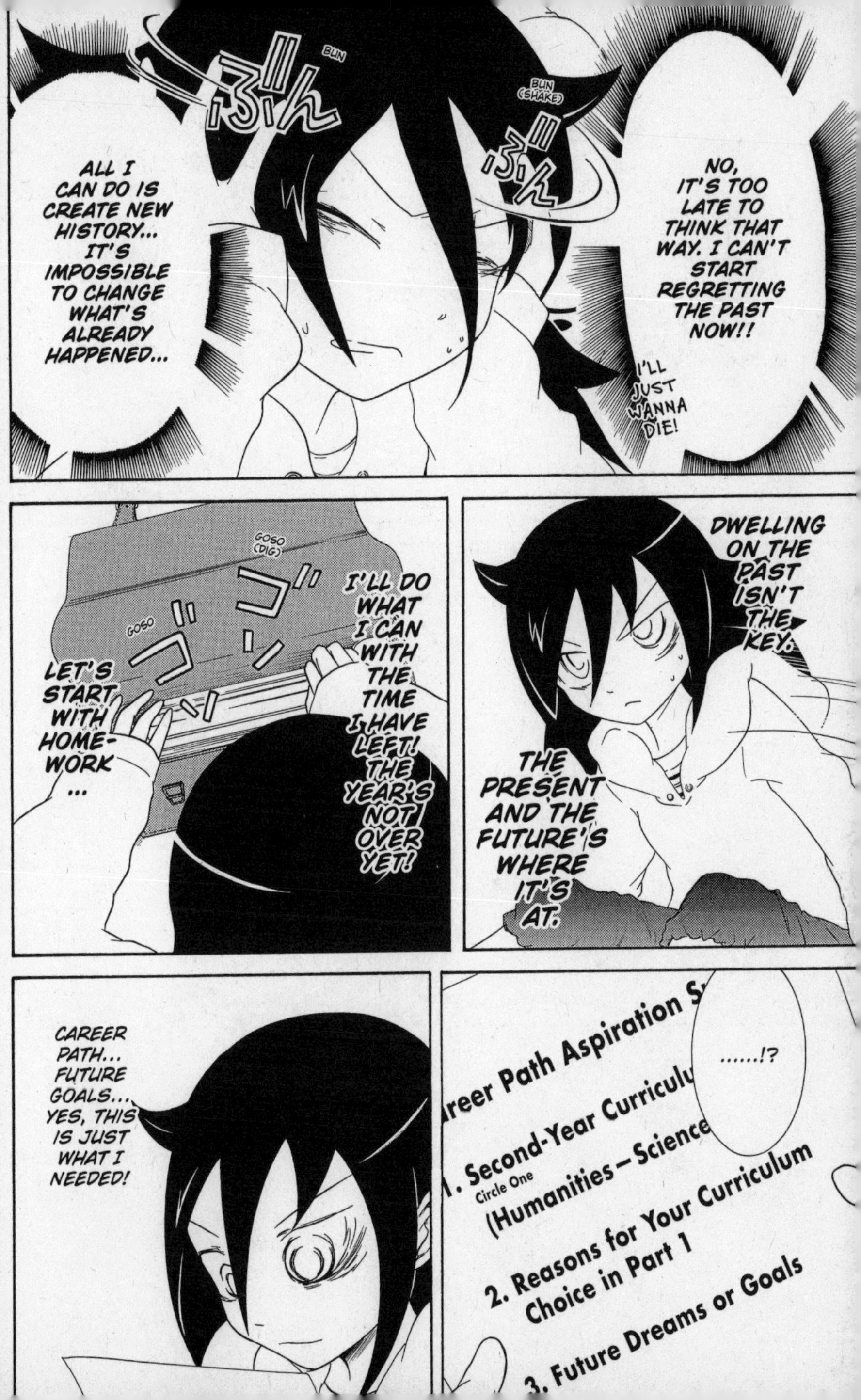
NO, IT'S TOO LATE TO THINK THAT WAY. I CAN'T START REGRETTING THE PAST NOW!!
I'LL JUST WANNA DIE!
BUN (SHAKE)
BUN
ALL I CAN DO IS CREATE NEW HISTORY... IT'S IMPOSSIBLE TO CHANGE WHAT'S ALREADY HAPPENED...
DWELLING ON THE PAST ISN'T THE KEY.
THE PRESENT AND THE FUTURE'S WHERE IT'S AT.
I'LL DO WHAT I CAN WITH THE TIME I HAVE LEFT! THE YEAR'S NOT OVER YET!
GOSO (DIG)
GOSO
LET'S START WITH HOME-WORK...
......!?
areer Path Aspiration S
Second-Year Curriculu
1. Second-
Circle One
(Humanities – Science
2. Reasons for Your Curriculum Choice in Part 1
3. Future Dreams or Goals
CAREER PATH... FUTURE GOALS... YES, THIS IS JUST WHAT I NEEDED!

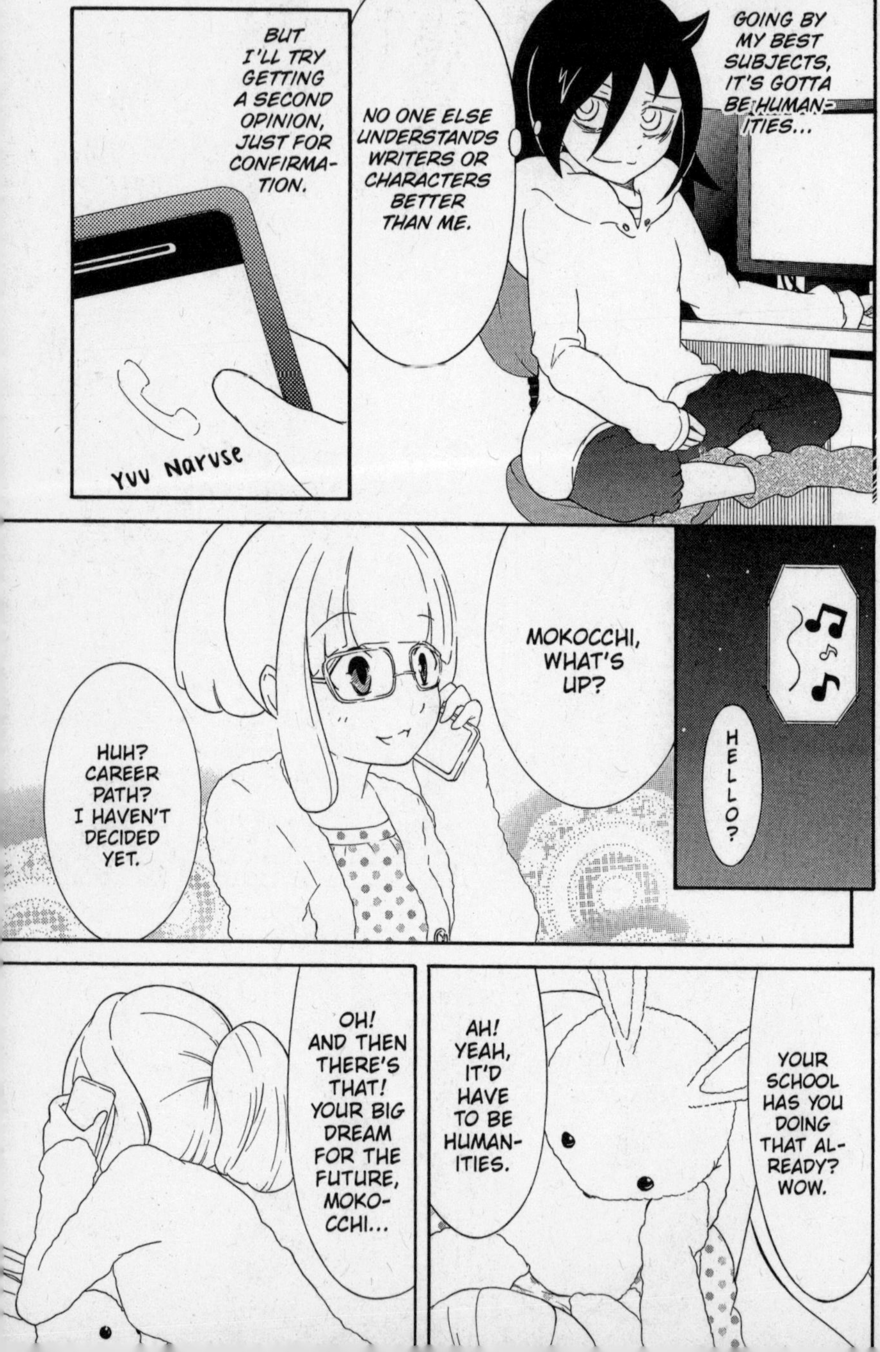
GOING BY MY BEST SUBJECTS, IT'S GOTTA BE HUMANITIES...
NO ONE ELSE UNDERSTANDS WRITERS OR CHARACTERS BETTER THAN ME.
BUT I'LL TRY GETTING A SECOND OPINION, JUST FOR CONFIRMATION.
Yuu Naruse
HELLO?
MOKOCCHI, WHAT'S UP?
HUH? CAREER PATH? I HAVEN'T DECIDED YET.
YOUR SCHOOL HAS YOU DOING THAT ALREADY? WOW.
AH! YEAH, IT'D HAVE TO BE HUMANITIES.
OH! AND THEN THERE'S THAT! YOUR BIG DREAM FOR THE FUTURE, MOKOCCHI...

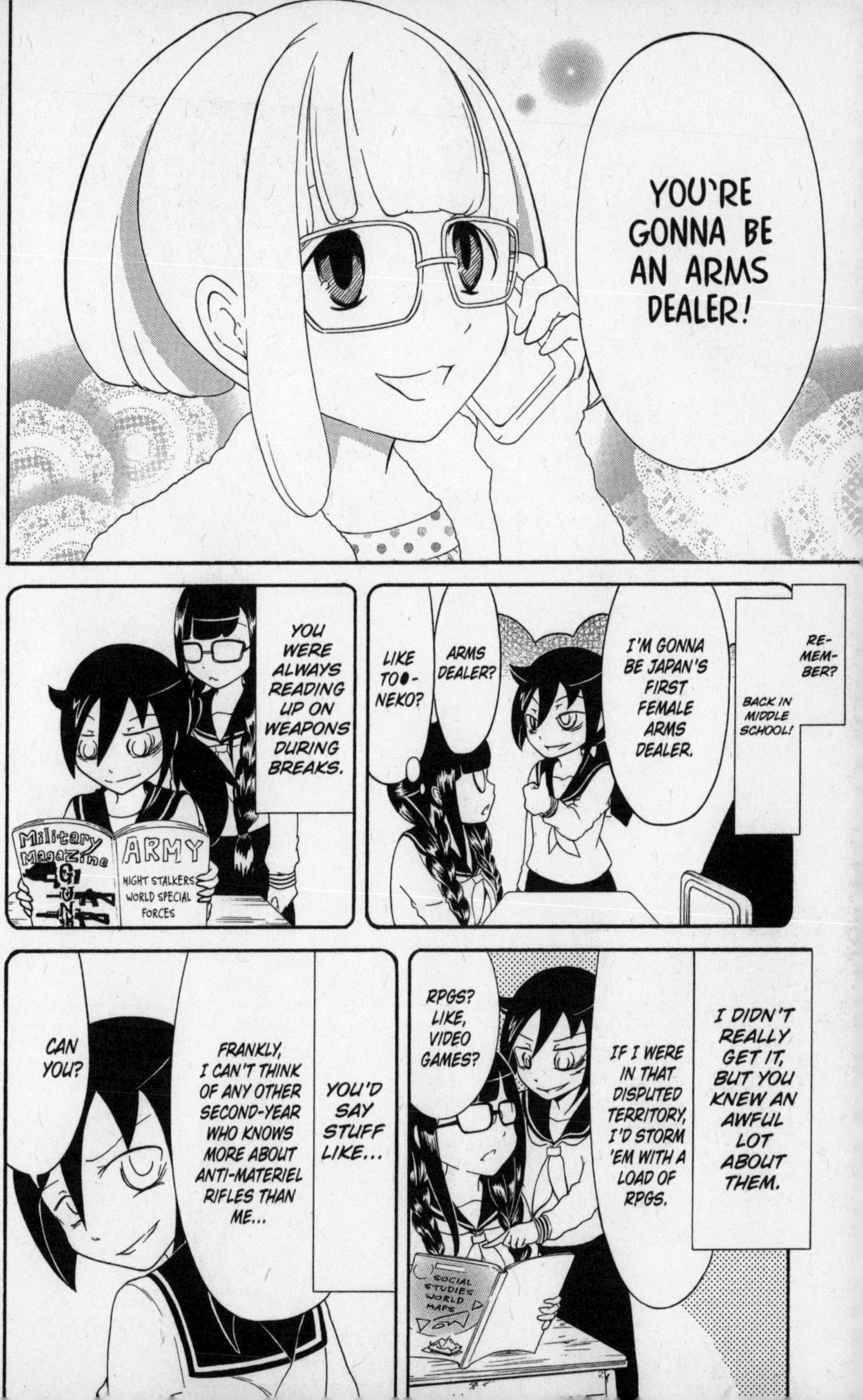
YOU'RE GONNA BE AN ARMS DEALER!
REMEMBER?
BACK IN MIDDLE SCHOOL!
I'M GONNA BE JAPAN'S FIRST FEMALE ARMS DEALER.
ARMS DEALER?
LIKE TO●-NEKO?
YOU WERE ALWAYS READING UP ON WEAPONS DURING BREAKS.
Military Magazine
GUN
ARMY
NIGHT STALKERS
WORLD SPECIAL FORCES
I DIDN'T REALLY GET IT, BUT YOU KNEW AN AWFUL LOT ABOUT THEM.
IF I WERE IN THAT DISPUTED TERRITORY, I'D STORM 'EM WITH A LOAD OF RPGS.
RPGS? LIKE, VIDEO GAMES?
SOCIAL STUDIES WORLD MAPS
YOU'D SAY STUFF LIKE...
FRANKLY, I CAN'T THINK OF ANY OTHER SECOND-YEAR WHO KNOWS MORE ABOUT ANTI-MATERIEL RIFLES THAN ME...
CAN YOU?

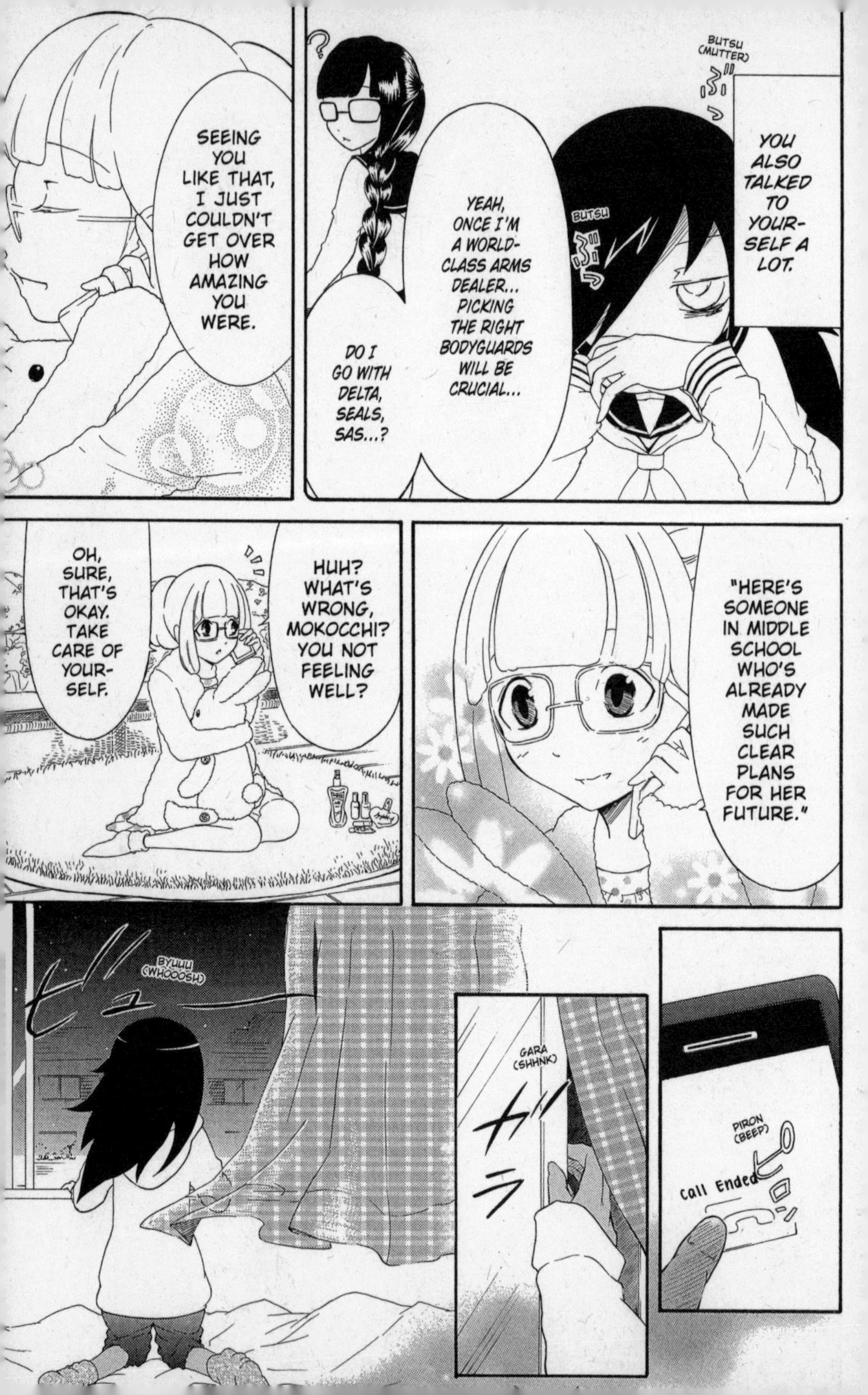
BUTSU (MUTTER)
YOU ALSO TALKED TO YOURSELF A LOT.
BUTSU
YEAH, ONCE I'M A WORLD-CLASS ARMS DEALER... PICKING THE RIGHT BODYGUARDS WILL BE CRUCIAL...
DO I GO WITH DELTA, SEALS, SAS...?
SEEING YOU LIKE THAT, I JUST COULDN'T GET OVER HOW AMAZING YOU WERE.
"HERE'S SOMEONE IN MIDDLE SCHOOL WHO'S ALREADY MADE SUCH CLEAR PLANS FOR HER FUTURE."
HUH? WHAT'S WRONG, MOKOCCHI? YOU NOT FEELING WELL?
OH, SURE, THAT'S OKAY. TAKE CARE OF YOURSELF.
PIRON (BEEP)
Call Ended
GARA (SHHNK)
BYUUU (WHOOOSH)

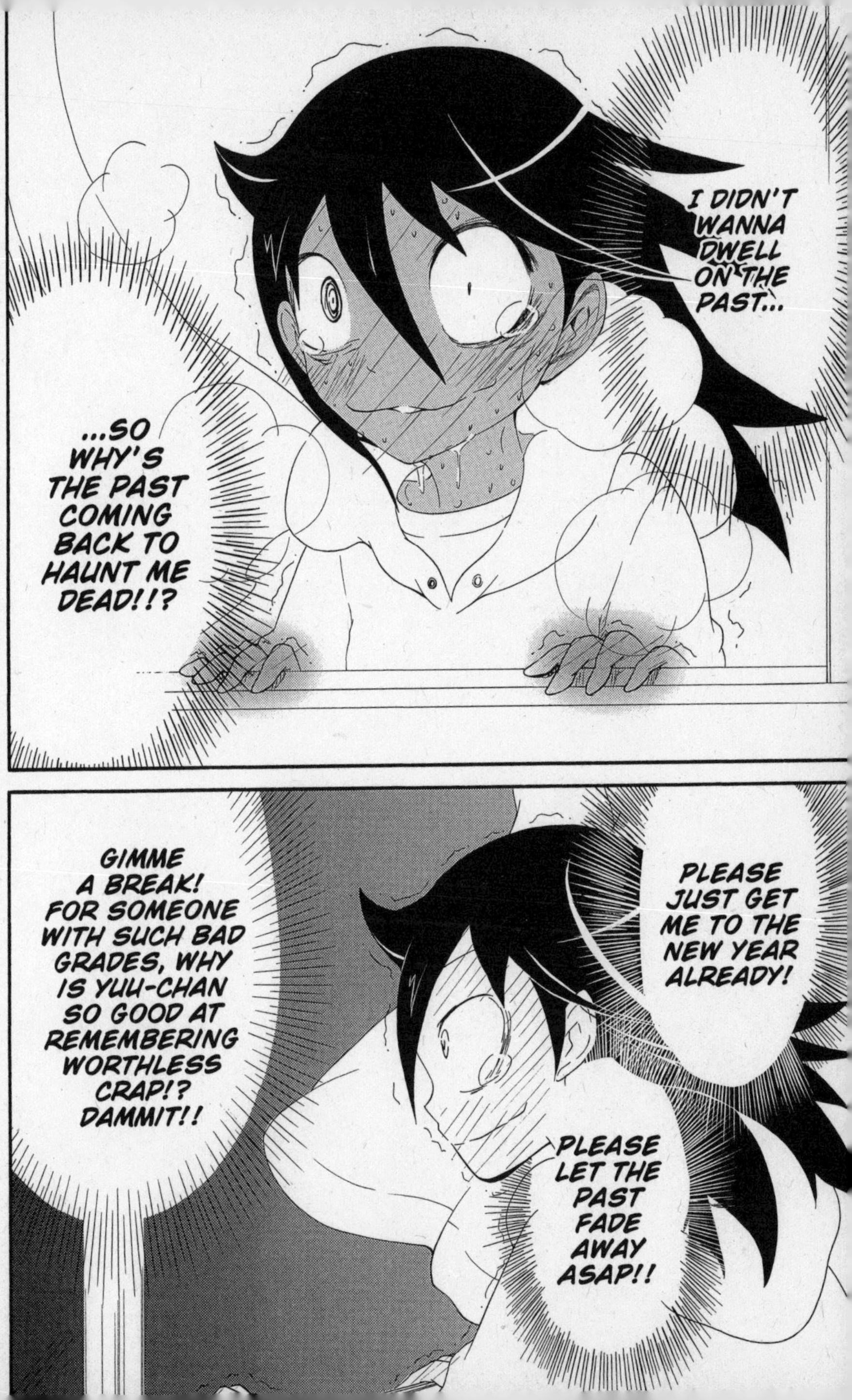
I DIDN'T WANNA DWELL ON THE PAST...
...SO WHY'S THE PAST COMING BACK TO HAUNT ME DEAD!!?
PLEASE JUST GET ME TO THE NEW YEAR ALREADY!
GIMME A BREAK! FOR SOMEONE WITH SUCH BAD GRADES, WHY IS YUU-CHAN SO GOOD AT REMEMBERING WORTHLESS CRAP!? DAMMIT!!
PLEASE LET THE PAST FADE AWAY ASAP!!

No Matter How I Look at It, It's You Guys' Fault I'm Not Popular!

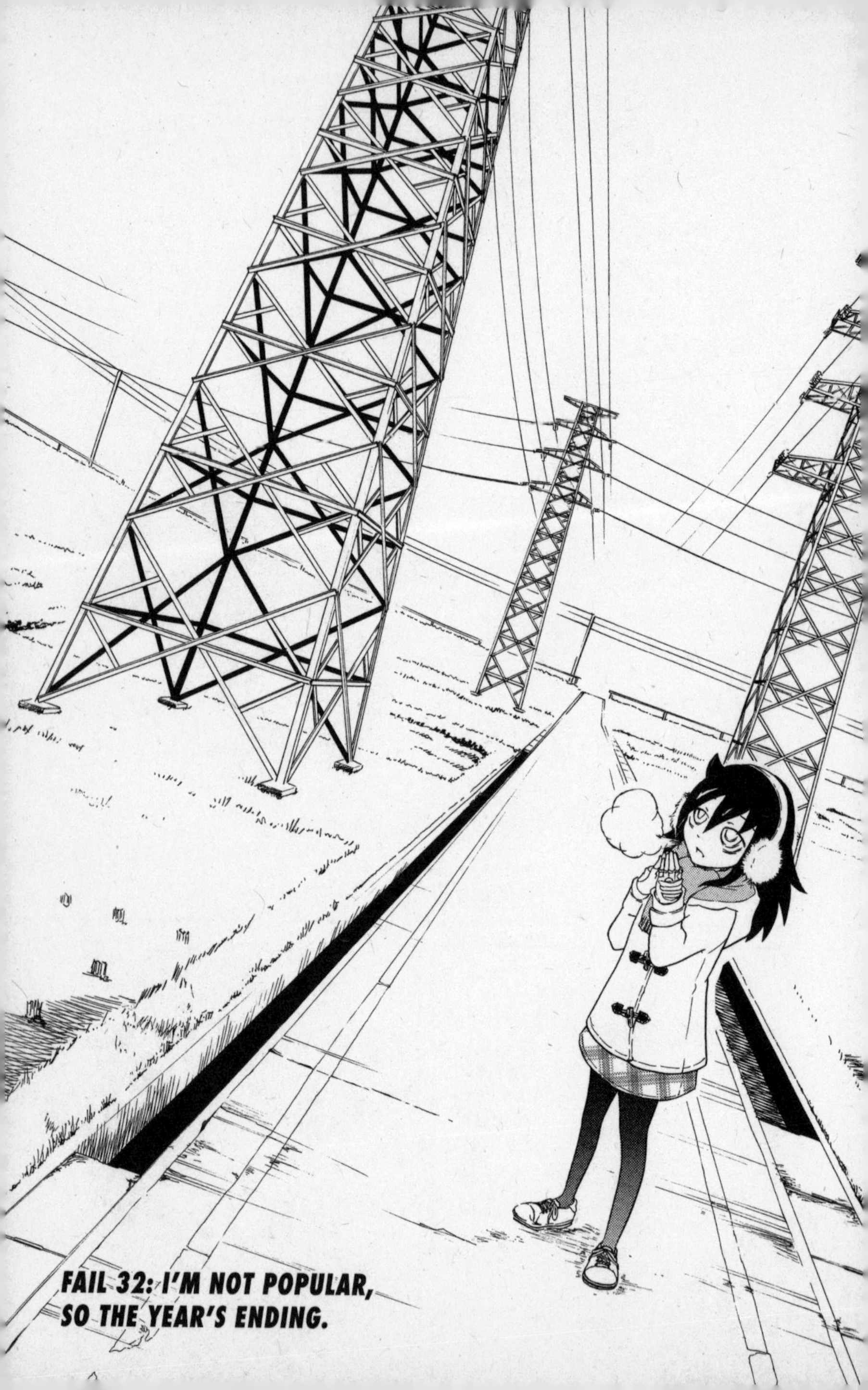
FAIL 32: I'M NOT POPULAR, SO THE YEAR'S ENDING.

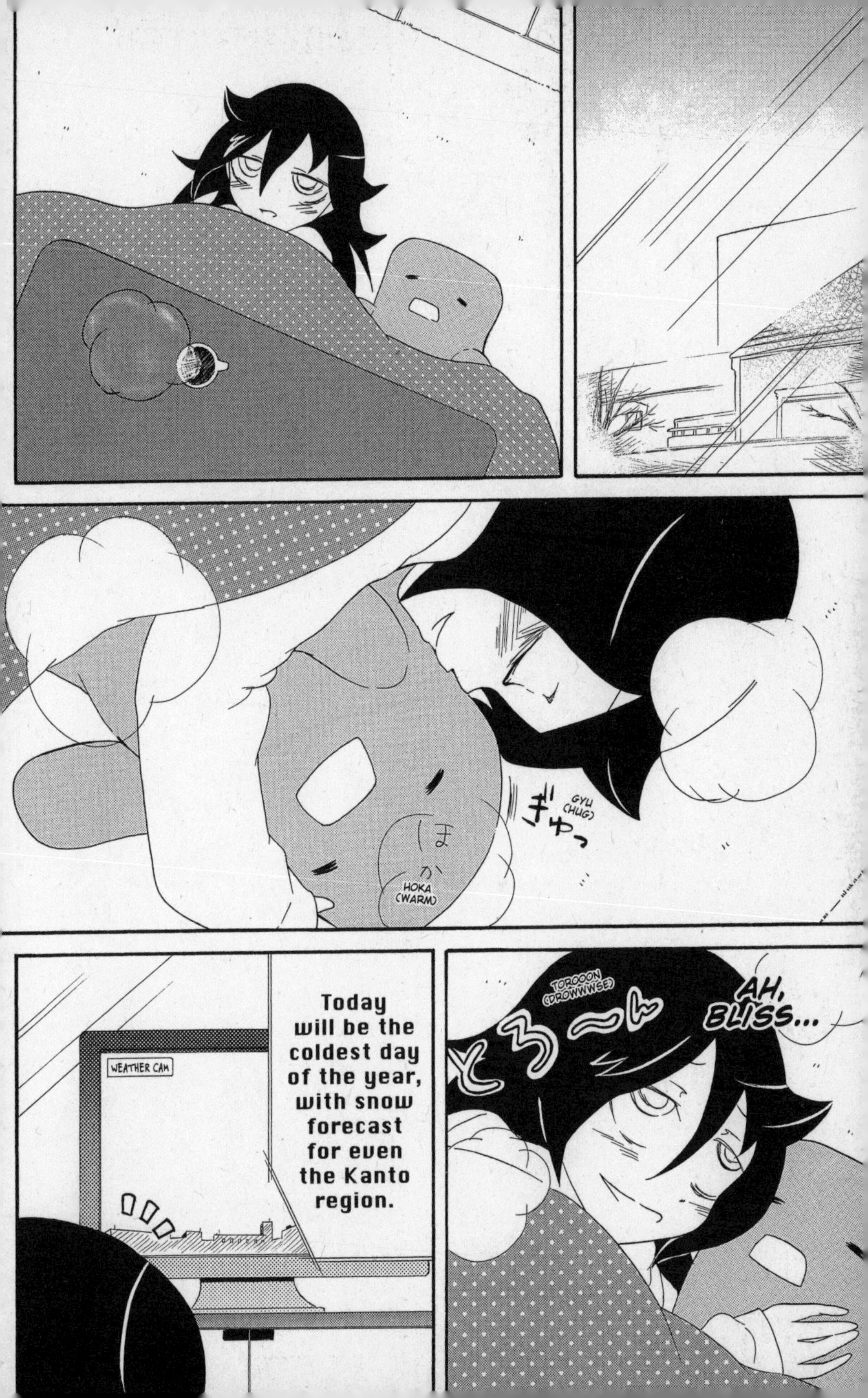
ぎゅっ
GYU (HUG)
ほか
HOKA (WARM)
とろ～ん
TOROOON (DROWWWSE)
AH, BLISS...
Today will be the coldest day of the year, with snow forecast for even the Kanto region.
WEATHER CAM

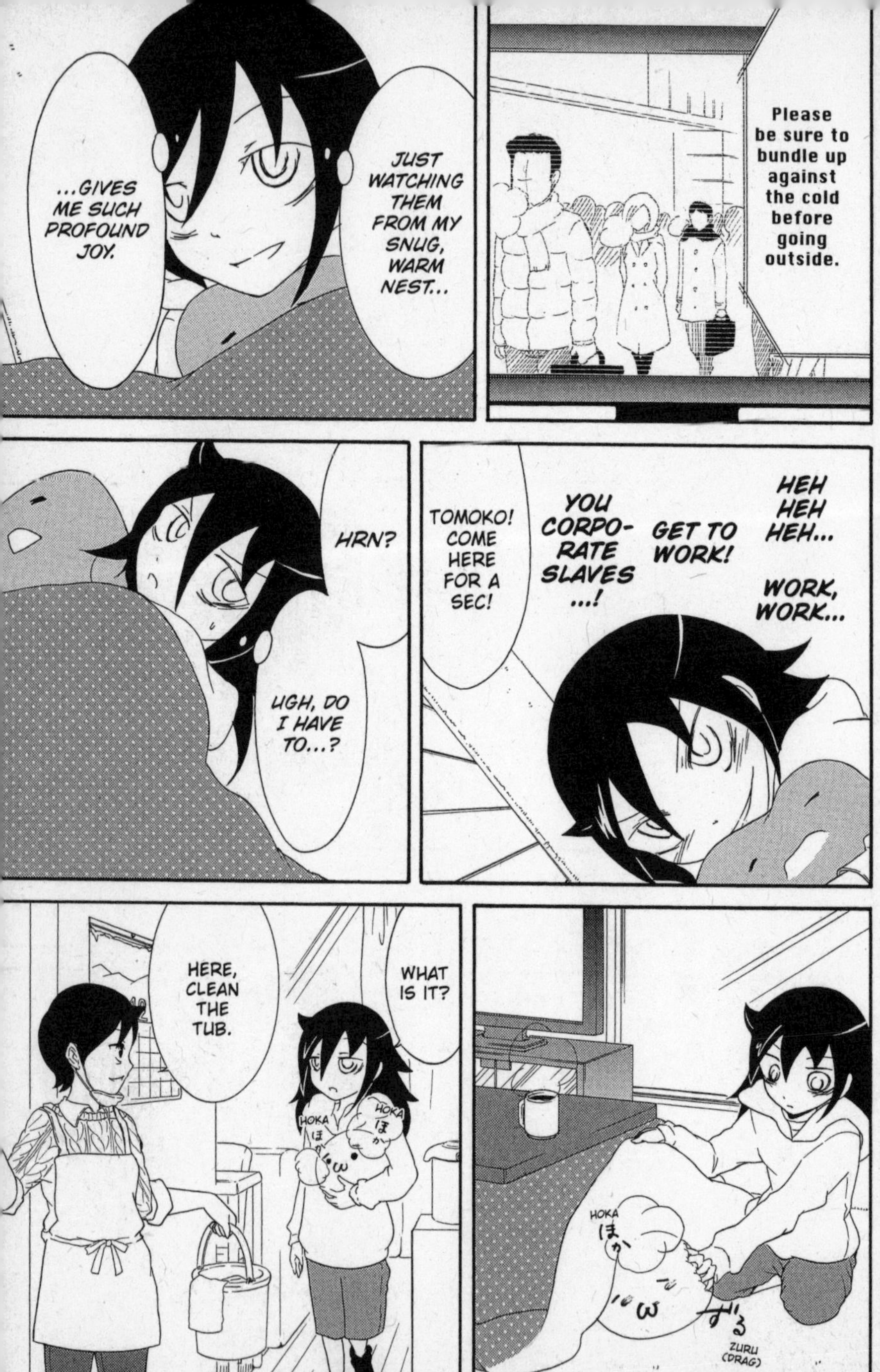

Please be sure to bundle up against the cold before going outside.
JUST WATCHING THEM FROM MY SNUG, WARM NEST...
...GIVES ME SUCH PROFOUND JOY.
HEH HEH HEH...
WORK, WORK...
GET TO WORK!
YOU CORPORATE SLAVES...!
TOMOKO! COME HERE FOR A SEC!
HRN?
UGH, DO I HAVE TO...?
HOKA ほか
ずる ZURU (DRAG)
WHAT IS IT?
HOKA ほか
HOKA ほか
HERE, CLEAN THE TUB.

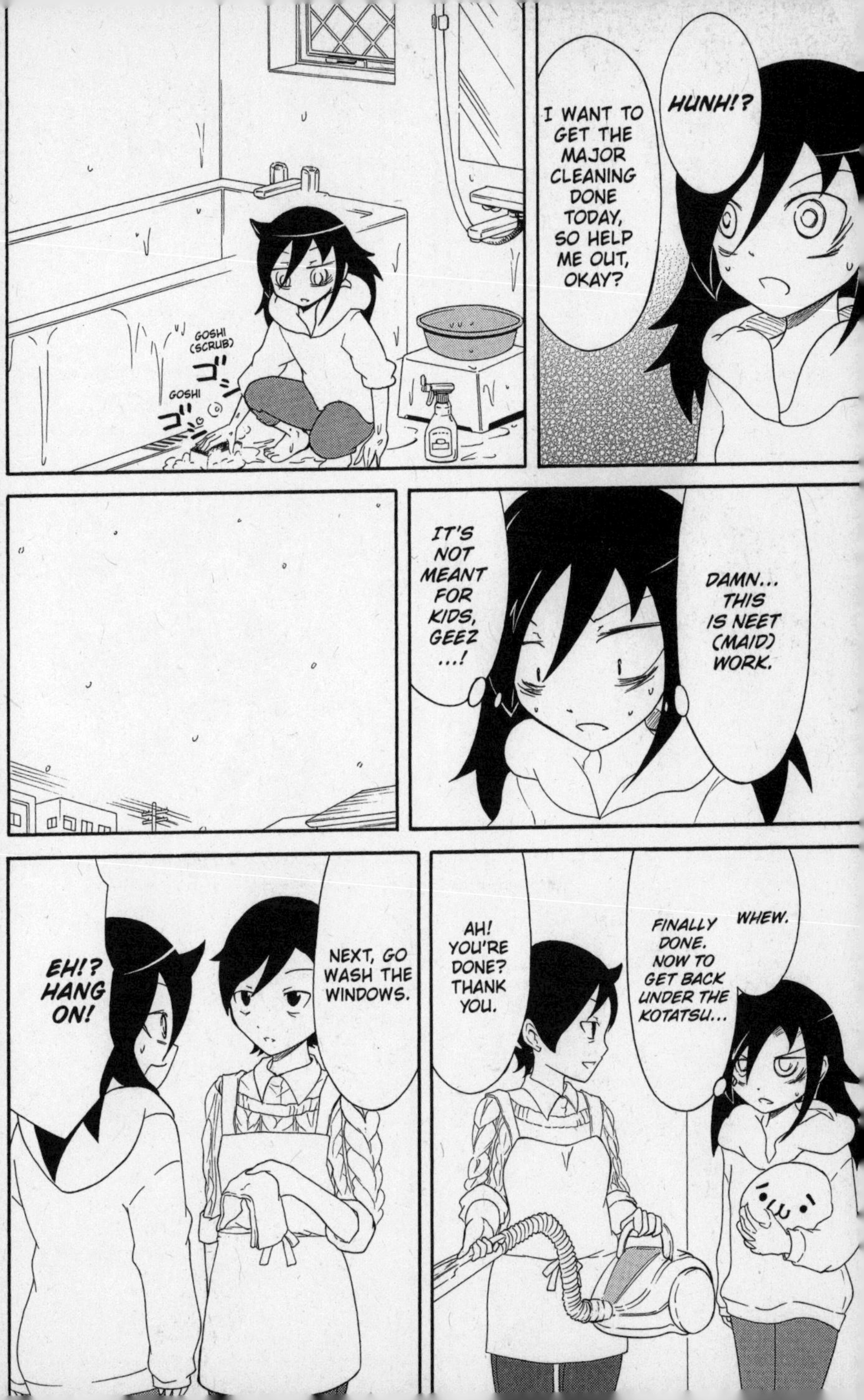

HUNH!?
I WANT TO GET THE MAJOR CLEANING DONE TODAY, SO HELP ME OUT, OKAY?
GOSHI (SCRUB)
ゴシ
GOSHI
ゴシ
DAMN... THIS IS NEET (MAID) WORK.
IT'S NOT MEANT FOR KIDS, GEEZ...!
WHEW.
FINALLY DONE. NOW TO GET BACK UNDER THE KOTATSU...
AH! YOU'RE DONE? THANK YOU.
NEXT, GO WASH THE WINDOWS.
EH!? HANG ON!

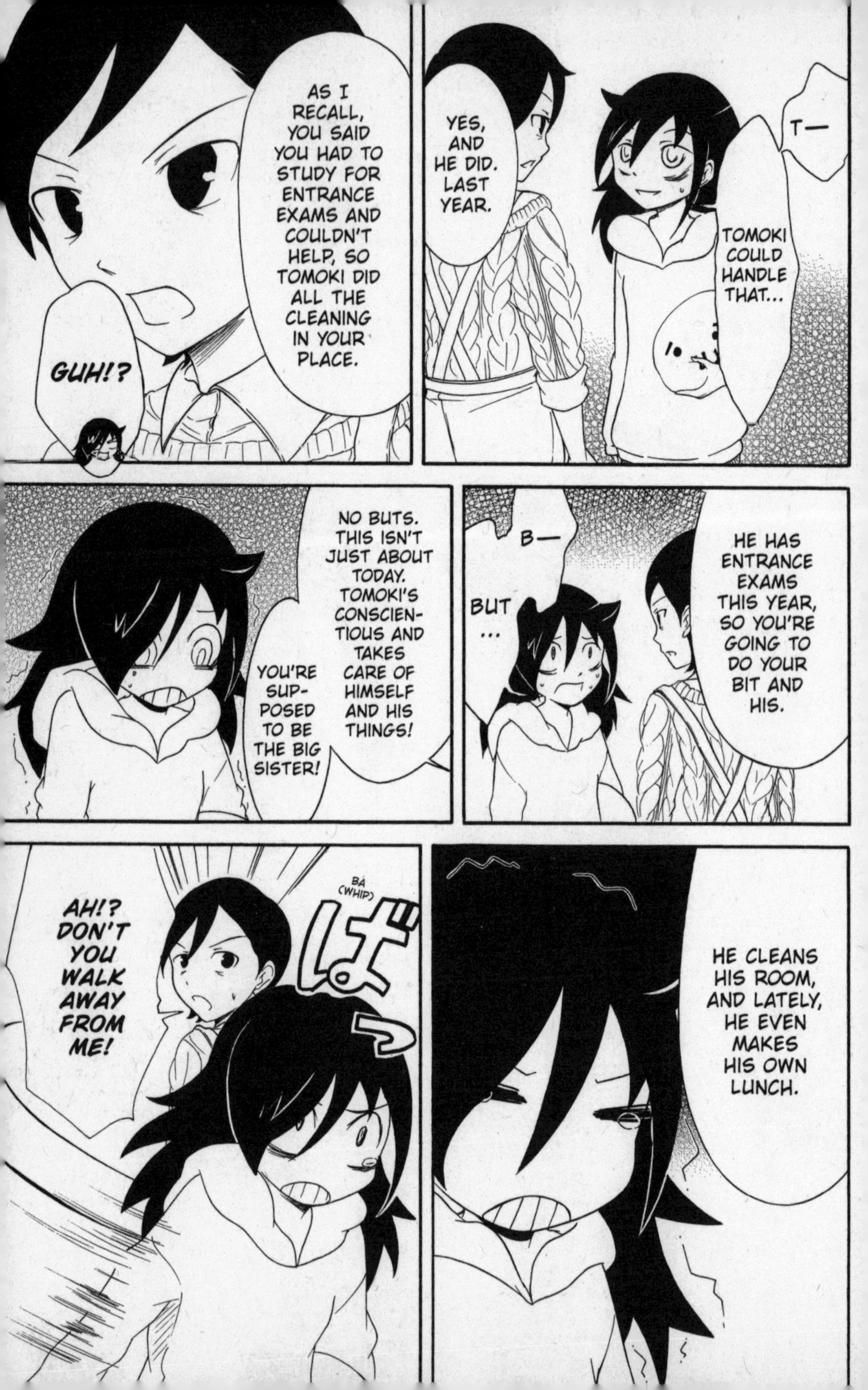
T—
TOMOKI COULD HANDLE THAT...
YES, AND HE DID. LAST YEAR.
AS I RECALL, YOU SAID YOU HAD TO STUDY FOR ENTRANCE EXAMS AND COULDN'T HELP, SO TOMOKI DID ALL THE CLEANING IN YOUR PLACE.
GUH!?
HE HAS ENTRANCE EXAMS THIS YEAR, SO YOU'RE GOING TO DO YOUR BIT AND HIS.
B—
BUT...
NO BUTS. THIS ISN'T JUST ABOUT TODAY. TOMOKI'S CONSCIEN-TIOUS AND TAKES CARE OF HIMSELF AND HIS THINGS!
YOU'RE SUP-POSED TO BE THE BIG SISTER!
HE CLEANS HIS ROOM, AND LATELY, HE EVEN MAKES HIS OWN LUNCH.
BA (WHIP)
ば
AH!? DON'T YOU WALK AWAY FROM ME!

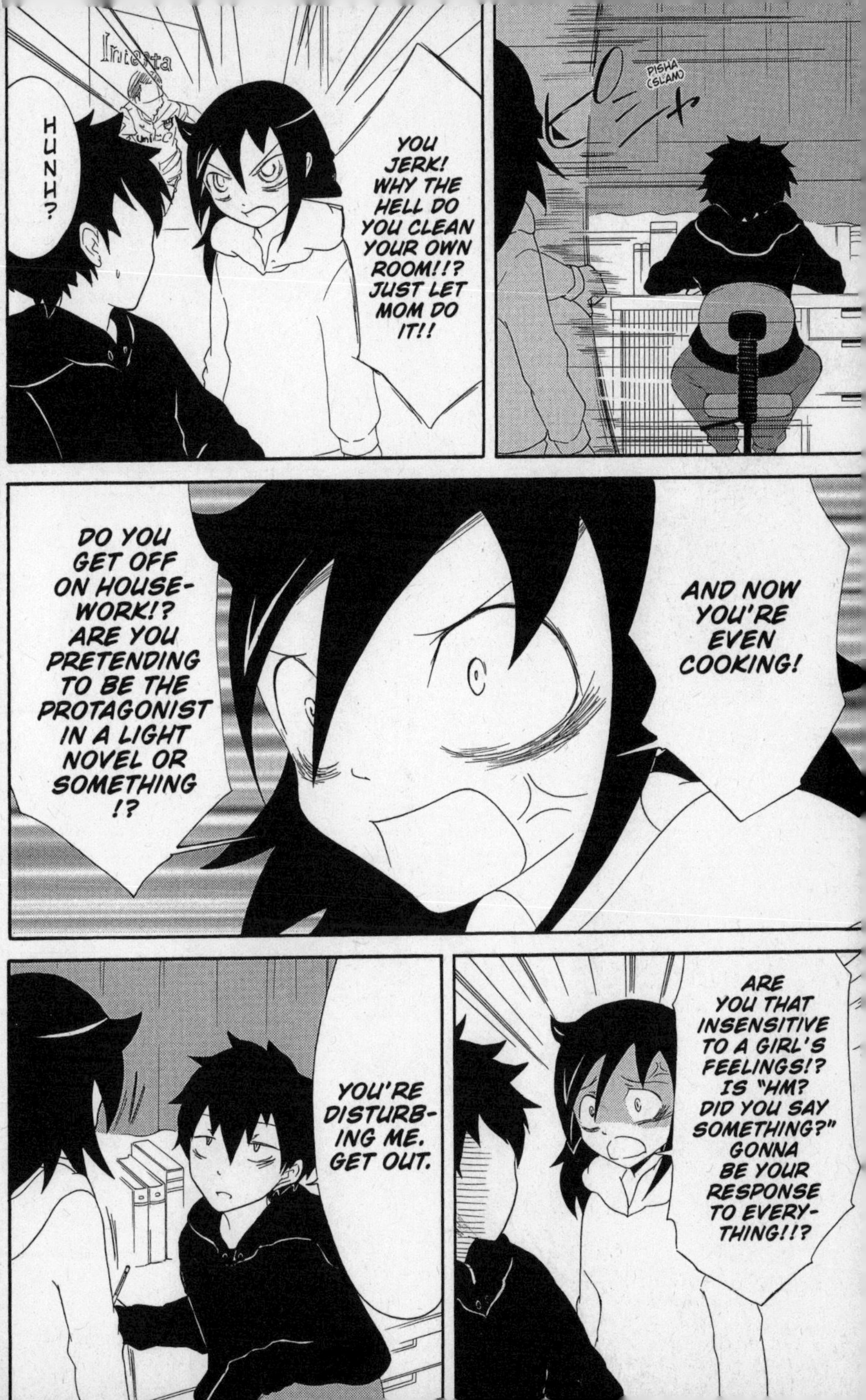
PISHA (SLAM)
YOU JERK! WHY THE HELL DO YOU CLEAN YOUR OWN ROOM!!? JUST LET MOM DO IT!!
HUNH?
AND NOW YOU'RE EVEN COOKING!
DO YOU GET OFF ON HOUSE-WORK!? ARE YOU PRETENDING TO BE THE PROTAGONIST IN A LIGHT NOVEL OR SOMETHING !?
ARE YOU THAT INSENSITIVE TO A GIRL'S FEELINGS!? IS "HM? DID YOU SAY SOMETHING?" GONNA BE YOUR RESPONSE TO EVERY-THING!!?
YOU'RE DISTURB-ING ME. GET OUT.

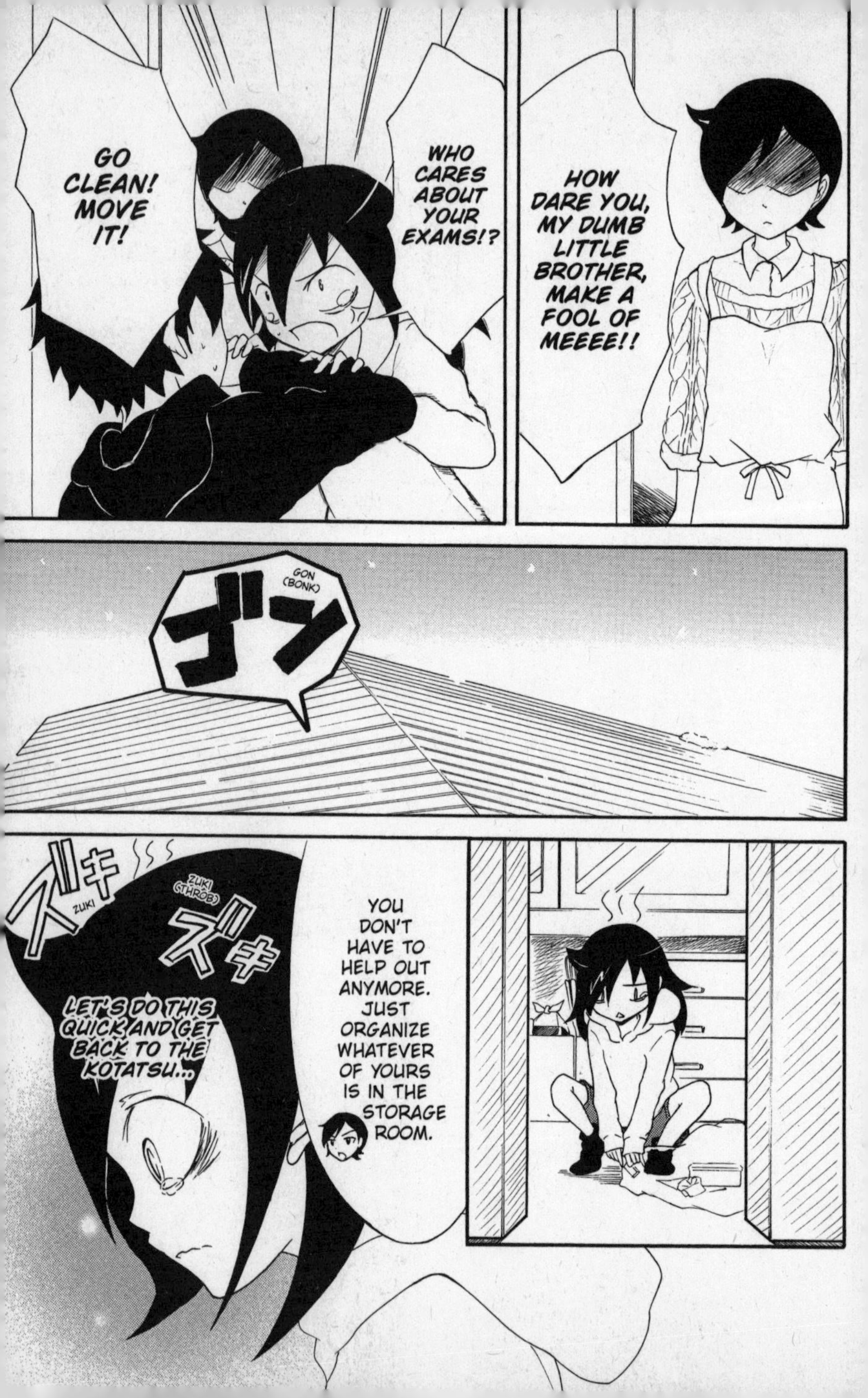
HOW DARE YOU, MY DUMB LITTLE BROTHER, MAKE A FOOL OF MEEEE!!
WHO CARES ABOUT YOUR EXAMS!?
GO CLEAN! MOVE IT!
ゴン
GON (BONK)
YOU DON'T HAVE TO HELP OUT ANYMORE. JUST ORGANIZE WHATEVER OF YOURS IS IN THE STORAGE ROOM.
ズキ
ZUKI (THROB)
ズキ
ZUKI
LET'S DO THIS QUICK AND GET BACK TO THE KOTATSU...

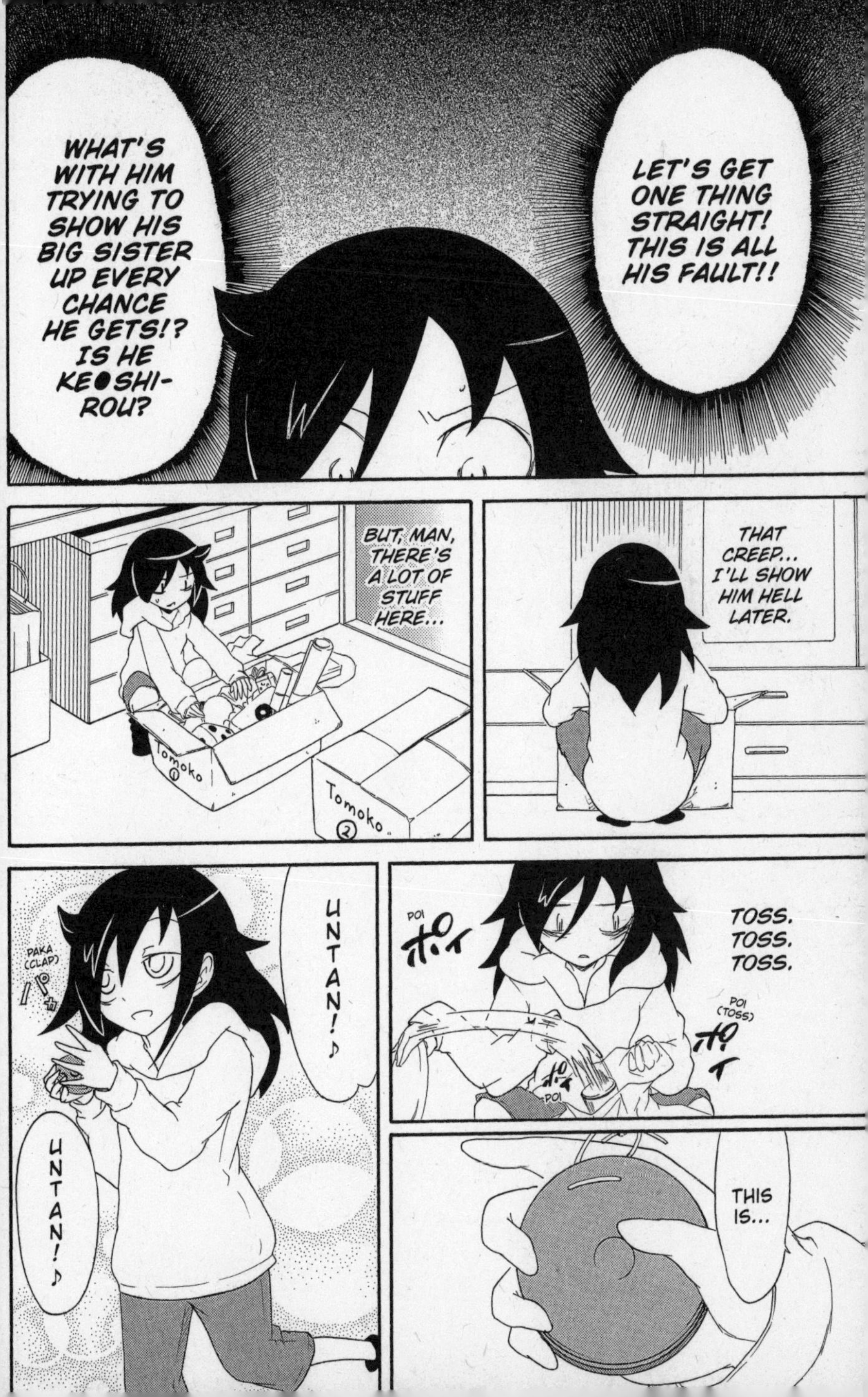
LET'S GET ONE THING STRAIGHT! THIS IS ALL HIS FAULT!!
WHAT'S WITH HIM TRYING TO SHOW HIS BIG SISTER UP EVERY CHANCE HE GETS!? IS HE KE●SHIROU?
THAT CREEP... I'LL SHOW HIM HELL LATER.
BUT, MAN, THERE'S A LOT OF STUFF HERE...
Tomoko ①
Tomoko ②
POI
ポイ
TOSS. TOSS. TOSS.
POI (TOSS)
ポイ
ポイ
POI
THIS IS...
UNTAN!♪
PAKA (CLAP)
パカ
UNTAN!♪

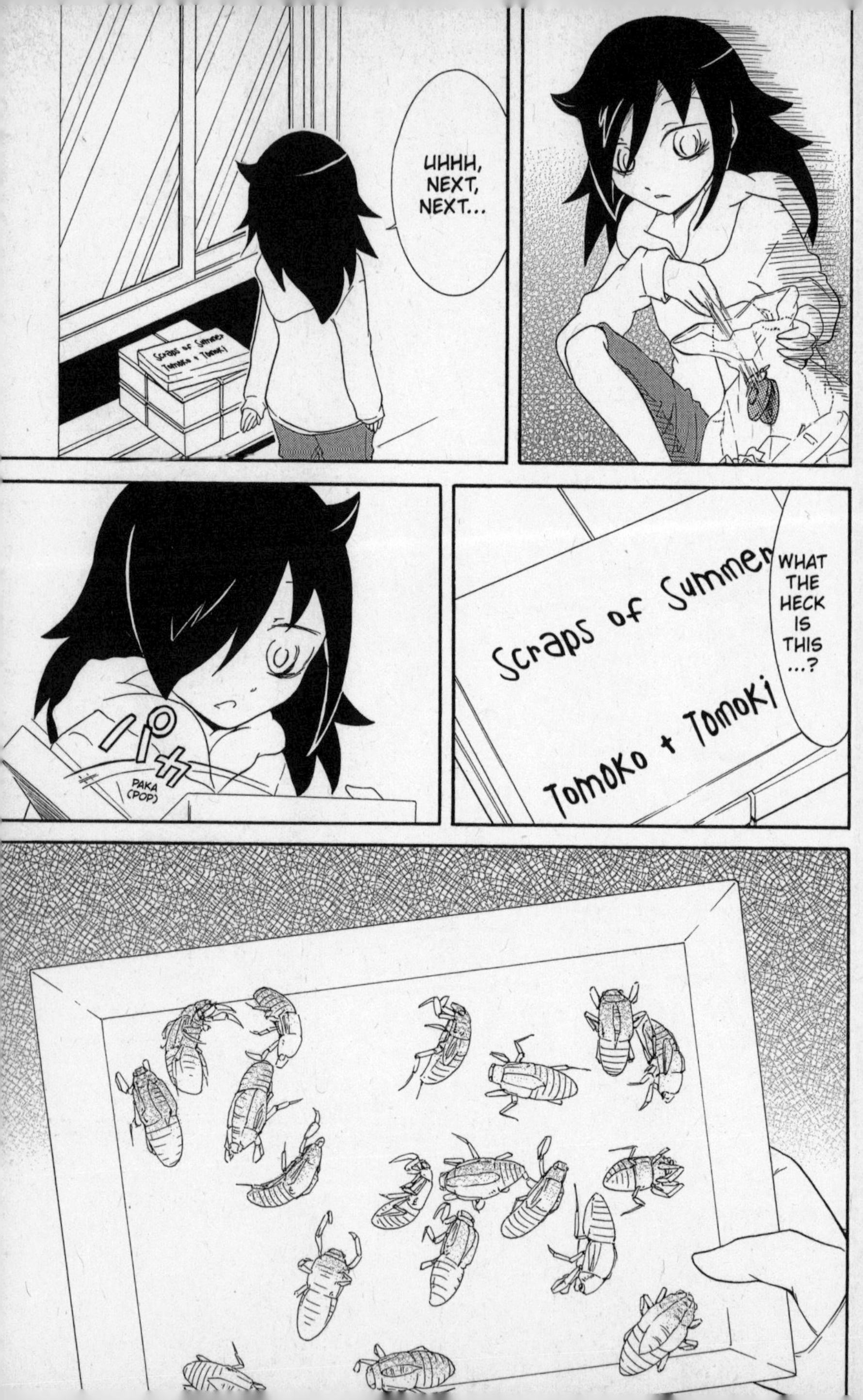
UHHH, NEXT, NEXT...
Scraps of Summer
Tomoko + Tomoki
WHAT THE HECK IS THIS ...?
Scraps of Summer
Tomoko + Tomoki
PAKA (POP)

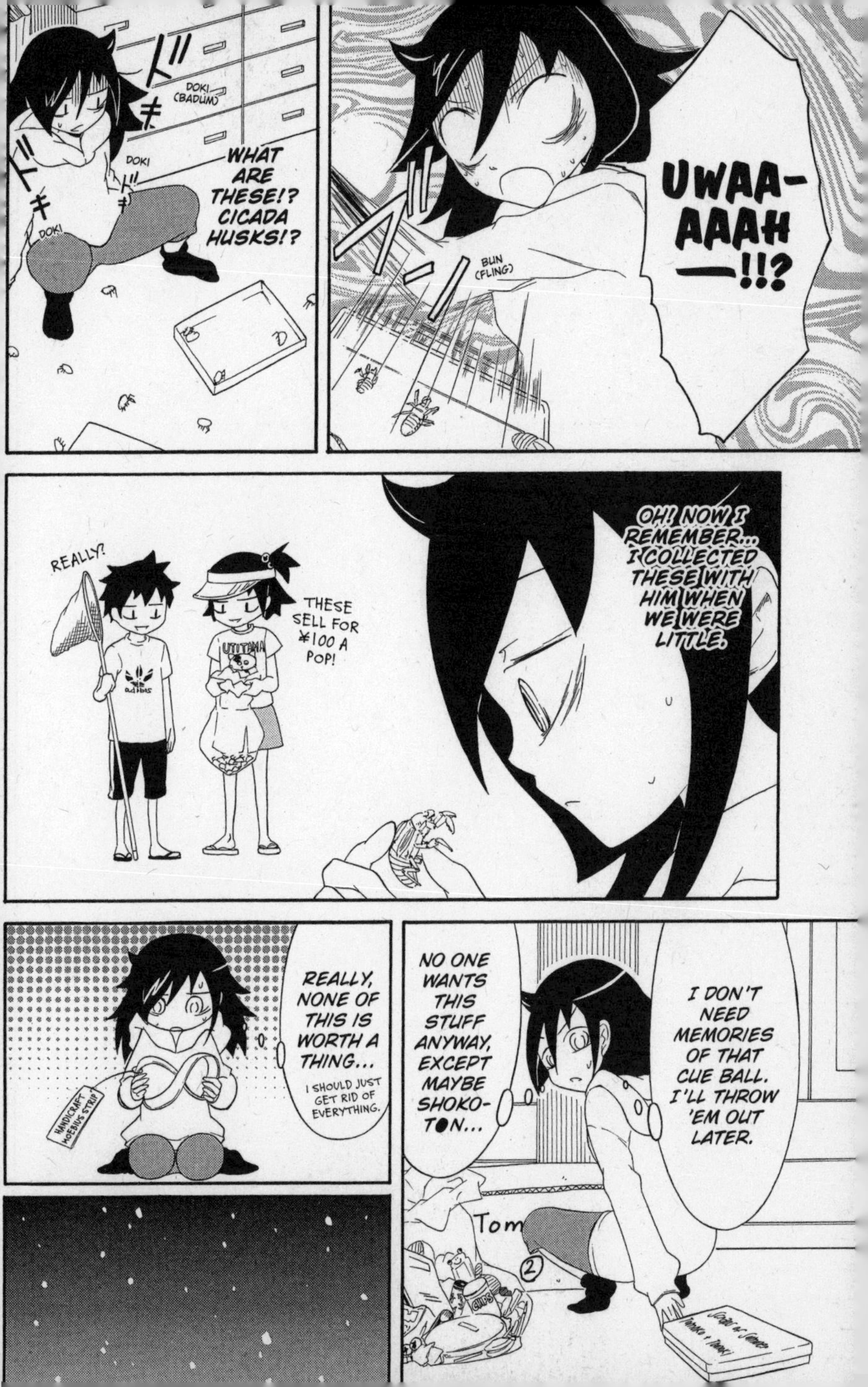
UWAA-AAAH—!!?
BUN (FLING)
DOKI (BADUM)
DOKI
DOKI
WHAT ARE THESE!? CICADA HUSKS!?
OH! NOW I REMEMBER... I COLLECTED THESE WITH HIM WHEN WE WERE LITTLE.
THESE SELL FOR ¥100 A POP!
REALLY?
UTITAMA
I DON'T NEED MEMORIES OF THAT CUE BALL. I'LL THROW 'EM OUT LATER.
NO ONE WANTS THIS STUFF ANYWAY, EXCEPT MAYBE SHOKO-TON...
Tom
CHIPS
REALLY, NONE OF THIS IS WORTH A THING...
I SHOULD JUST GET RID OF EVERYTHING.
HANDICRAFT MOEBIUS STRIP

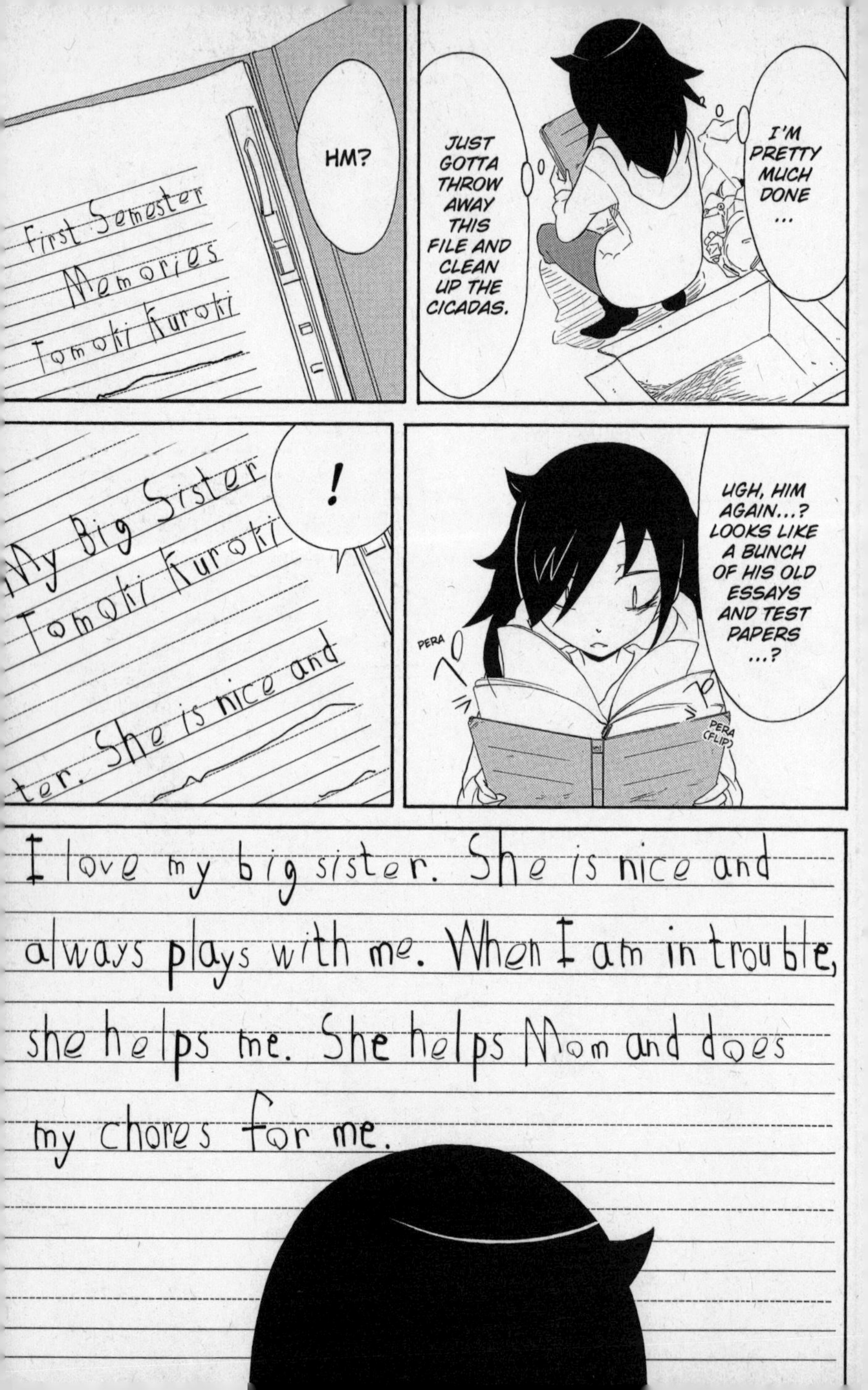
I'M PRETTY MUCH DONE ...
JUST GOTTA THROW AWAY THIS FILE AND CLEAN UP THE CICADAS.
HM?
First Semester Memories
Tomoki Kuroki
UGH, HIM AGAIN...? LOOKS LIKE A BUNCH OF HIS OLD ESSAYS AND TEST PAPERS ...?
PERA (FLIP)
PERA
!
My Big Sister
Tomoki Kuroki
ter. She is nice and
I love my big sister. She is nice and always plays with me. When I am in trouble, she helps me. She helps Mom and does my chores for me.

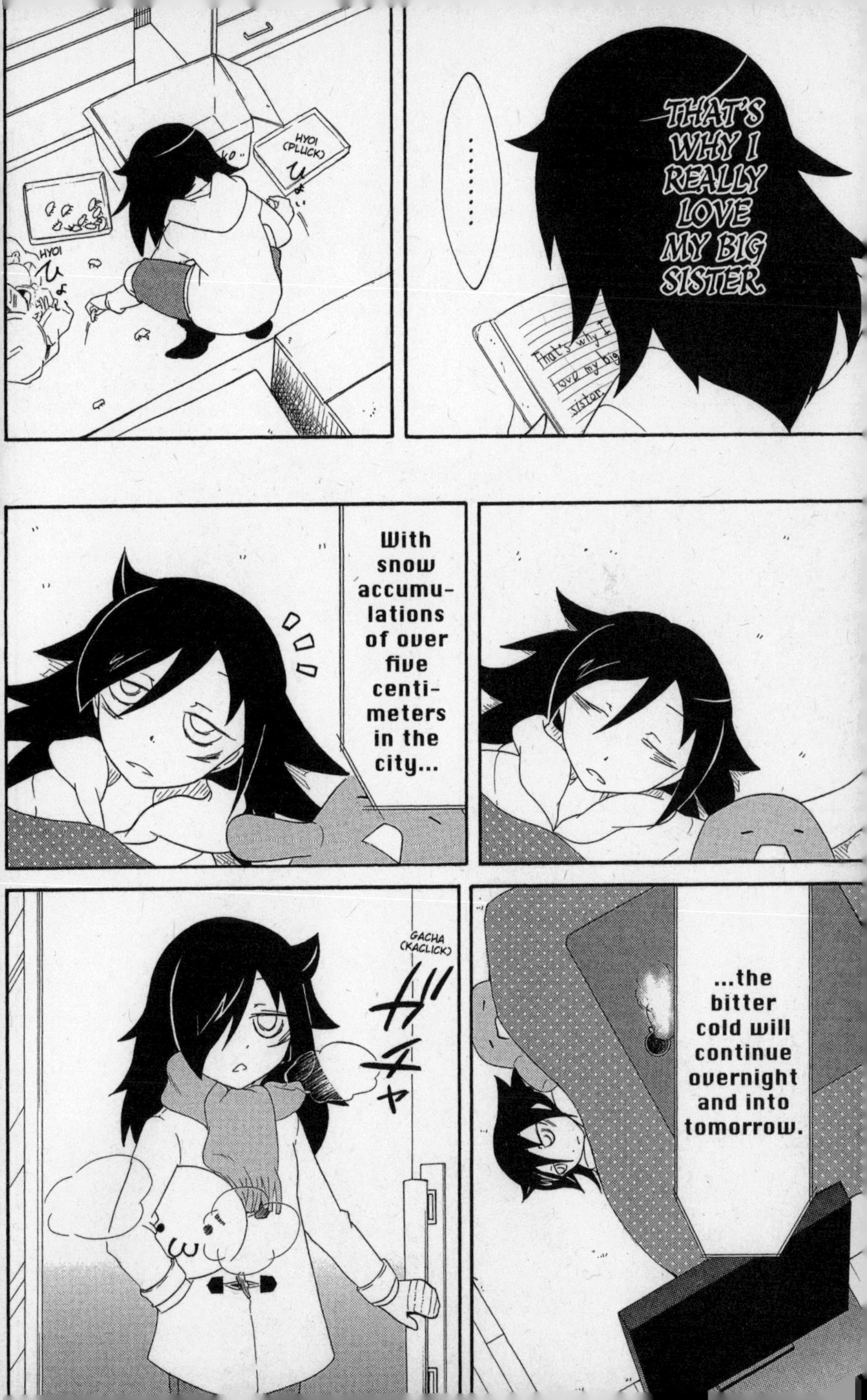
THAT'S WHY I REALLY LOVE MY BIG SISTER
That's why I love my big sister.
......
HYOI (PLUCK)
HYOI
With snow accumulations of over five centimeters in the city...
...the bitter cold will continue overnight and into tomorrow.
GACHA (KACLICK)

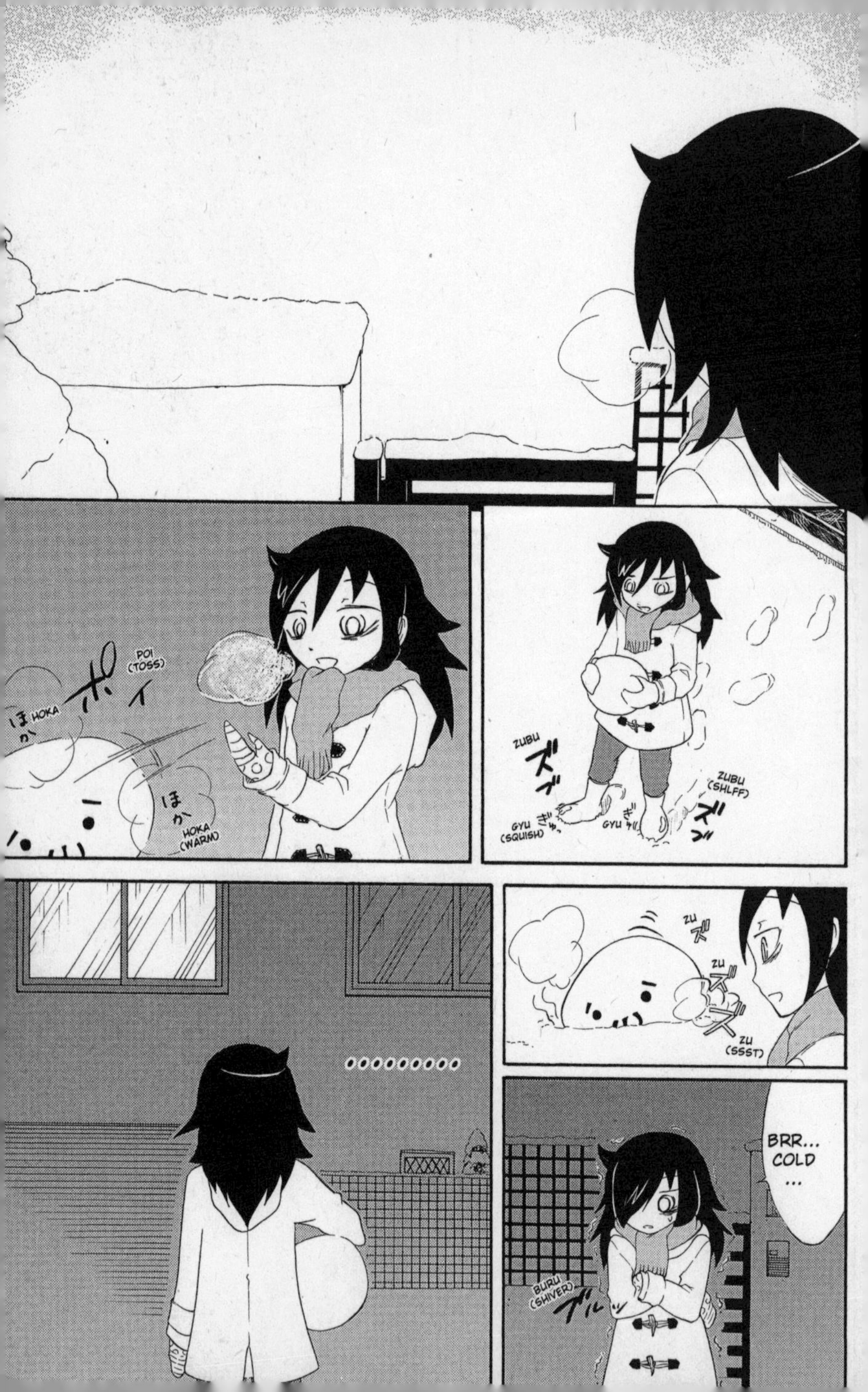
ZUBU
ズブ
ZUBU (SHLFF)
ズブ
GYU (SQUISH)
ぎゅ
GYU
ぎゅ
POI (TOSS)
ポイ
ほか HOKA
ほか
HOKA (WARM)
ZU
ズ
ZU
ズ
ズ
ZU (SSST)
BRR... COLD ...
BURU (SHIVER)
ブルッ
OOOOOOOOO

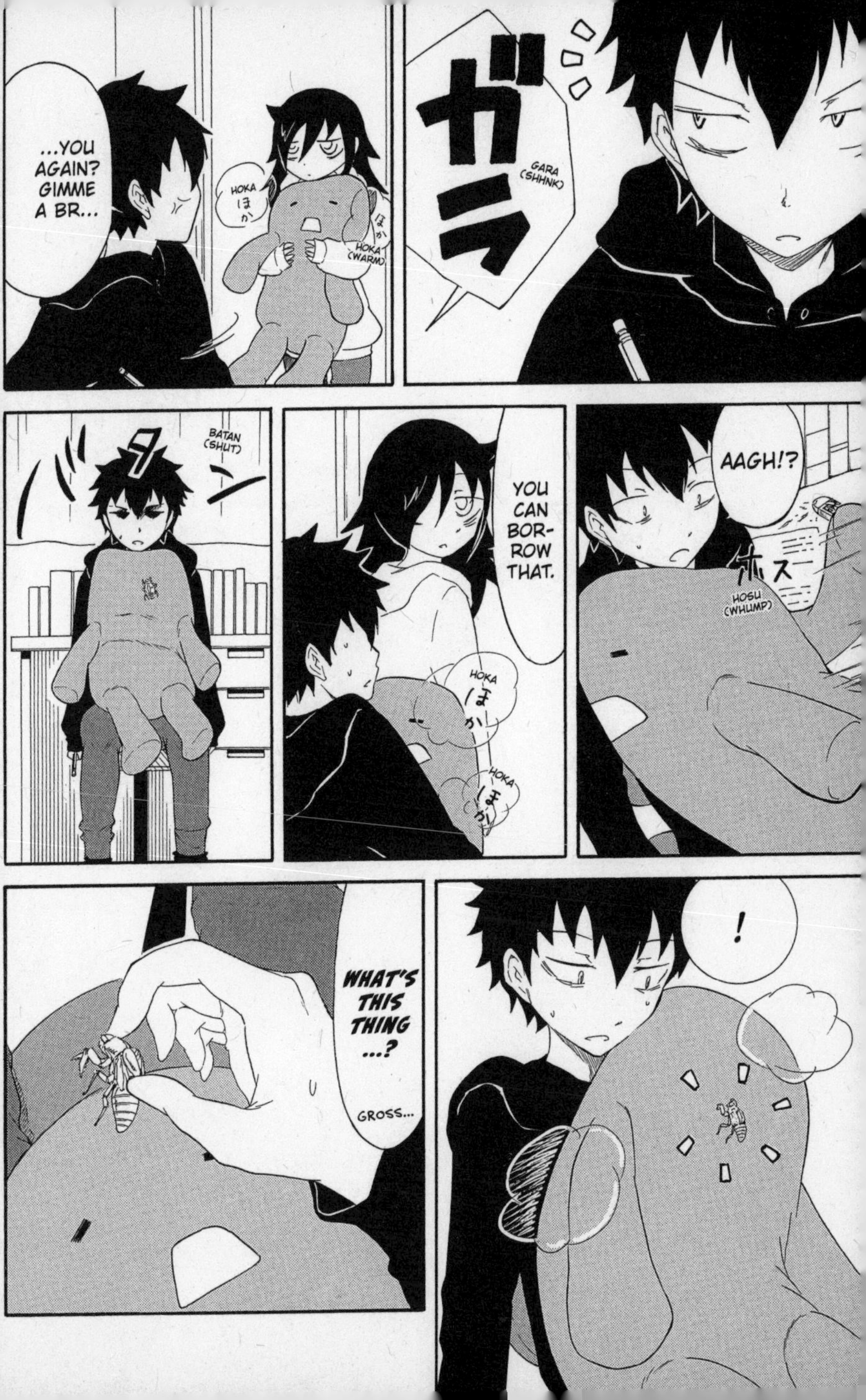
ガラ
GARA (SHHNK)
...YOU AGAIN? GIMME A BR...
HOKA ほか
ほか HOKA (WARM)
AAGH!?
ホス
HOSU (WHUMP)
YOU CAN BORROW THAT.
HOKA ほか
HOKA ほか
BATAN (SHUT)
!
WHAT'S THIS THING ...?
GROSS...

No Matter How I Look at It, It's You Guys' Fault I'm Not Popular!

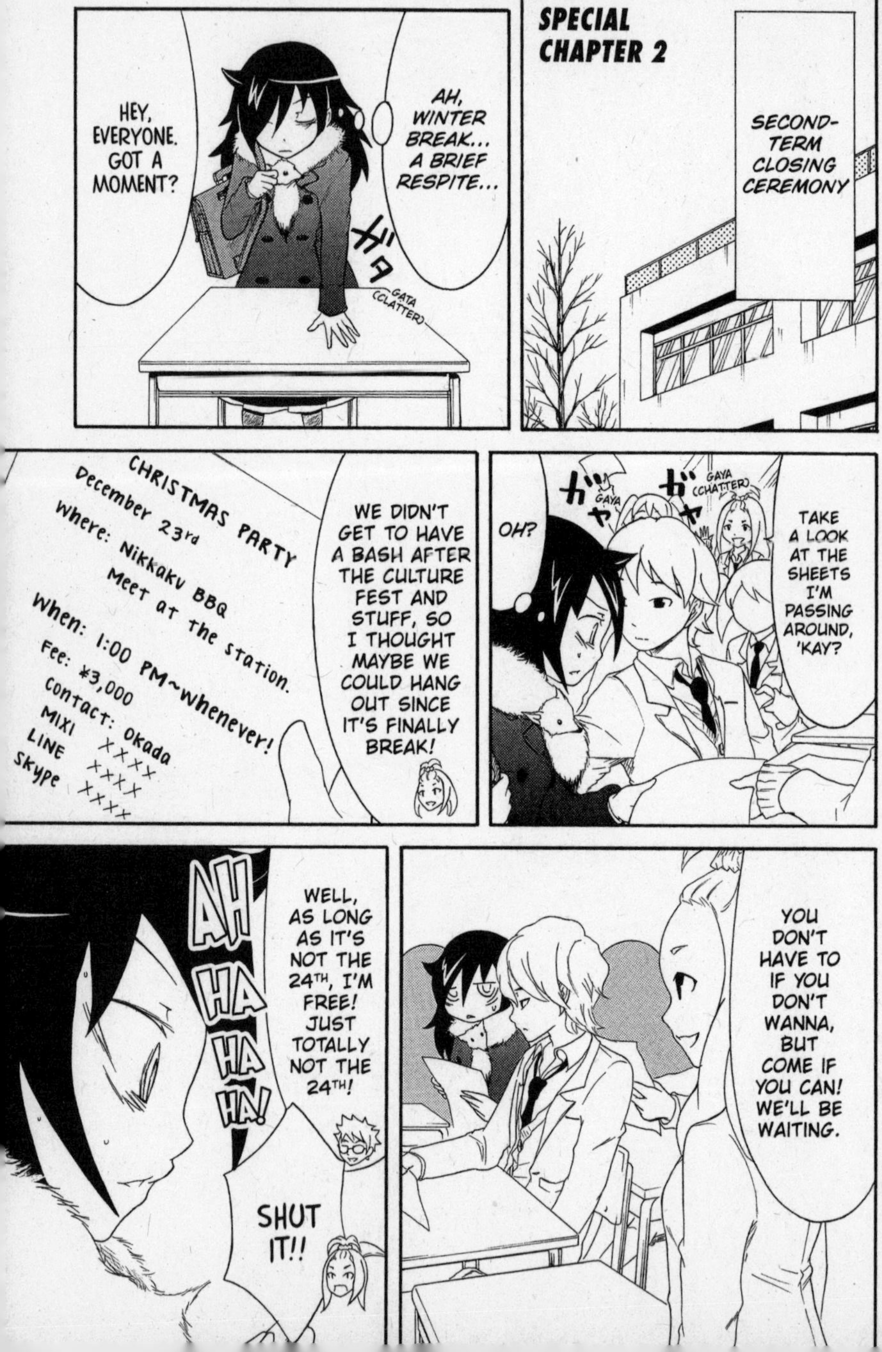
SPECIAL CHAPTER 2
SECOND-TERM CLOSING CEREMONY
AH, WINTER BREAK... A BRIEF RESPITE...
GATA (CLATTER)
HEY, EVERYONE. GOT A MOMENT?
GAYA (CHATTER)
GAYA
OH?
TAKE A LOOK AT THE SHEETS I'M PASSING AROUND, 'KAY?
WE DIDN'T GET TO HAVE A BASH AFTER THE CULTURE FEST AND STUFF, SO I THOUGHT MAYBE WE COULD HANG OUT SINCE IT'S FINALLY BREAK!
CHRISTMAS PARTY
December 23rd
Where: Nikkaku BBQ
Meet at the station.
When: 1:00 PM~whenever!
Fee: ¥3,000
Contact: Okada
MIXI XXXX
LINE XXXX
Skype XXXX
YOU DON'T HAVE TO IF YOU DON'T WANNA, BUT COME IF YOU CAN! WE'LL BE WAITING.
WELL, AS LONG AS IT'S NOT THE 24TH, I'M FREE! JUST TOTALLY NOT THE 24TH!
AH HA HA HA HA!
SHUT IT!!

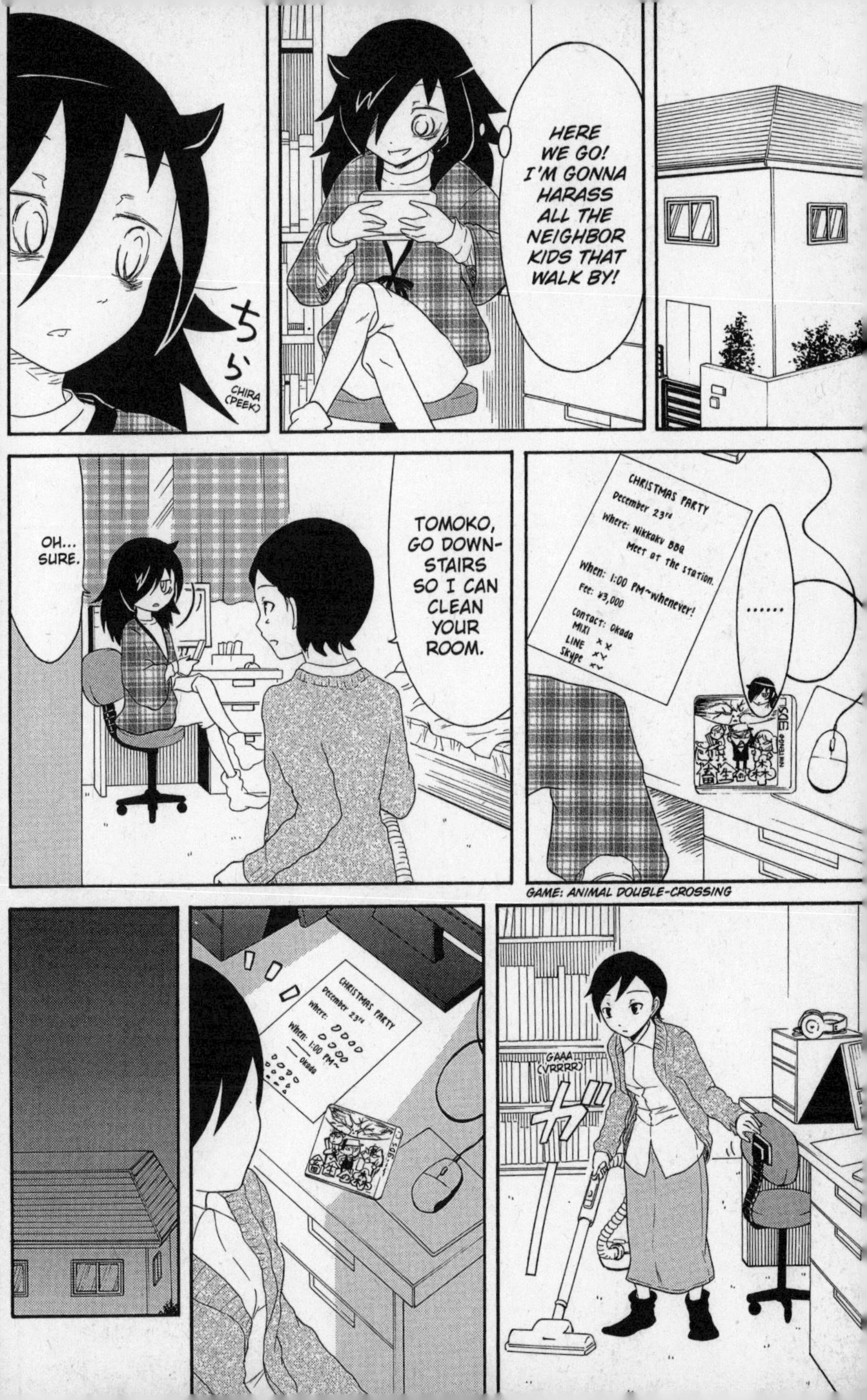
HERE WE GO! I'M GONNA HARASS ALL THE NEIGHBOR KIDS THAT WALK BY!
ちら
CHIRA (PEEK)
CHRISTMAS PARTY
December 23rd
Where: Nikkaku BBQ
Meet at the station.
When: 1:00 PM~whenever!
Fee: ¥3,000
Contact: Okada
MIXI ××
LINE ××
Skype ××
......
GAME: ANIMAL DOUBLE-CROSSING
TOMOKO, GO DOWNSTAIRS SO I CAN CLEAN YOUR ROOM.
OH... SURE.
GAAA (VRRRR)
CHRISTMAS PARTY
December 23rd
Where:
When: 1:00 PM~
Okada

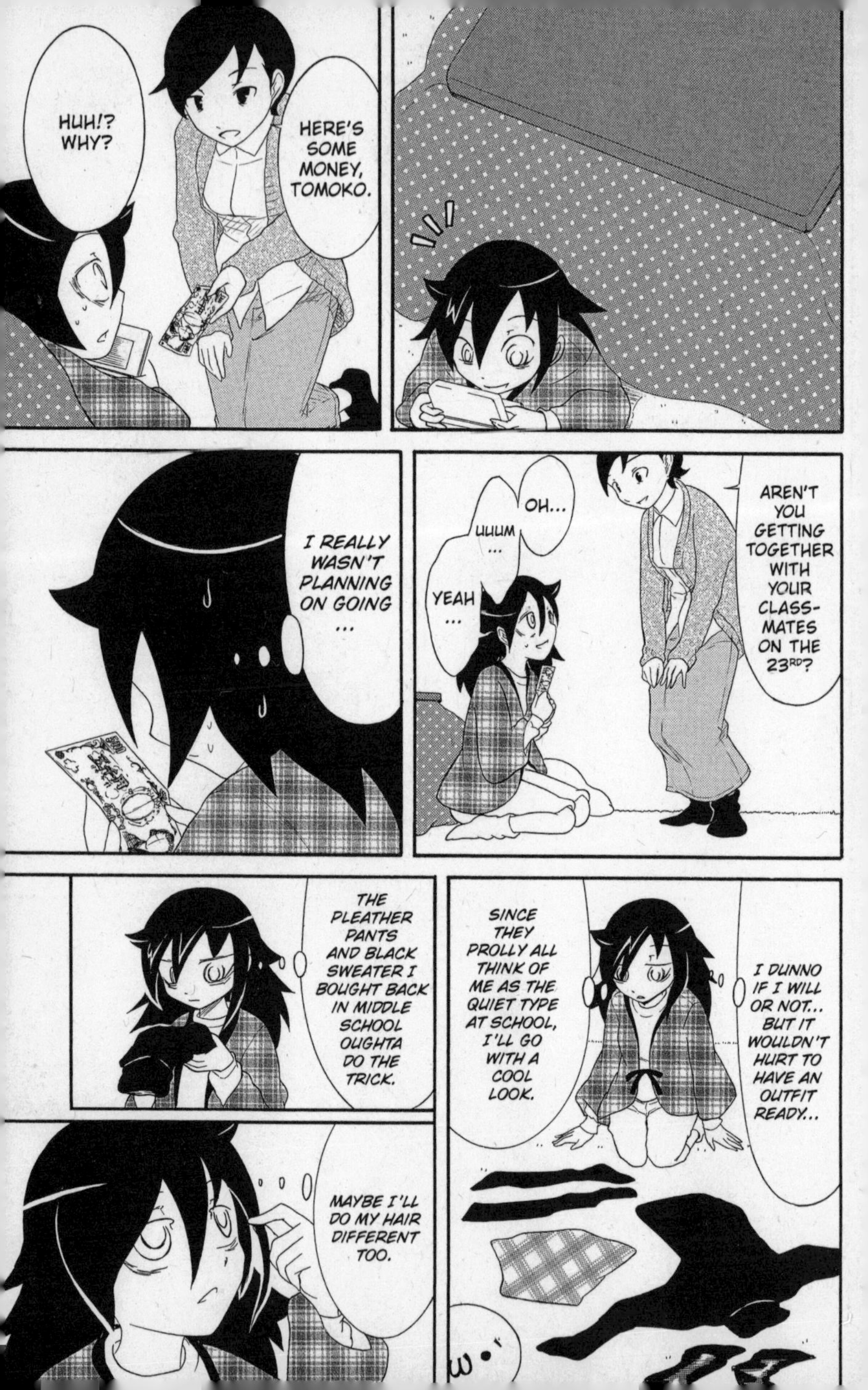
HERE'S SOME MONEY, TOMOKO.
HUH!? WHY?
AREN'T YOU GETTING TOGETHER WITH YOUR CLASSMATES ON THE 23RD?
OH...
UUUM ...
YEAH ...
I REALLY WASN'T PLANNING ON GOING ...
I DUNNO IF I WILL OR NOT... BUT IT WOULDN'T HURT TO HAVE AN OUTFIT READY...
SINCE THEY PROLLY ALL THINK OF ME AS THE QUIET TYPE AT SCHOOL, I'LL GO WITH A COOL LOOK.
THE PLEATHER PANTS AND BLACK SWEATER I BOUGHT BACK IN MIDDLE SCHOOL OUGHTA DO THE TRICK.
MAYBE I'LL DO MY HAIR DIFFERENT TOO.

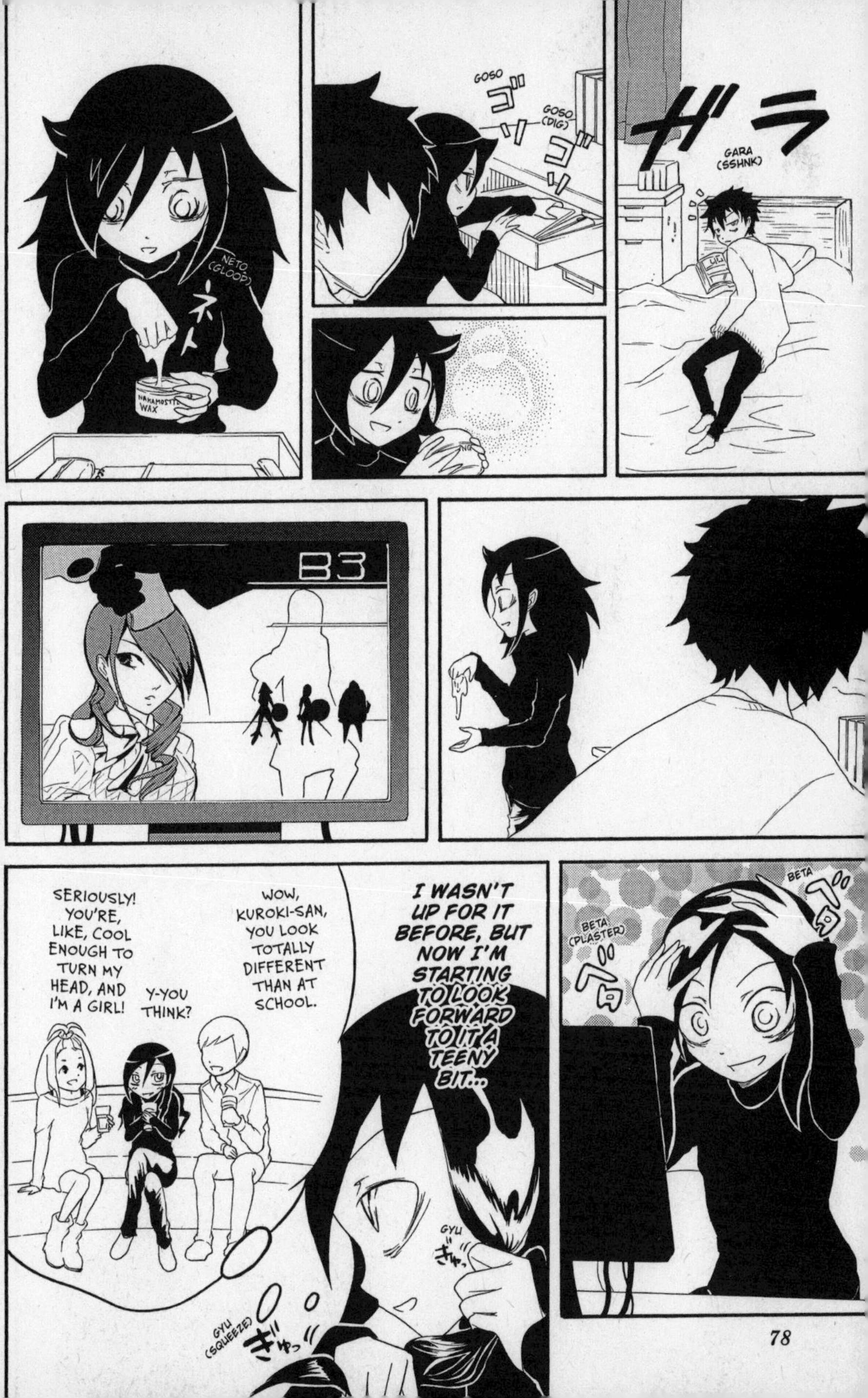
ガラ
GARA (SSHNK)
ゴソ
GOSO
ゴソ
GOSO (DIG)
ネト
NETO (GLOOP)
NAKAMOSTTI WAX
B3
ベタ
BETA
ベタ
BETA (PLASTER)
I WASN'T UP FOR IT BEFORE, BUT NOW I'M STARTING TO LOOK FORWARD TO IT A TEENY BIT...
WOW, KUROKI-SAN, YOU LOOK TOTALLY DIFFERENT THAN AT SCHOOL.
SERIOUSLY! YOU'RE, LIKE, COOL ENOUGH TO TURN MY HEAD, AND I'M A GIRL!
Y-YOU THINK?
ぎゅっ
GYU
ぎゅっ
GYU (SQUEEZE)

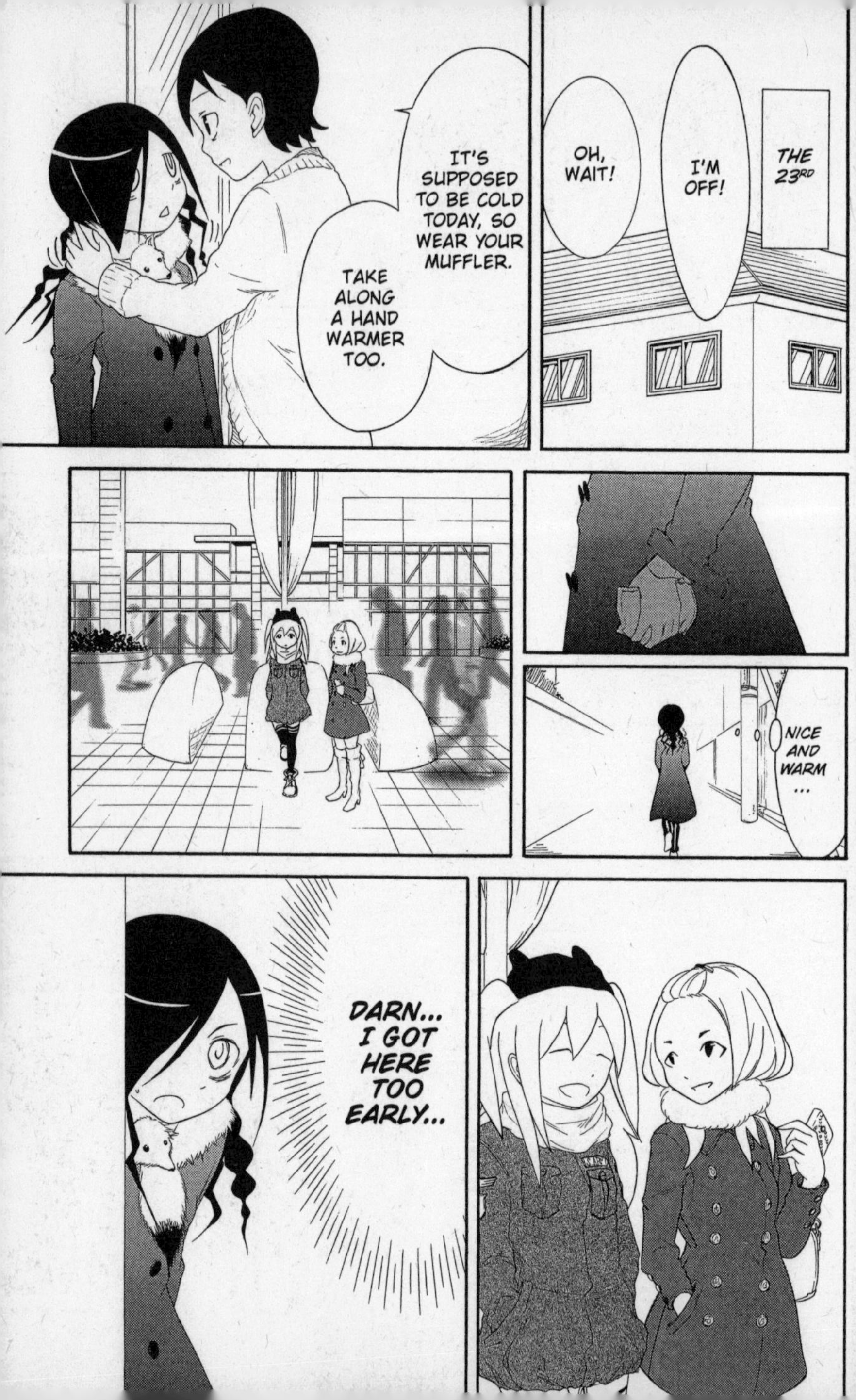
THE 23RD
I'M OFF!
OH, WAIT!
IT'S SUPPOSED TO BE COLD TODAY, SO WEAR YOUR MUFFLER.
TAKE ALONG A HAND WARMER TOO.
NICE AND WARM ...
DARN... I GOT HERE TOO EARLY...

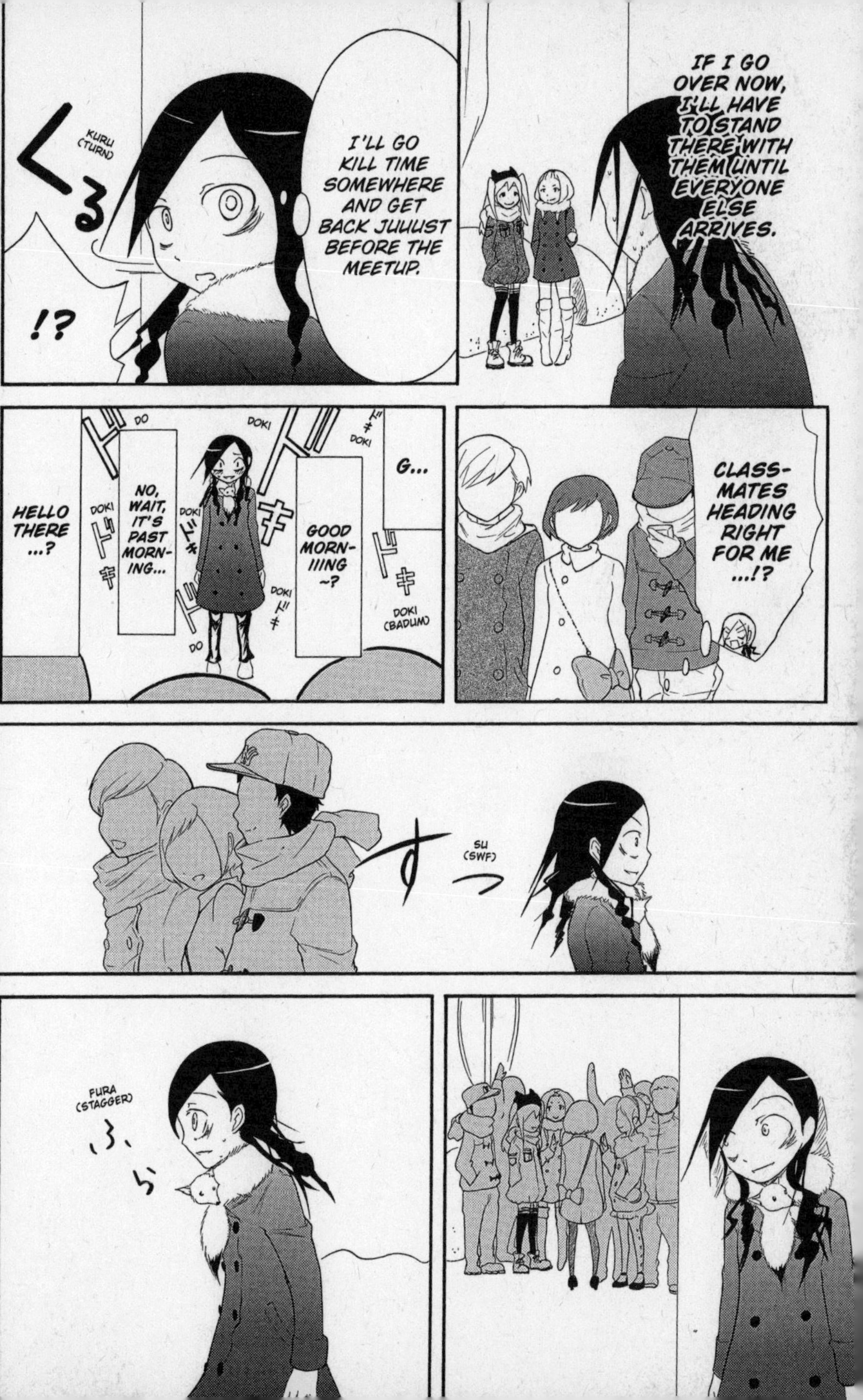
IF I GO OVER NOW, I'LL HAVE TO STAND THERE WITH THEM UNTIL EVERYONE ELSE ARRIVES.
I'LL GO KILL TIME SOMEWHERE AND GET BACK JUUUST BEFORE THE MEETUP.
KURU (TURN)
!?
CLASS-MATES HEADING RIGHT FOR ME ...!?
DOKI
DOKI
G...
GOOD MORN-IIING ~?
DOKI
DOKI (BADUM)
DO
NO, WAIT, IT'S PAST MORN-ING...
DOKI
DOKI
HELLO THERE ...?
DO
SU (SWF)
FURA (STAGGER)

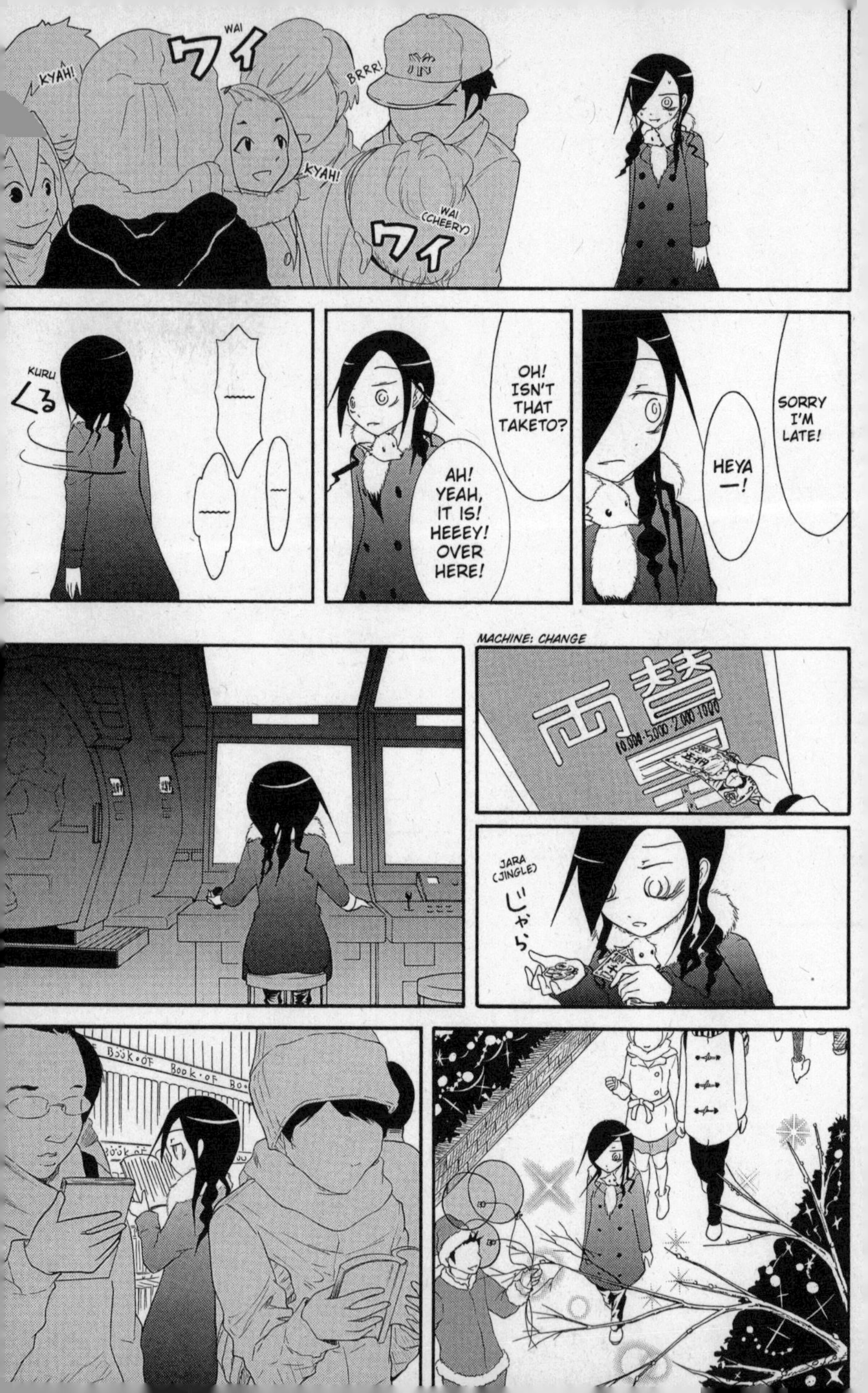
BRRR!
WAI
ワイ
KYAH!
KYAH!
WAI (CHEERY)
ワイ
SORRY I'M LATE!
HEYA—!
OH! ISN'T THAT TAKETO?
AH! YEAH, IT IS! HEEEY! OVER HERE!
KURU
くる
MACHINE: CHANGE
両替
10,000・5,000・2,000・1000
JARA (JINGLE)
じゃら

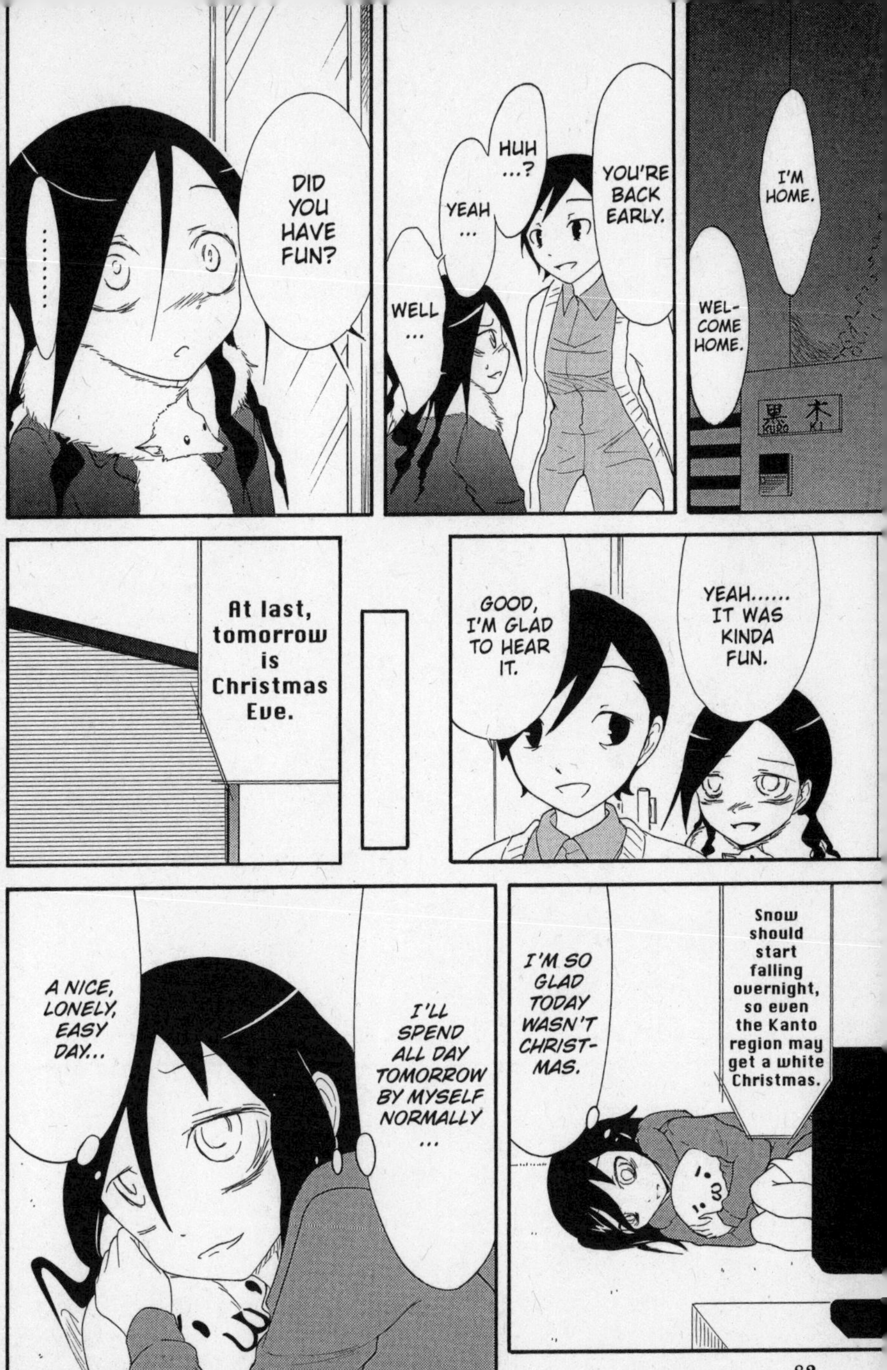
I'M HOME.
WEL-COME HOME.
黒木 KURO KI
YOU'RE BACK EARLY.
HUH ...?
YEAH ...
WELL ...
DID YOU HAVE FUN?
......
YEAH...... IT WAS KINDA FUN.
GOOD, I'M GLAD TO HEAR IT.
At last, tomorrow is Christmas Eve.
Snow should start falling overnight, so even the Kanto region may get a white Christmas.
I'M SO GLAD TODAY WASN'T CHRIST-MAS.
I'LL SPEND ALL DAY TOMORROW BY MYSELF NORMALLY ...
A NICE, LONELY, EASY DAY...

No Matter How I Look at It, It's You Guys' Fault I'm Not Popular!

NEW YEAR

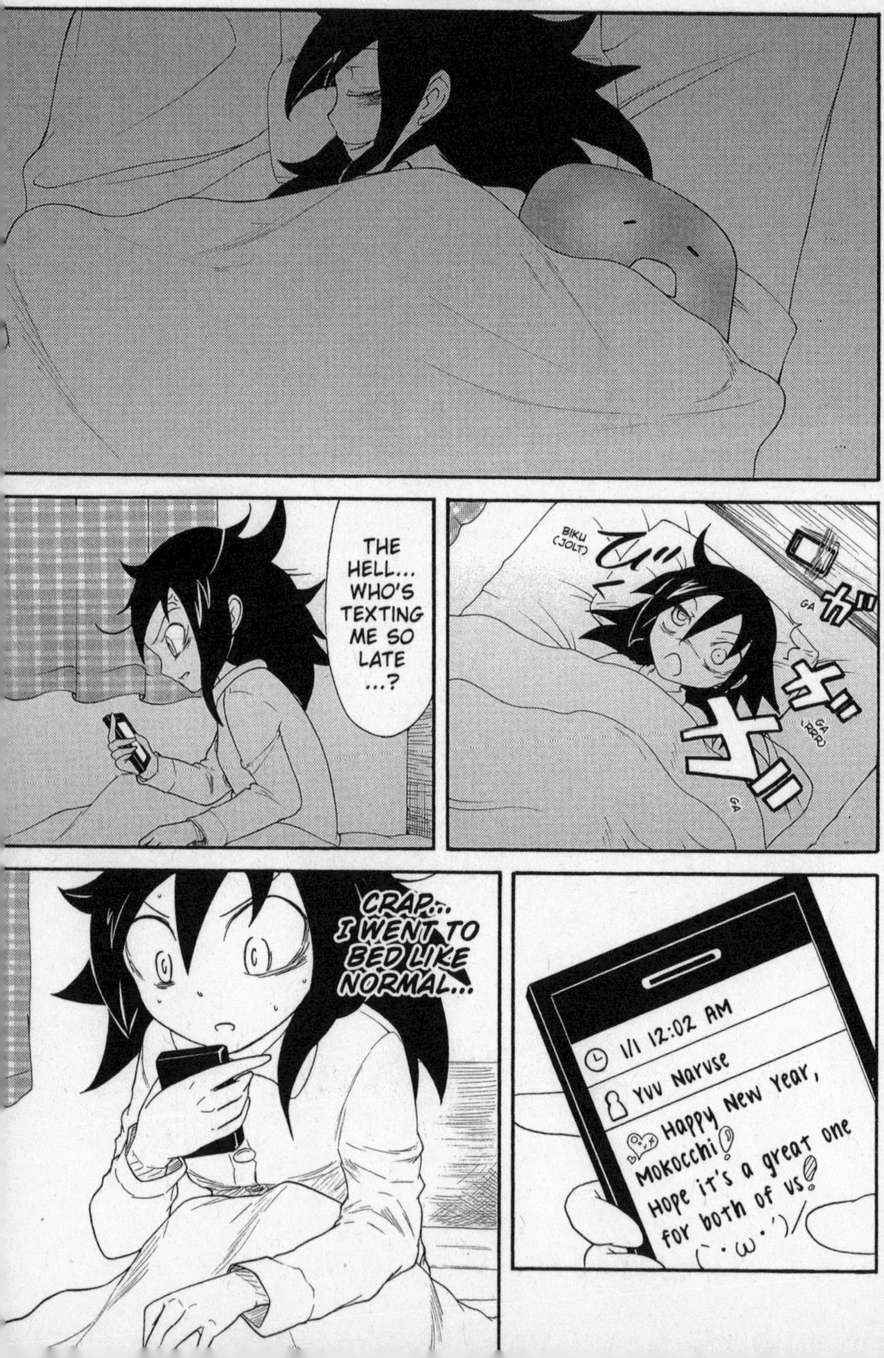
BIKU (JOLT)
GA
GA (RRR)
GA
THE HELL... WHO'S TEXTING ME SO LATE ...?
1/1 12:02 AM
Yuu Naruse
Happy New Year, Mokocchi! Hope it's a great one for both of us! (´・ω・)/
CRAP... I WENT TO BED LIKE NORMAL...

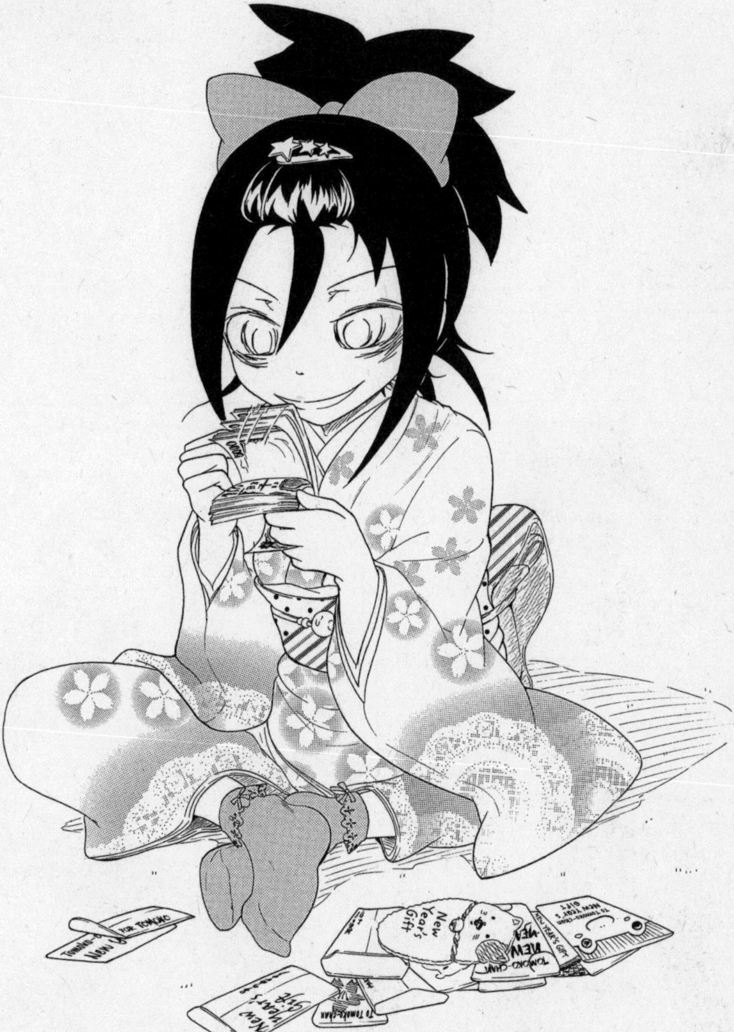
FOR TOMOKO
New Year's Gift
New Year's Gift
TO TOMOKO-CHAN
TOMOKO-CHAN
NEW YEAR'S GIFT

FAIL 33: I'M NOT POPULAR, SO I'LL GREET THE NEW YEAR.

NEW YEAR'S GREETINGS

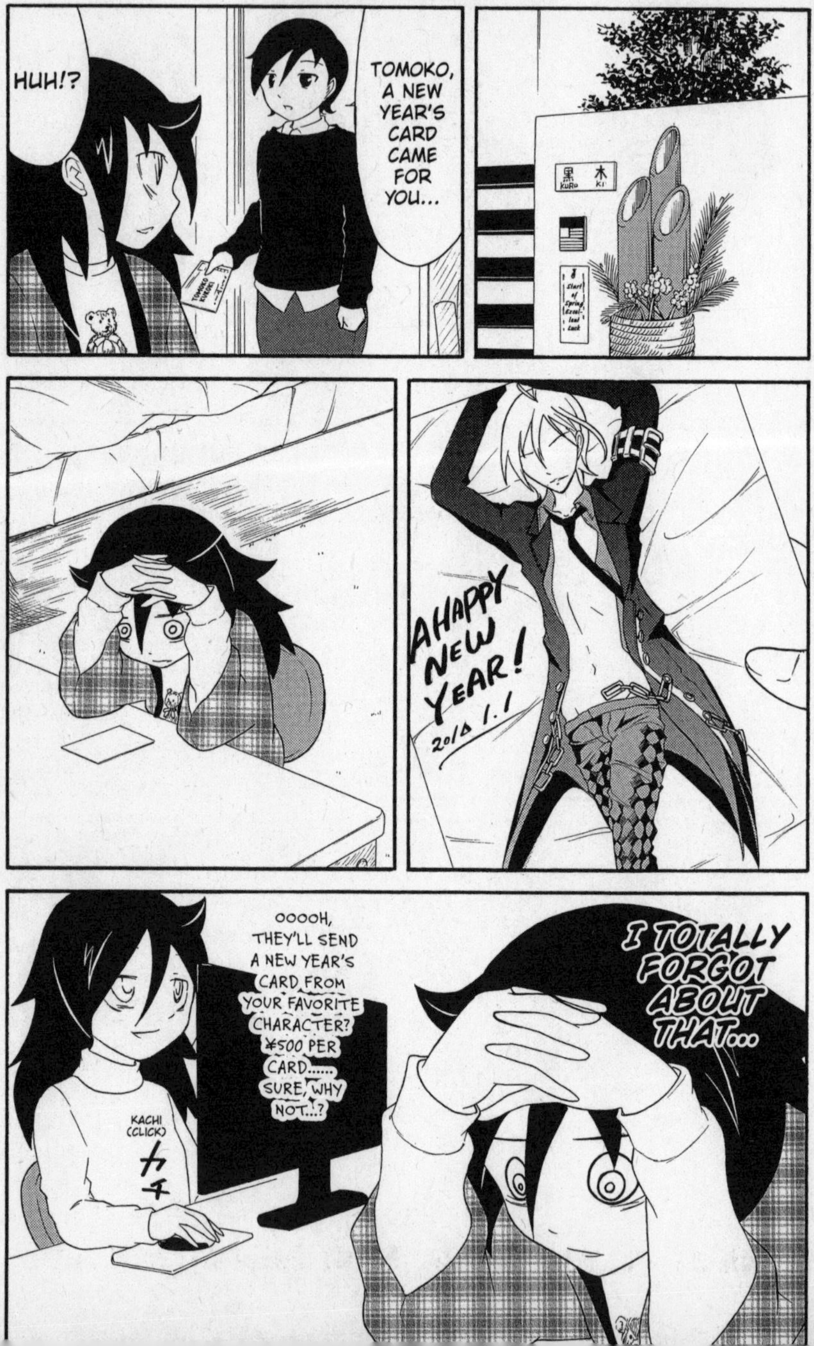
黒 木
KURO KI
Start of Spring Excellent Luck
TOMOKO, A NEW YEAR'S CARD CAME FOR YOU...
HUH!?
A HAPPY NEW YEAR!
2014 1.1
I TOTALLY FORGOT ABOUT THAT...
OOOOH, THEY'LL SEND A NEW YEAR'S CARD FROM YOUR FAVORITE CHARACTER? ¥500 PER CARD...... SURE, WHY NOT...?
KACHI (CLICK)
カチ

NEW YEAR'S GIFTS AND HOW TO USE THEM

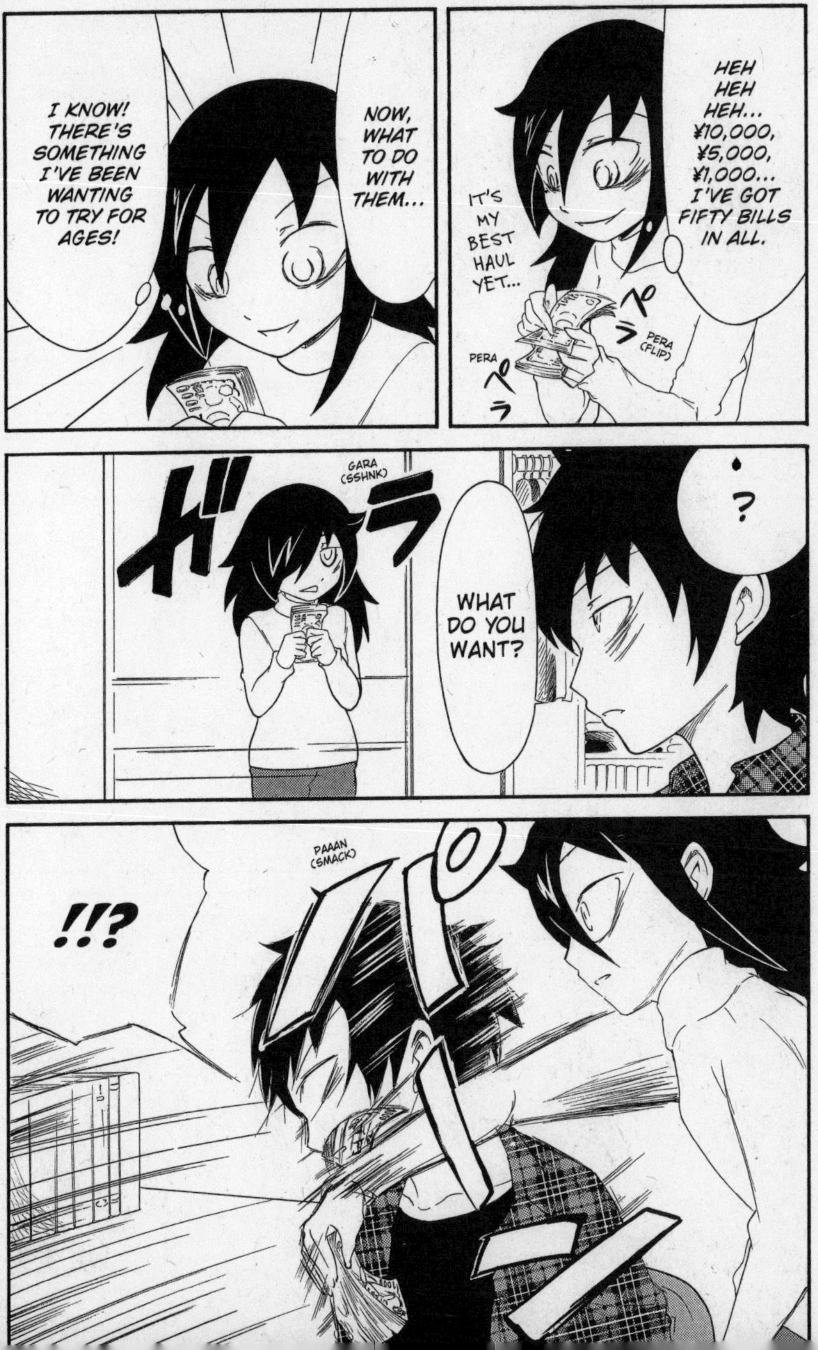
HEH HEH HEH... ¥10,000, ¥5,000, ¥1,000... I'VE GOT FIFTY BILLS IN ALL.
IT'S MY BEST HAUL YET...
PERA (FLIP)
PERA
NOW, WHAT TO DO WITH THEM...
I KNOW! THERE'S SOMETHING I'VE BEEN WANTING TO TRY FOR AGES!
?
GARA (SSHNK)
WHAT DO YOU WANT?
PAAAN (SMACK)
!!?

SIBLING RIVALRY

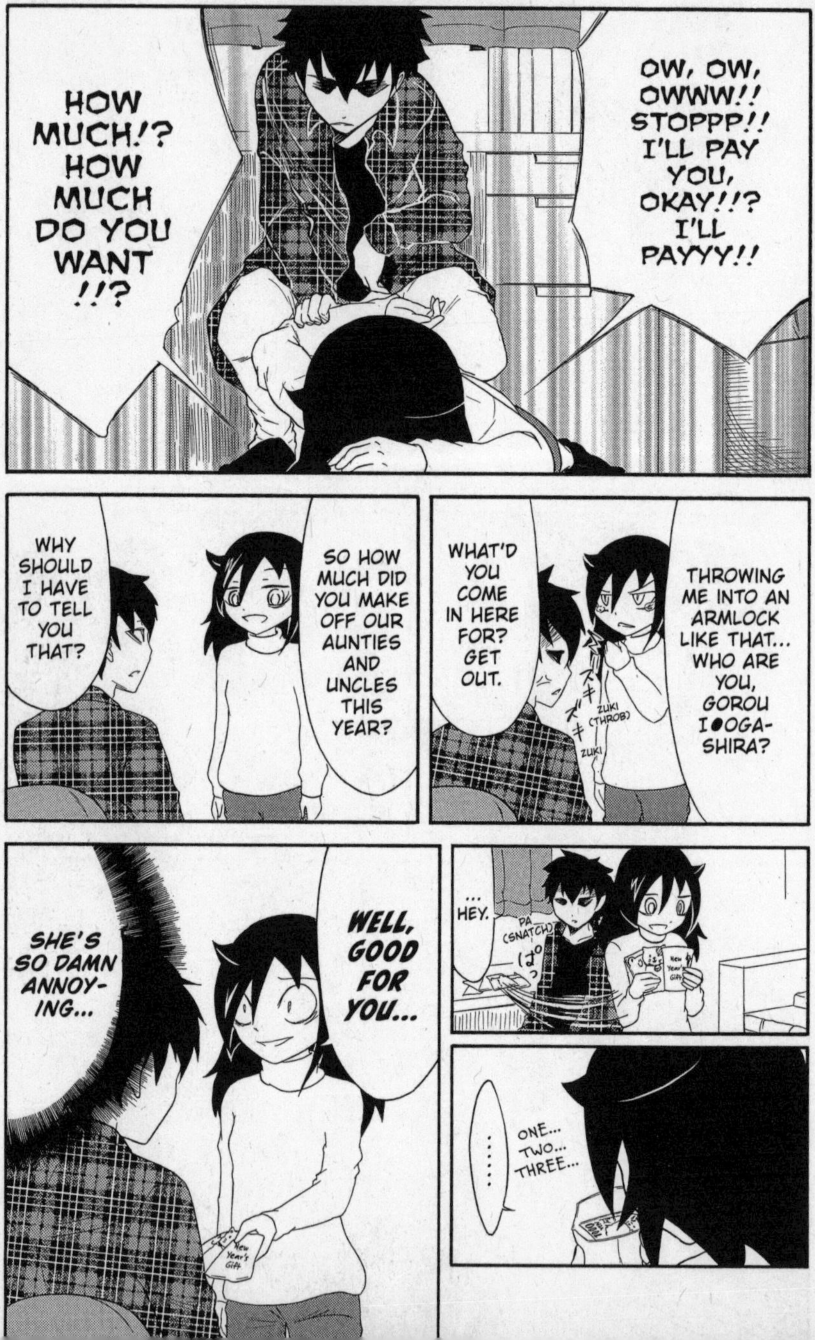
OW, OW, OWWW!! STOPPP!! I'LL PAY YOU, OKAY!!? I'LL PAYYY!!
HOW MUCH!? HOW MUCH DO YOU WANT!!?
THROWING ME INTO AN ARMLOCK LIKE THAT... WHO ARE YOU, GOROU I●OGA-SHIRA?
ZUKI (THROB)
ZUKI
WHAT'D YOU COME IN HERE FOR? GET OUT.
SO HOW MUCH DID YOU MAKE OFF OUR AUNTIES AND UNCLES THIS YEAR?
WHY SHOULD I HAVE TO TELL YOU THAT?
New Year's Gift
PA (SNATCH)
... HEY.
ONE... TWO... THREE...
......
WELL, GOOD FOR YOU...
SHE'S SO DAMN ANNOY-ING...
New Year's Gift

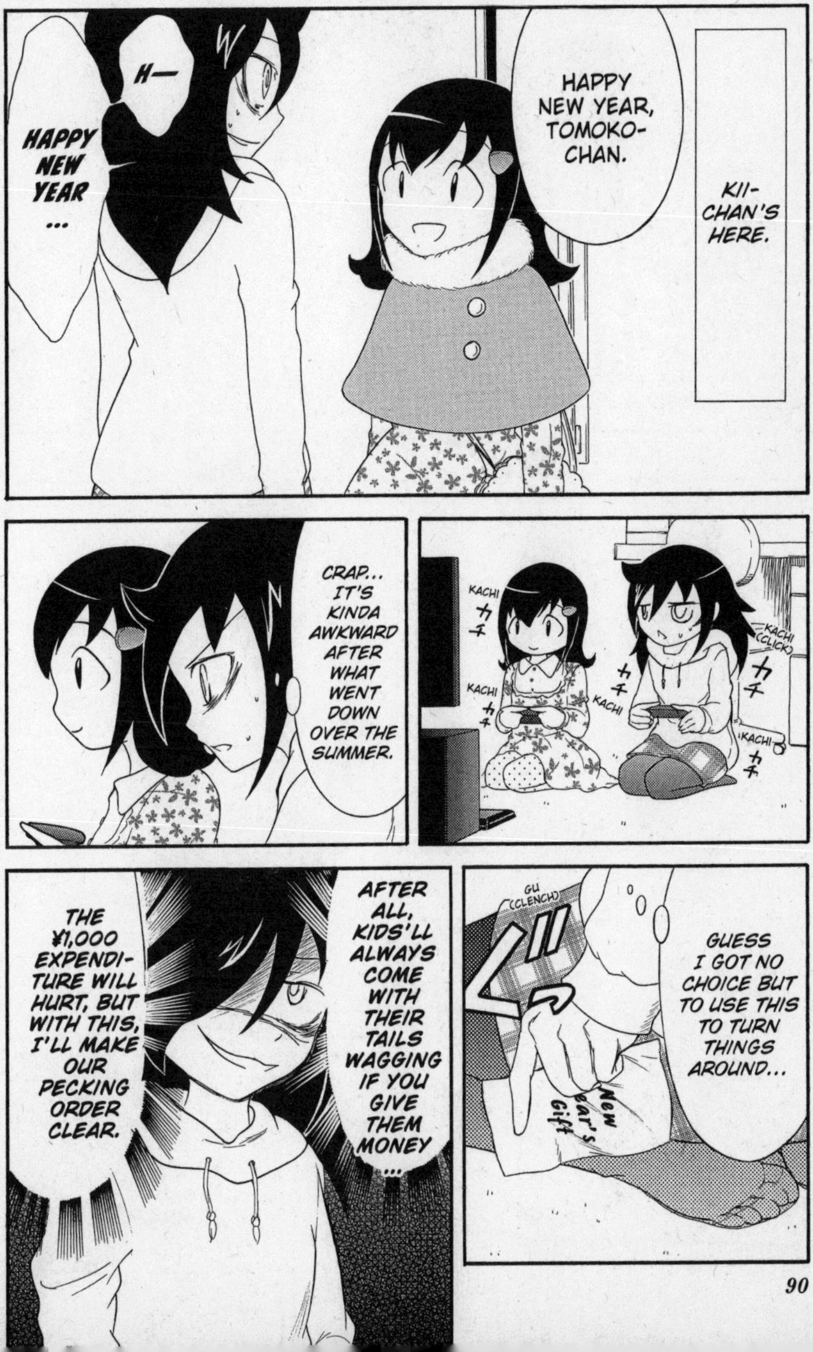
KII-CHAN'S HERE.
HAPPY NEW YEAR, TOMOKO-CHAN.
H—
HAPPY NEW YEAR ...
KACHI (CLICK)
KACHI
KACHI
KACHI
KACHI
CRAP... IT'S KINDA AWKWARD AFTER WHAT WENT DOWN OVER THE SUMMER.
GU (CLENCH)
GUESS I GOT NO CHOICE BUT TO USE THIS TO TURN THINGS AROUND...
New ear's Gift
AFTER ALL, KIDS'LL ALWAYS COME WITH THEIR TAILS WAGGING IF YOU GIVE THEM MONEY...
THE ¥1,000 EXPENDITURE WILL HURT, BUT WITH THIS, I'LL MAKE OUR PECKING ORDER CLEAR.

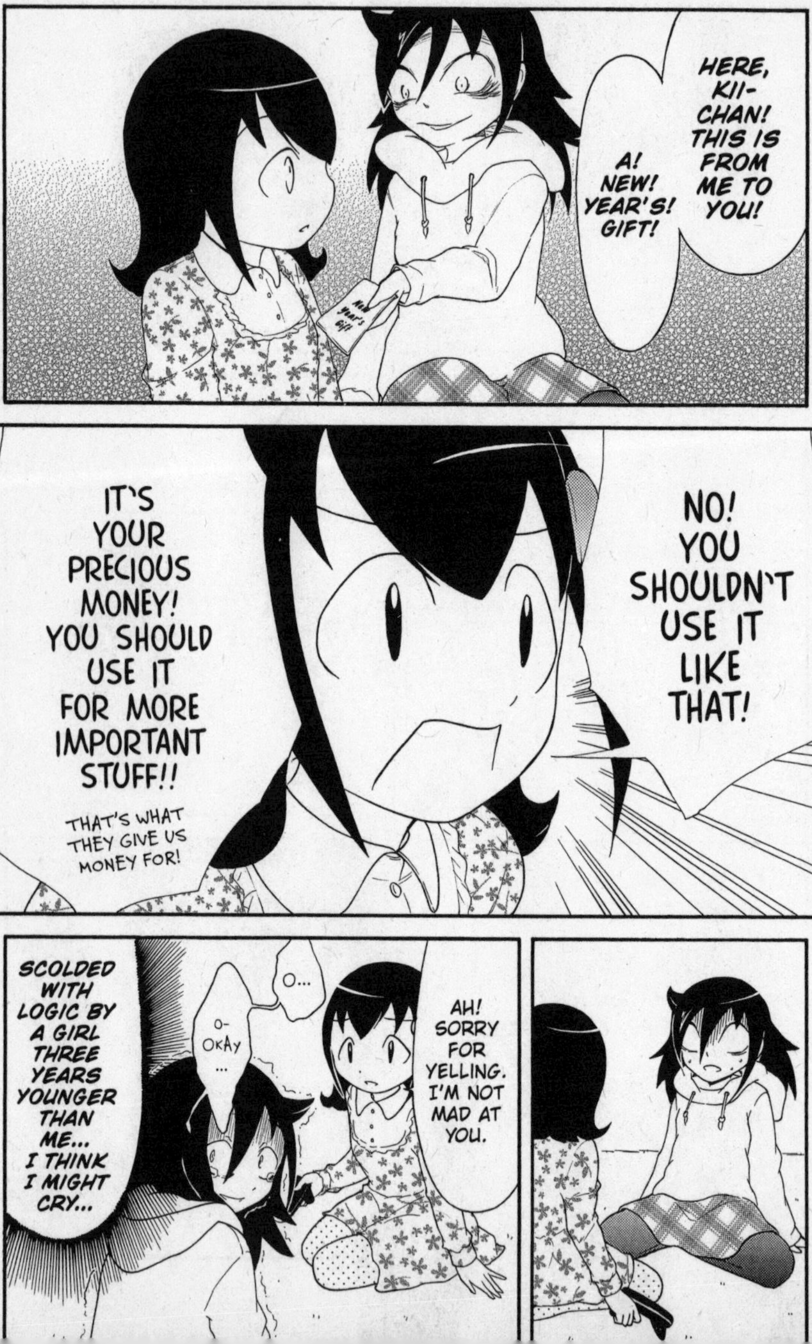
HERE, KII-CHAN! THIS IS FROM ME TO YOU!
A! NEW! YEAR'S! GIFT!
New Year's Gift
NO! YOU SHOULDN'T USE IT LIKE THAT!
IT'S YOUR PRECIOUS MONEY! YOU SHOULD USE IT FOR MORE IMPORTANT STUFF!!
THAT'S WHAT THEY GIVE US MONEY FOR!
AH! SORRY FOR YELLING. I'M NOT MAD AT YOU.
O...
O-OKAY...
SCOLDED WITH LOGIC BY A GIRL THREE YEARS YOUNGER THAN ME... I THINK I MIGHT CRY...

THOUGHTFULNESS

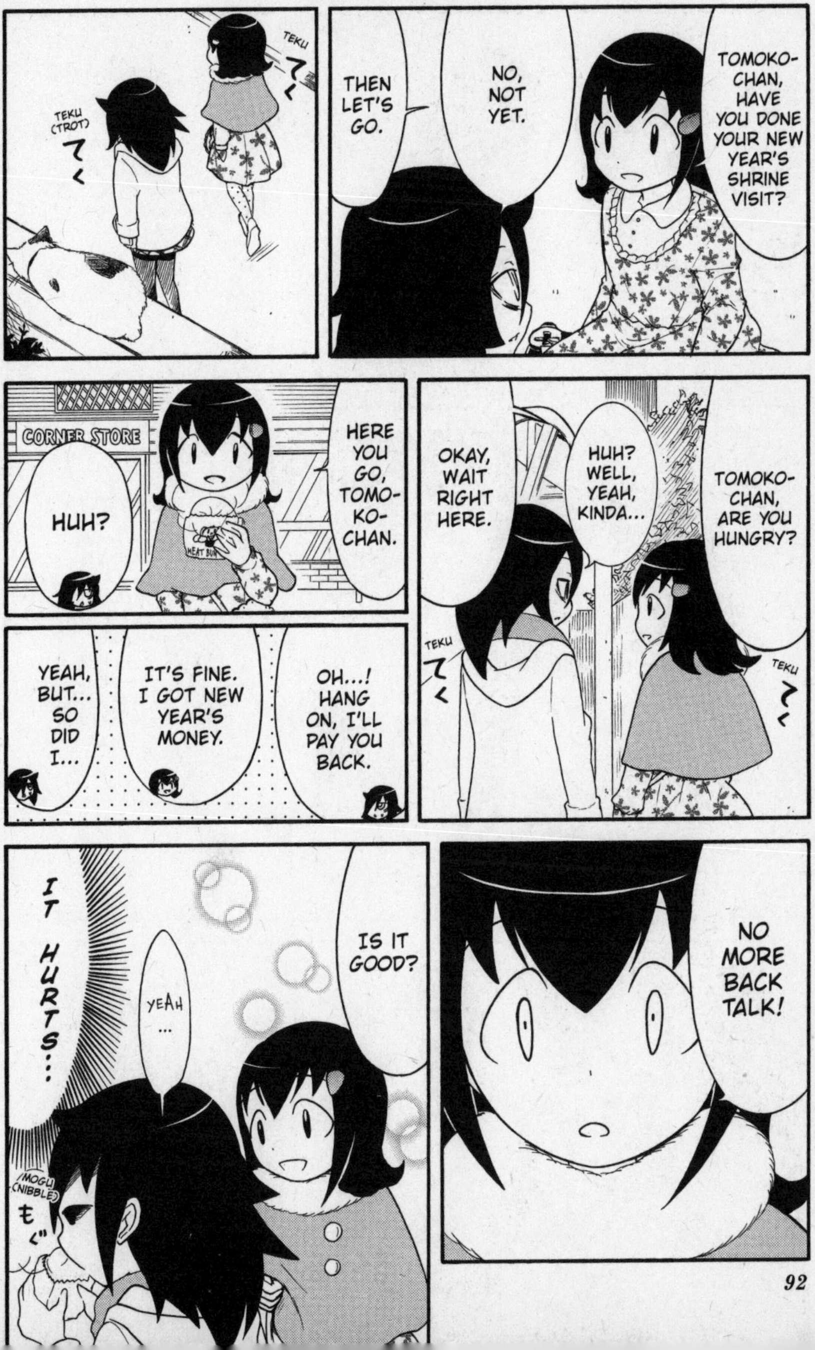
TOMOKO-CHAN, HAVE YOU DONE YOUR NEW YEAR'S SHRINE VISIT?
NO, NOT YET.
THEN LET'S GO.
TEKU てく
TEKU (TROT) てく
TOMOKO-CHAN, ARE YOU HUNGRY?
HUH? WELL, YEAH, KINDA...
OKAY, WAIT RIGHT HERE.
TEKU てく
TEKU てく
HERE YOU GO, TOMO-KO-CHAN.
CORNER STORE
MEAT BUN
HUH?
OH...! HANG ON, I'LL PAY YOU BACK.
IT'S FINE. I GOT NEW YEAR'S MONEY.
YEAH, BUT... SO DID I...
NO MORE BACK TALK!
IS IT GOOD?
YEAH...
IT HURTS...
MOGU (NIBBLE) もぐ

WISHES

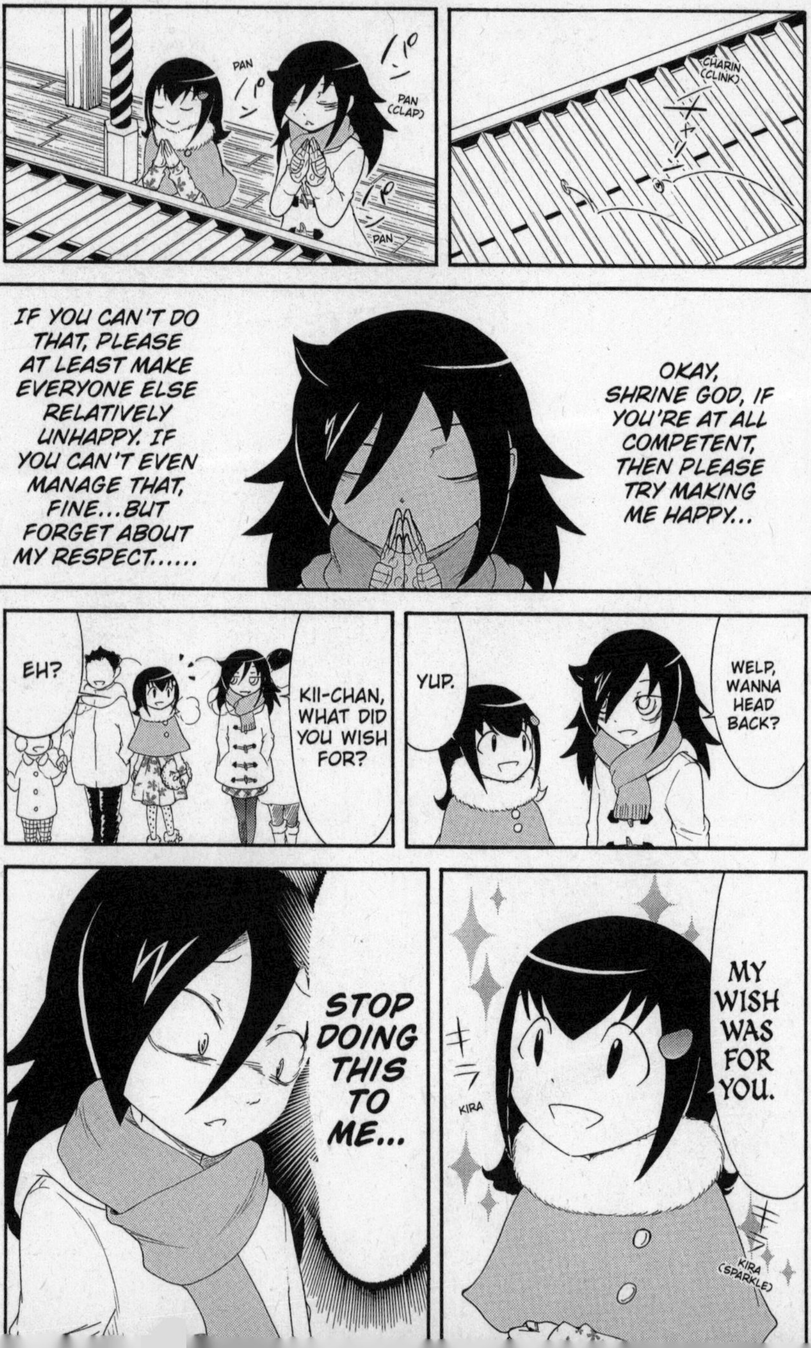
CHARIN (CLINK)
PAN (CLAP)
PAN
PAN
OKAY, SHRINE GOD, IF YOU'RE AT ALL COMPETENT, THEN PLEASE TRY MAKING ME HAPPY...
IF YOU CAN'T DO THAT, PLEASE AT LEAST MAKE EVERYONE ELSE RELATIVELY UNHAPPY. IF YOU CAN'T EVEN MANAGE THAT, FINE...BUT FORGET ABOUT MY RESPECT......
WELP, WANNA HEAD BACK?
YUP.
KII-CHAN, WHAT DID YOU WISH FOR?
EH?
MY WISH WAS FOR YOU.
KIRA
KIRA (SPARKLE)
STOP DOING THIS TO ME...

FIRST DREAM OF THE YEAR

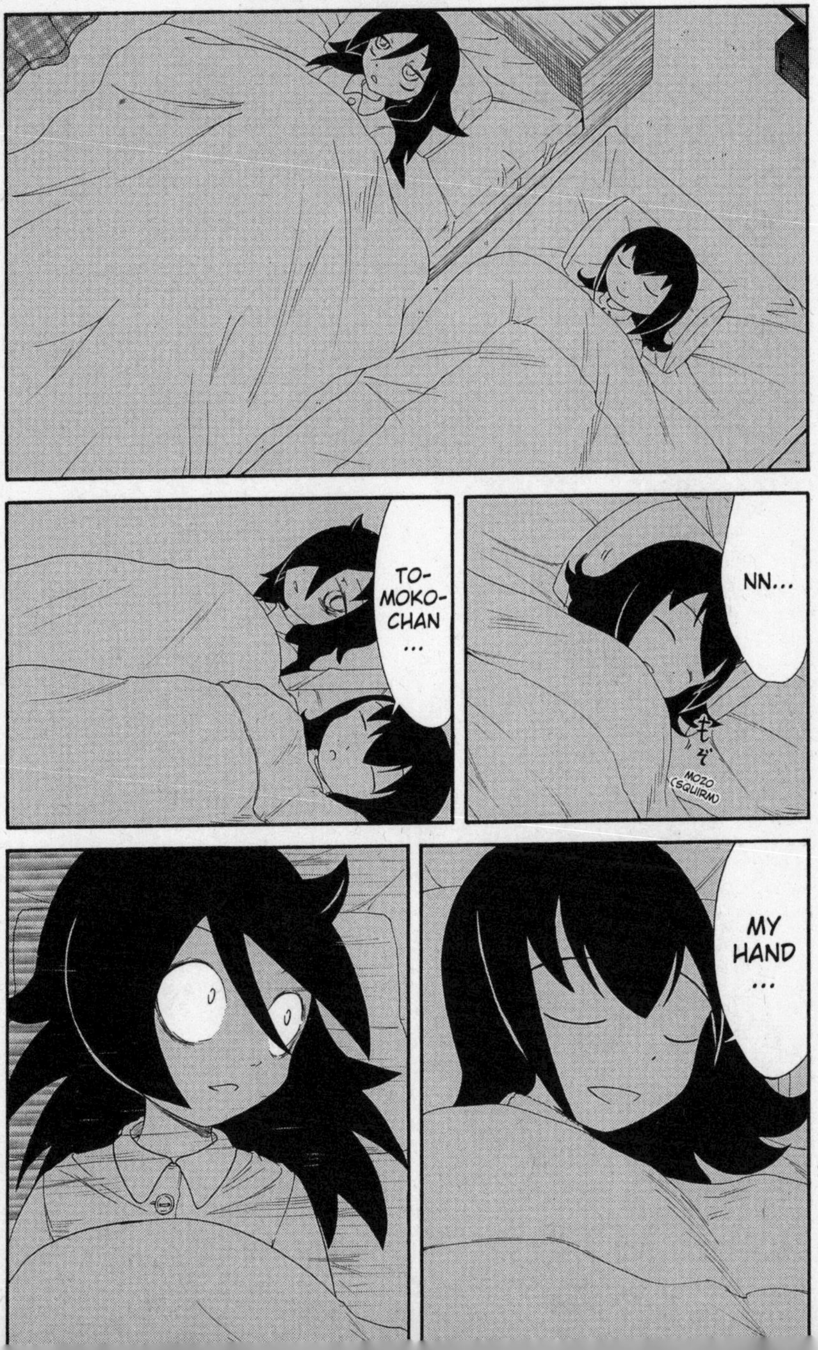
NN...
もぞ
MOZO (SQUIRM)
TO-MOKO-CHAN ...
MY HAND ...

PLAYING SOLO

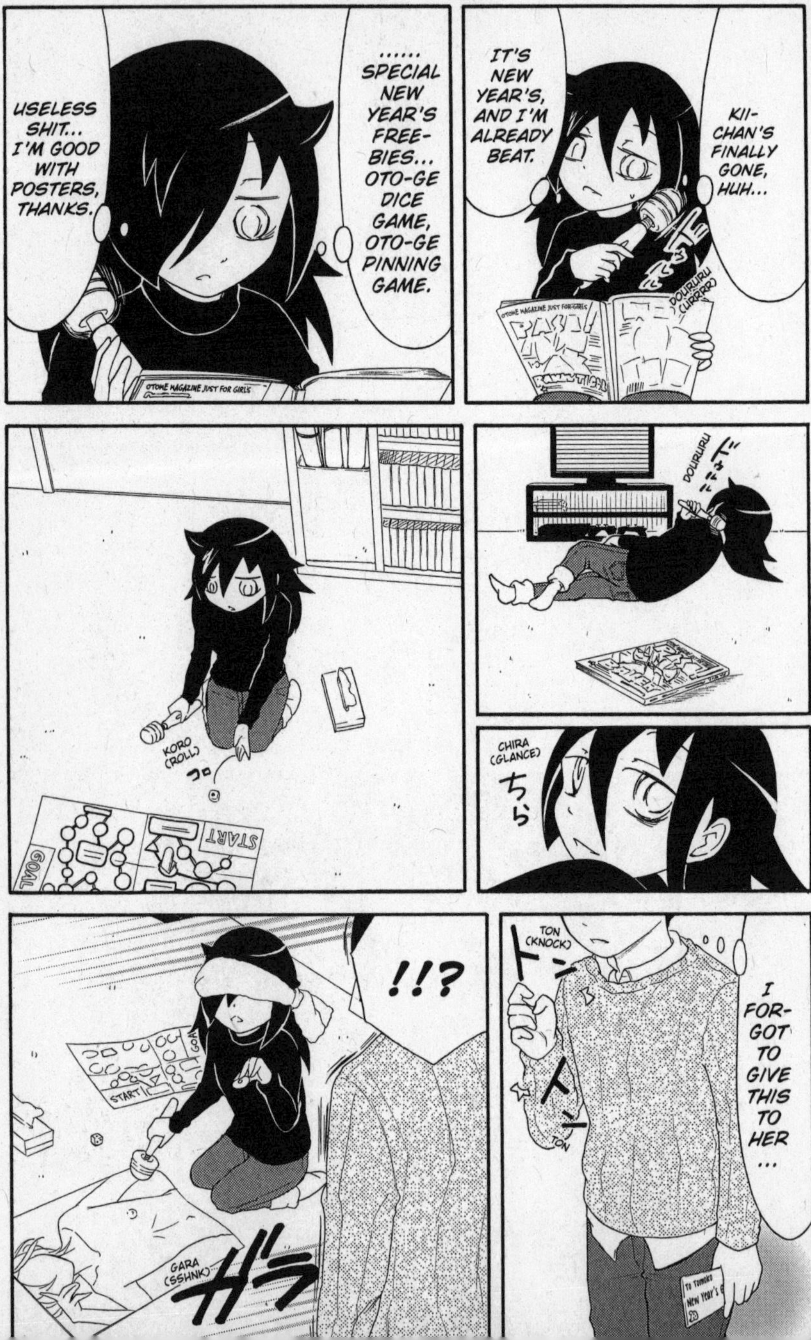
KII-CHAN'S FINALLY GONE, HUH...
IT'S NEW YEAR'S, AND I'M ALREADY BEAT.
DOURURU (URRRR)
OTOME MAGAZINE JUST FOR GIRLS
......SPECIAL NEW YEAR'S FREEBIES... OTO-GE DICE GAME, OTO-GE PINNING GAME.
USELESS SHIT... I'M GOOD WITH POSTERS, THANKS.
OTOME MAGAZINE JUST FOR GIRLS
DOURURU
CHIRA (GLANCE)
KORO (ROLL)
START
GOAL
TON (KNOCK)
TON
I FORGOT TO GIVE THIS TO HER...
!!?
START
GOAL
GARA (SSHNK)

GOOD TIDINGS

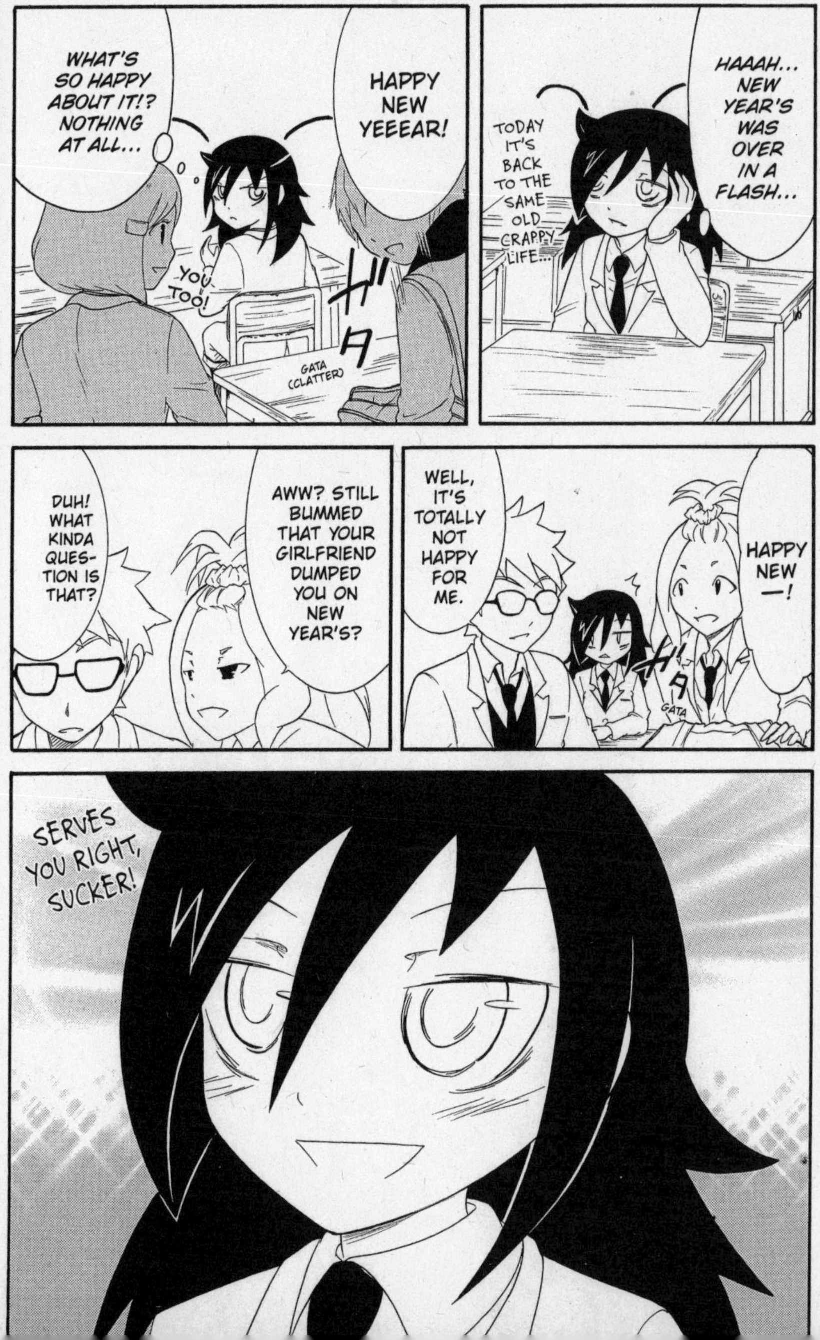
HAAAH... NEW YEAR'S WAS OVER IN A FLASH...
TODAY IT'S BACK TO THE SAME OLD CRAPPY LIFE...
HAPPY NEW YEEEAR!
WHAT'S SO HAPPY ABOUT IT!? NOTHING AT ALL...
YOU TOO!
GATA (CLATTER)
HAPPY NEW—!
GATA
WELL, IT'S TOTALLY NOT HAPPY FOR ME.
AWW? STILL BUMMED THAT YOUR GIRLFRIEND DUMPED YOU ON NEW YEAR'S?
DUH! WHAT KINDA QUES-TION IS THAT?
SERVES YOU RIGHT, SUCKER!

No Matter How I Look at It, It's You Guys' Fault I'm Not Popular!

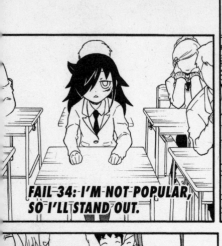

SEAT CHANGE
FAIL 34: I'M NOT POPULAR, SO I'LL STAND OUT.
TEACHER'S PODIUM
SMACK IN THE MIDDLE
BREAK TIME
ZAWA
ZAWA (CHATTER)
ザワ
ザワ
KOFF!
KOFF!
KOFF!!
KOFF!!
PI (BEEP)
ピ
PI
ピ
VIDEO RECORDER
REC
SA (SHFF)
Classical Japanese
1-10
Tomoko Kuroki

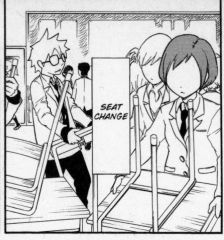

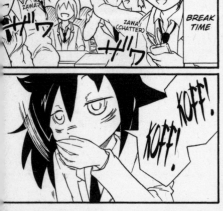

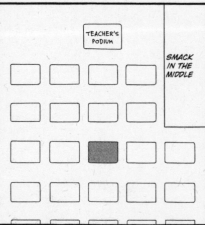

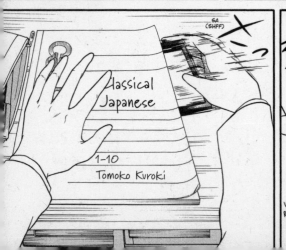

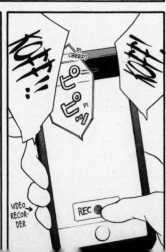

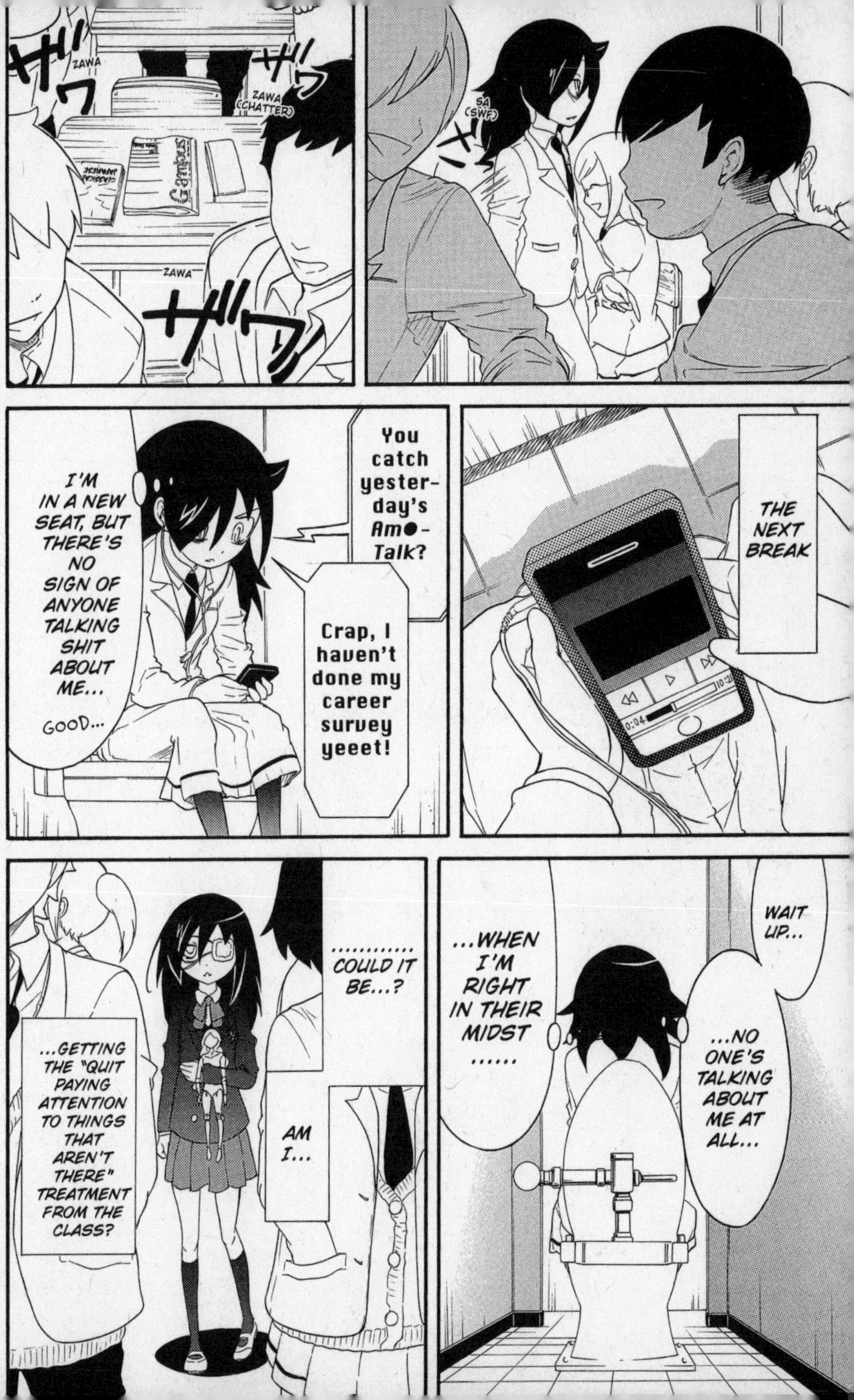
SA (SWF)
ZAWA
ZAWA (CHATTER)
ZAWA
THE NEXT BREAK
You catch yester-day's Am●-Talk?
Crap, I haven't done my career survey yeeet!
I'M IN A NEW SEAT, BUT THERE'S NO SIGN OF ANYONE TALKING SHIT ABOUT ME...
GOOD...
WAIT UP...
...NO ONE'S TALKING ABOUT ME AT ALL...
...WHEN I'M RIGHT IN THEIR MIDST ......
.... COULD IT BE...?
AM I...
...GETTING THE "QUIT PAYING ATTENTION TO THINGS THAT AREN'T THERE" TREATMENT FROM THE CLASS?

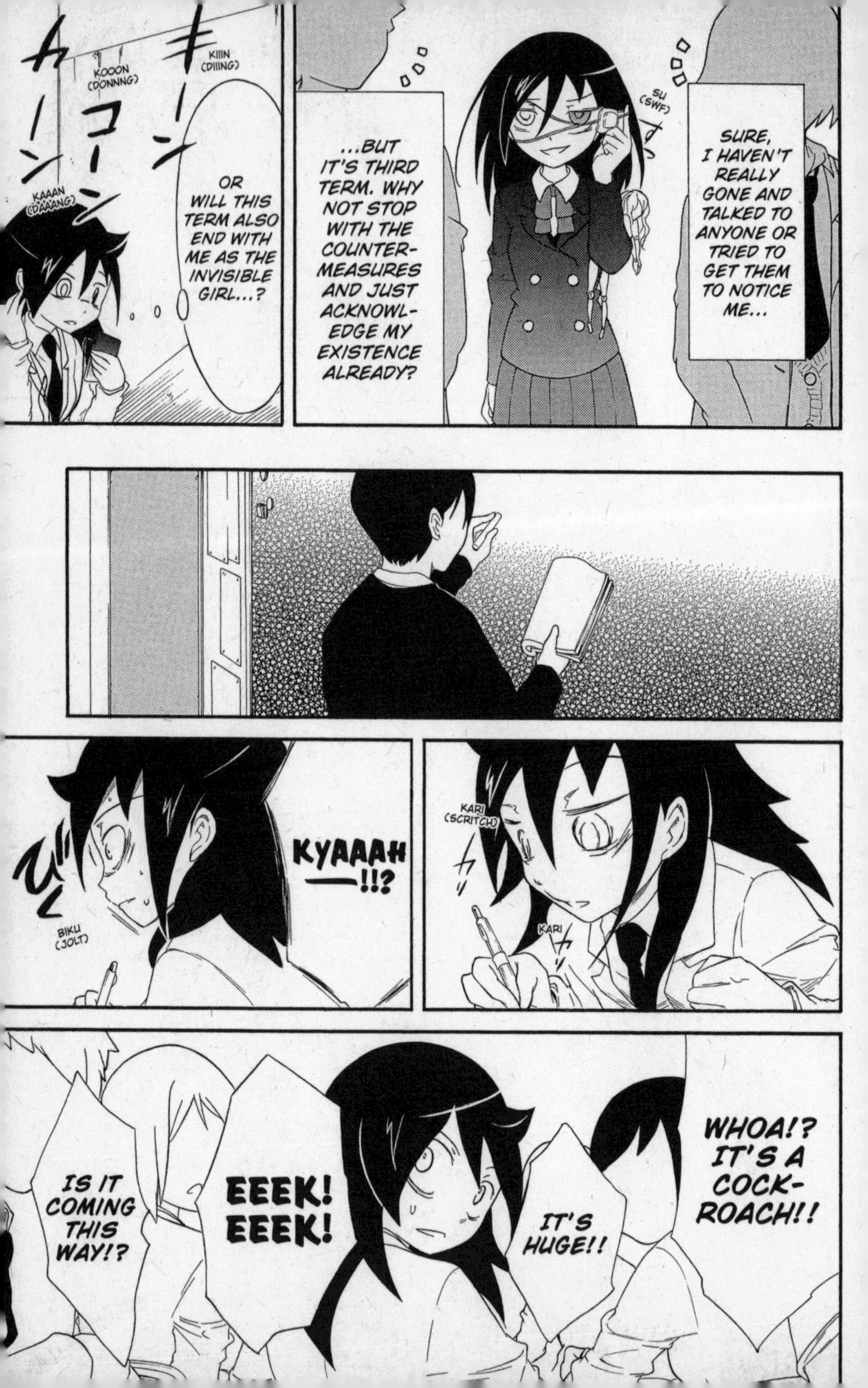
SURE, I HAVEN'T REALLY GONE AND TALKED TO ANYONE OR TRIED TO GET THEM TO NOTICE ME...
SU (SWF)
...BUT IT'S THIRD TERM. WHY NOT STOP WITH THE COUNTER-MEASURES AND JUST ACKNOWL-EDGE MY EXISTENCE ALREADY?
KIIIN (DIIING)
KOOON (DONNNG)
KAAAN (DAAANG)
OR WILL THIS TERM ALSO END WITH ME AS THE INVISIBLE GIRL...?
KARI (SCRITCH)
KARI
KYAAAH—!!?
BIKU (JOLT)
WHOA!? IT'S A COCK-ROACH!!
IT'S HUGE!!
EEEK! EEEK!
IS IT COMING THIS WAY!?

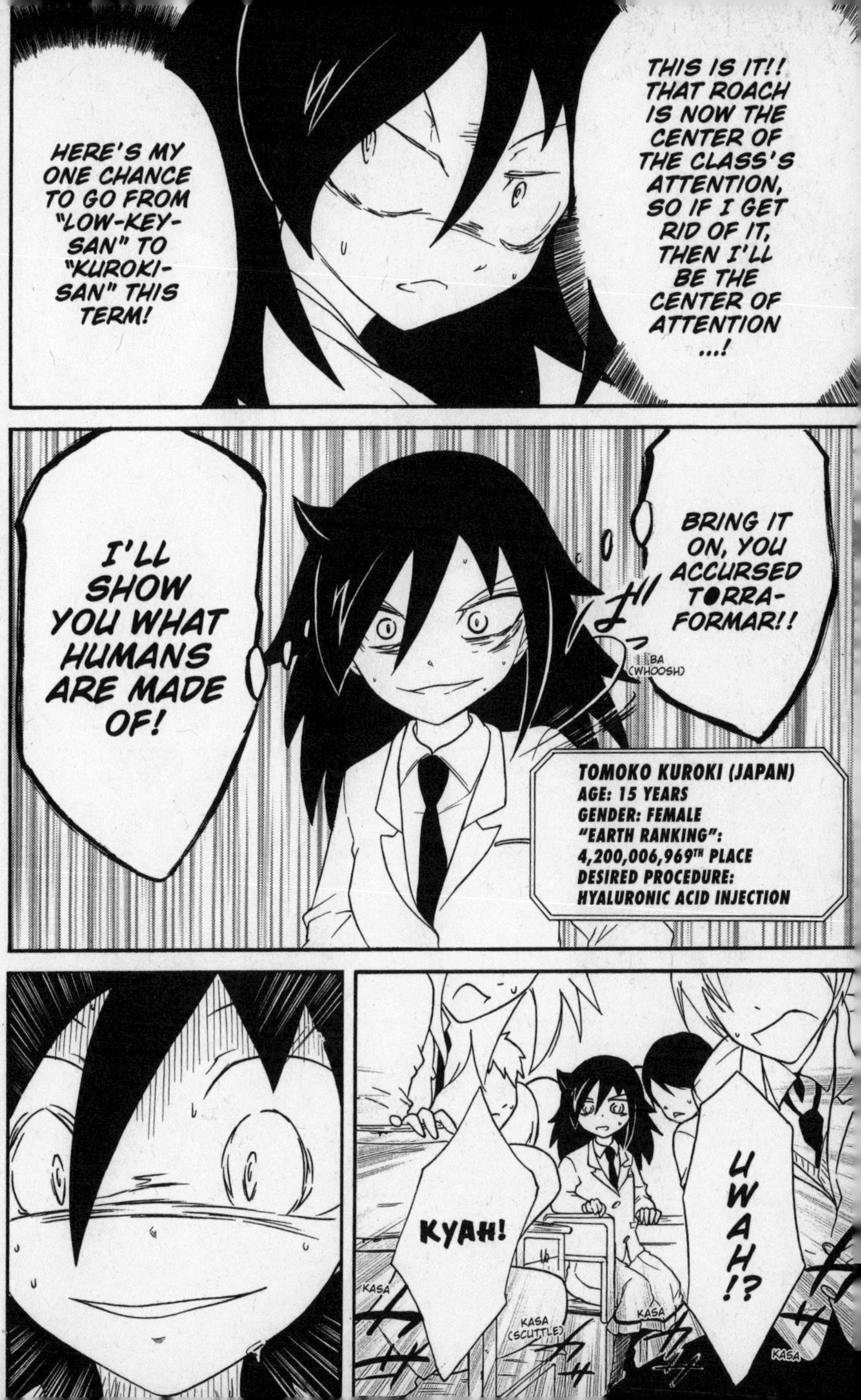
THIS IS IT!! THAT ROACH IS NOW THE CENTER OF THE CLASS'S ATTENTION, SO IF I GET RID OF IT, THEN I'LL BE THE CENTER OF ATTENTION ...!
HERE'S MY ONE CHANCE TO GO FROM "LOW-KEY-SAN" TO "KUROKI-SAN" THIS TERM!
BRING IT ON, YOU ACCURSED TORRA-FORMAR!!
BA (WHOOSH)
TOMOKO KUROKI (JAPAN)
AGE: 15 YEARS
GENDER: FEMALE
"EARTH RANKING": 4,200,006,969TH PLACE
DESIRED PROCEDURE: HYALURONIC ACID INJECTION
I'LL SHOW YOU WHAT HUMANS ARE MADE OF!
UWAH!?
KASA
KASA
KYAH!
KASA (SCUTTLE)
KASA

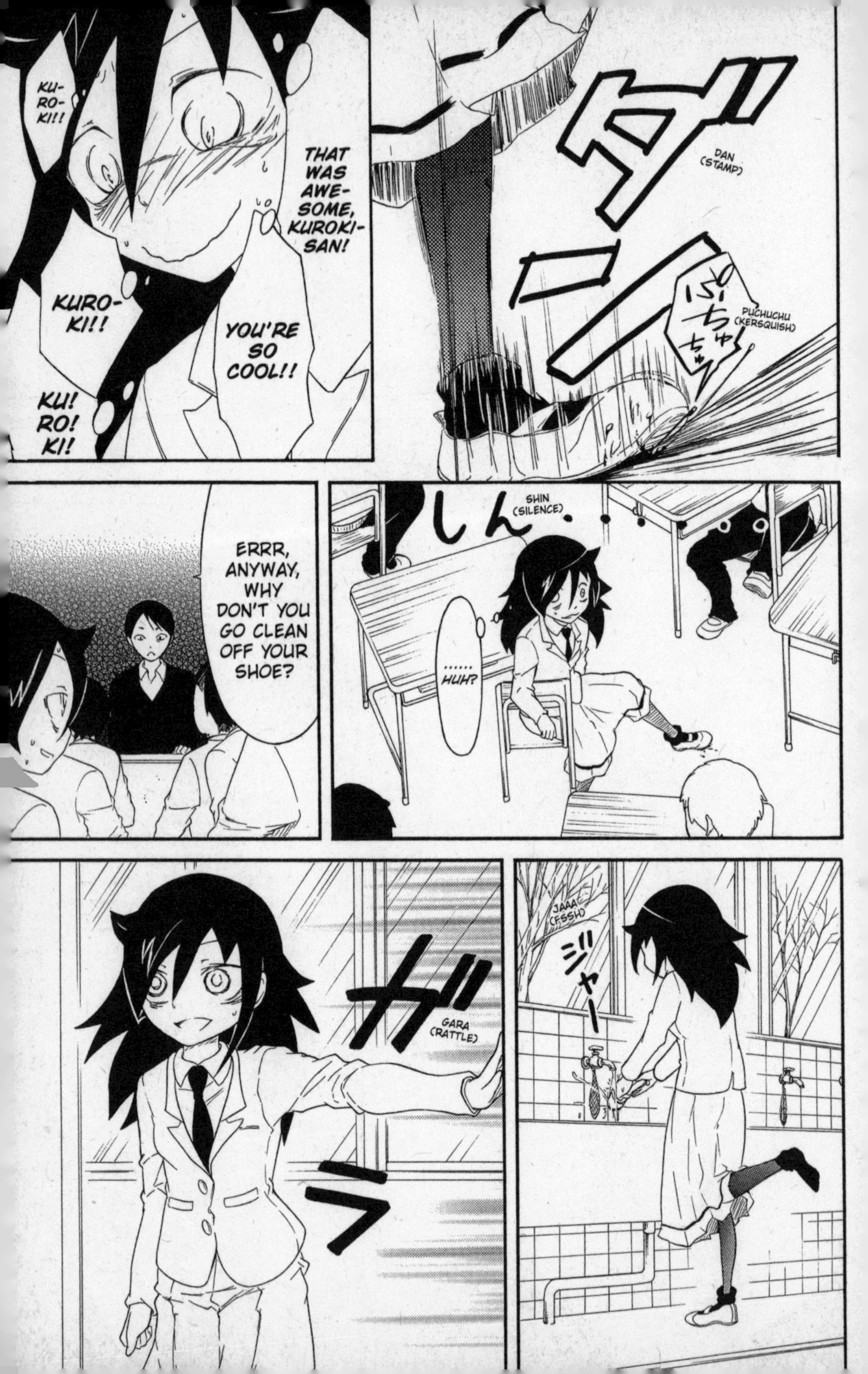
ダン
DAN (STAMP)
ぷちゅちゅ
PUCHUCHU (KERSQUISH)
THAT WAS AWESOME, KUROKI-SAN!
KU-RO-KI!!
YOU'RE SO COOL!!
KURO-KI!!
KU! RO! KI!
しん
SHIN (SILENCE)
...... HUH?
ERRR, ANYWAY, WHY DON'T YOU GO CLEAN OFF YOUR SHOE?
ジャー
JAAA (FSSH)
ガラ
GARA (RATTLE)

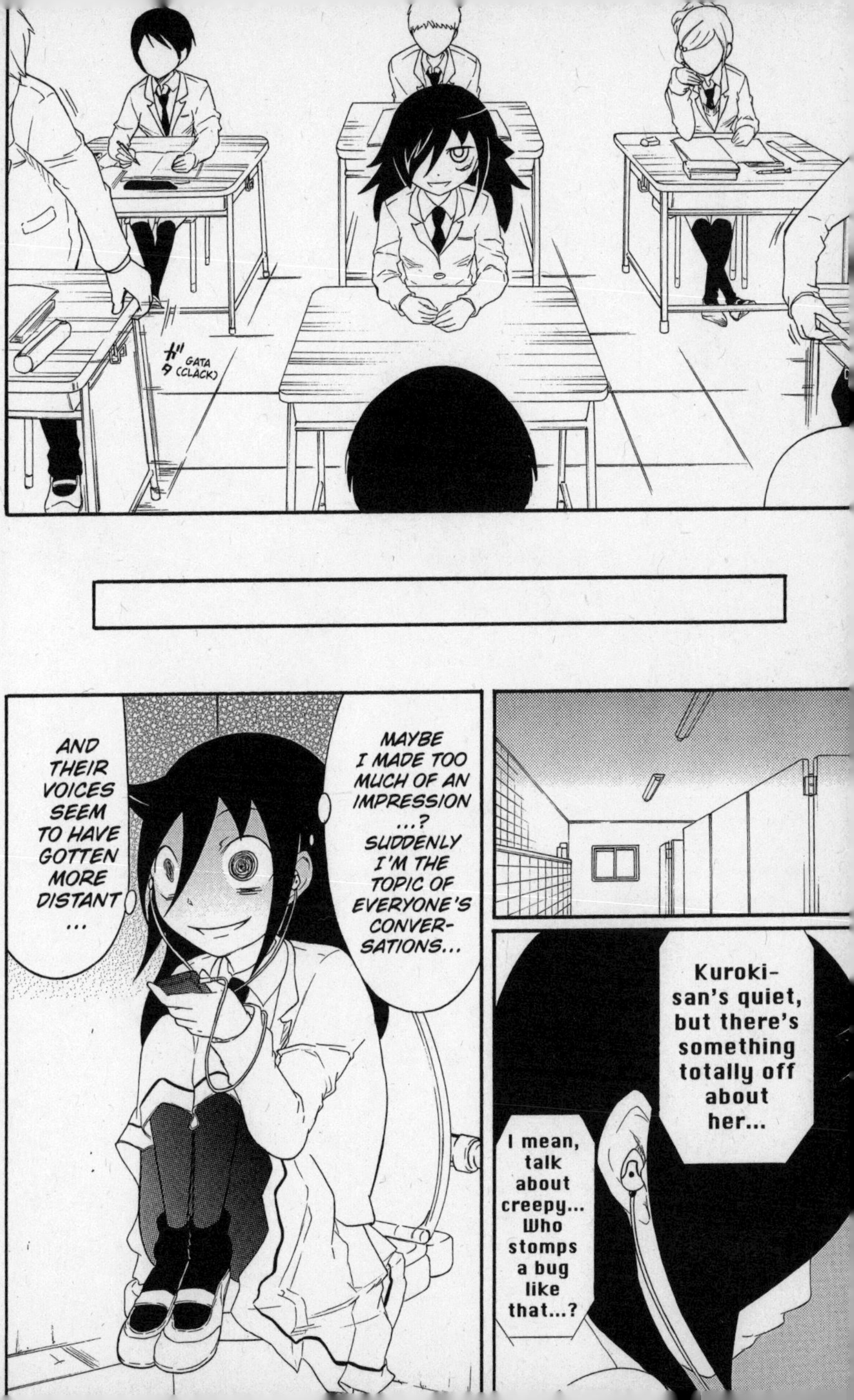
ガタ GATA (CLACK)
Kuroki-san's quiet, but there's something totally off about her...
I mean, talk about creepy... Who stomps a bug like that...?
MAYBE I MADE TOO MUCH OF AN IMPRESSION ...? SUDDENLY I'M THE TOPIC OF EVERYONE'S CONVERSATIONS...
AND THEIR VOICES SEEM TO HAVE GOTTEN MORE DISTANT ...

No Matter How I Look at It, It's You Guys' Fault I'm Not Popular!

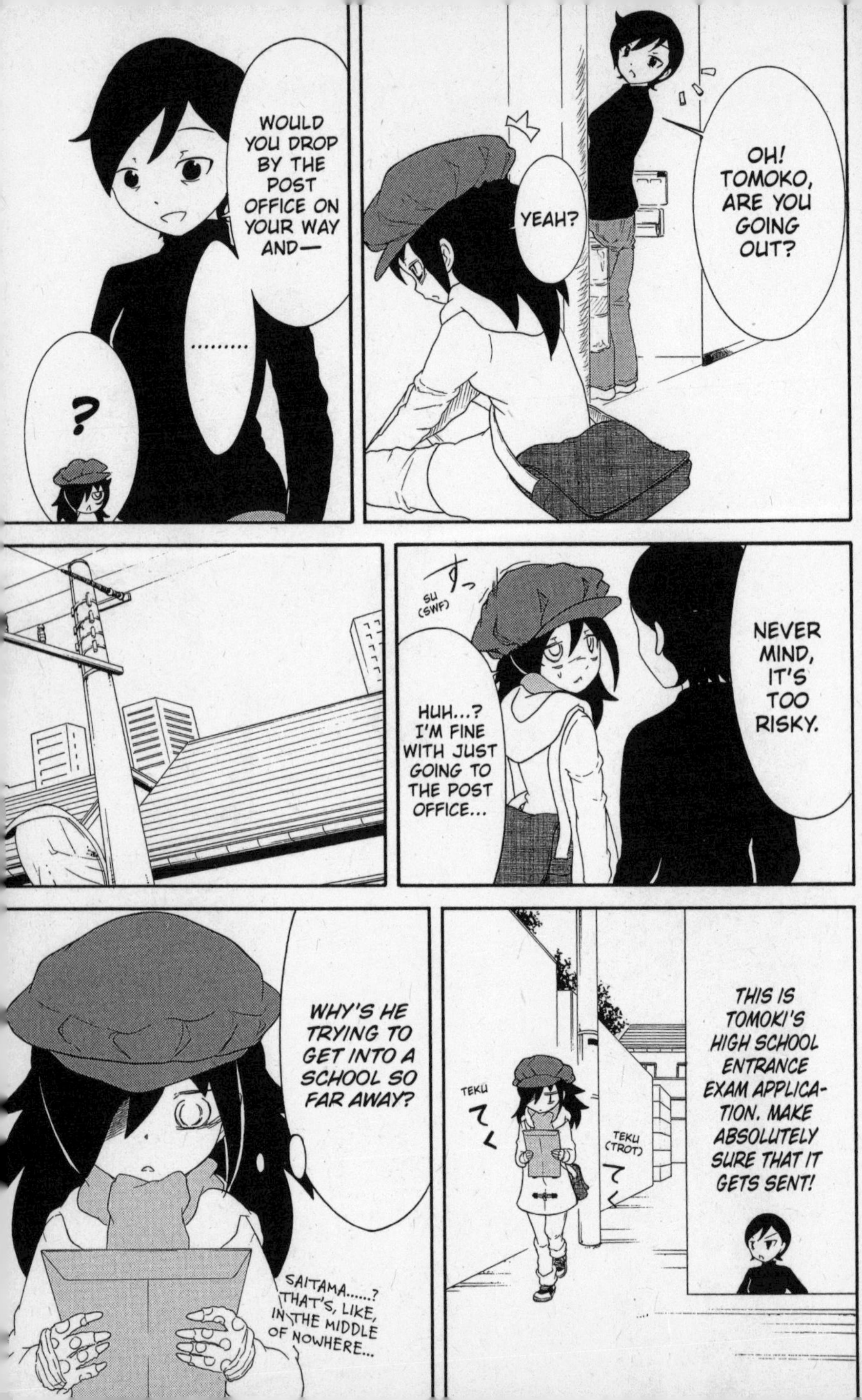
OH! TOMOKO, ARE YOU GOING OUT?
YEAH?
WOULD YOU DROP BY THE POST OFFICE ON YOUR WAY AND—
....
?
NEVER MIND, IT'S TOO RISKY.
すっ
SU (SWF)
HUH...? I'M FINE WITH JUST GOING TO THE POST OFFICE...
THIS IS TOMOKI'S HIGH SCHOOL ENTRANCE EXAM APPLICATION. MAKE ABSOLUTELY SURE THAT IT GETS SENT!
てく
TEKU (TROT)
てく
TEKU
WHY'S HE TRYING TO GET INTO A SCHOOL SO FAR AWAY?
SAITAMA......? THAT'S, LIKE, IN THE MIDDLE OF NOWHERE...

FAIL 35: I'M NOT POPULAR, SO I'LL MOTHER MY BROTHER.

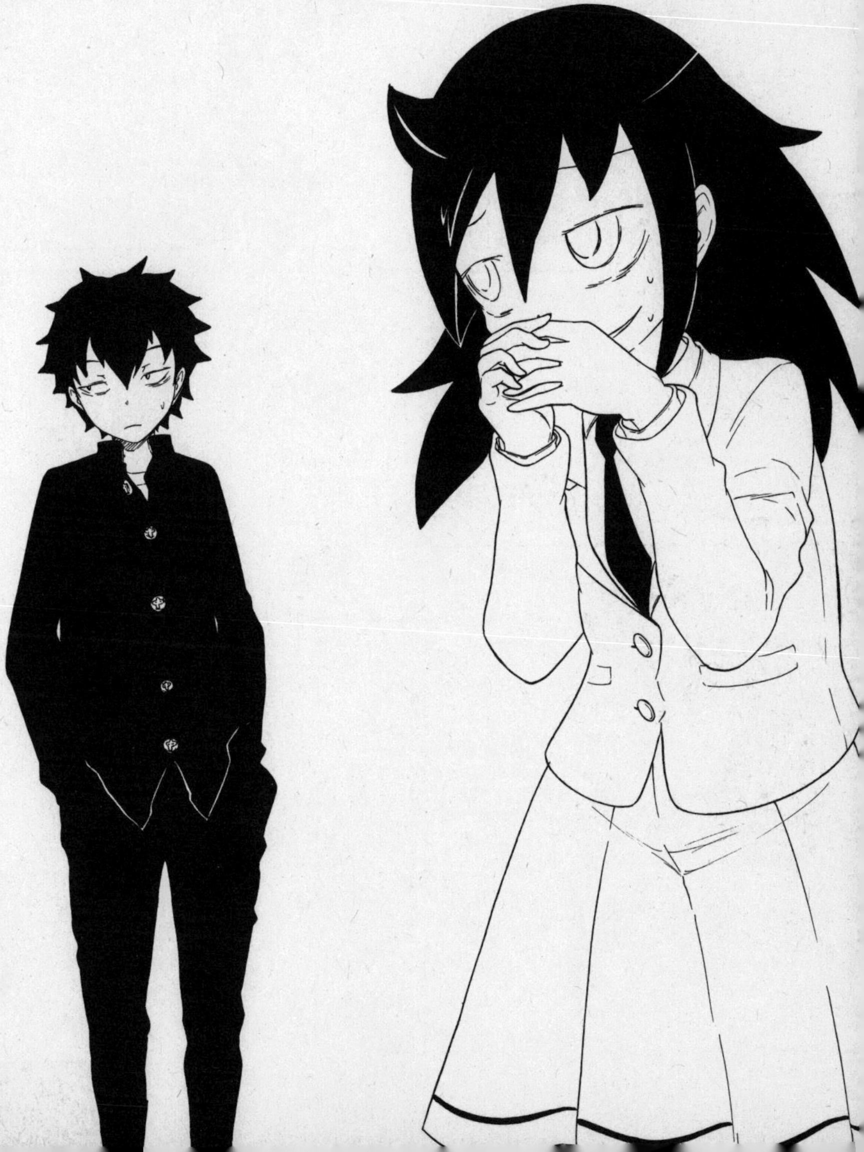

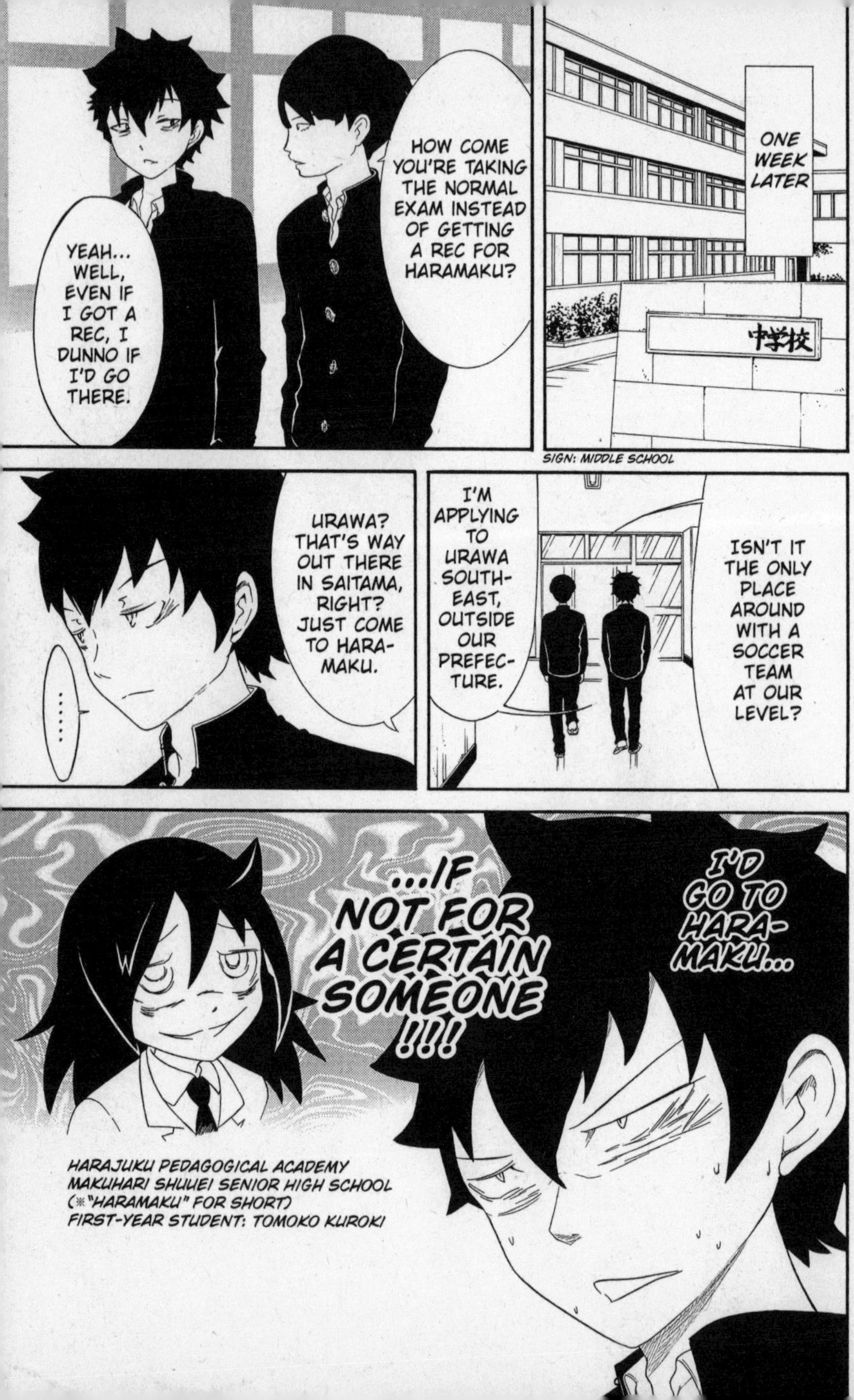
ONE WEEK LATER
中学校
SIGN: MIDDLE SCHOOL
HOW COME YOU'RE TAKING THE NORMAL EXAM INSTEAD OF GETTING A REC FOR HARAMAKU?
YEAH... WELL, EVEN IF I GOT A REC, I DUNNO IF I'D GO THERE.
ISN'T IT THE ONLY PLACE AROUND WITH A SOCCER TEAM AT OUR LEVEL?
I'M APPLYING TO URAWA SOUTH-EAST, OUTSIDE OUR PREFEC-TURE.
URAWA? THAT'S WAY OUT THERE IN SAITAMA, RIGHT? JUST COME TO HARA-MAKU.
......
I'D GO TO HARA-MAKU...
...IF NOT FOR A CERTAIN SOMEONE!!!
HARAJUKU PEDAGOGICAL ACADEMY MAKUHARI SHUUEI SENIOR HIGH SCHOOL (※"HARAMAKU" FOR SHORT) FIRST-YEAR STUDENT: TOMOKO KUROKI

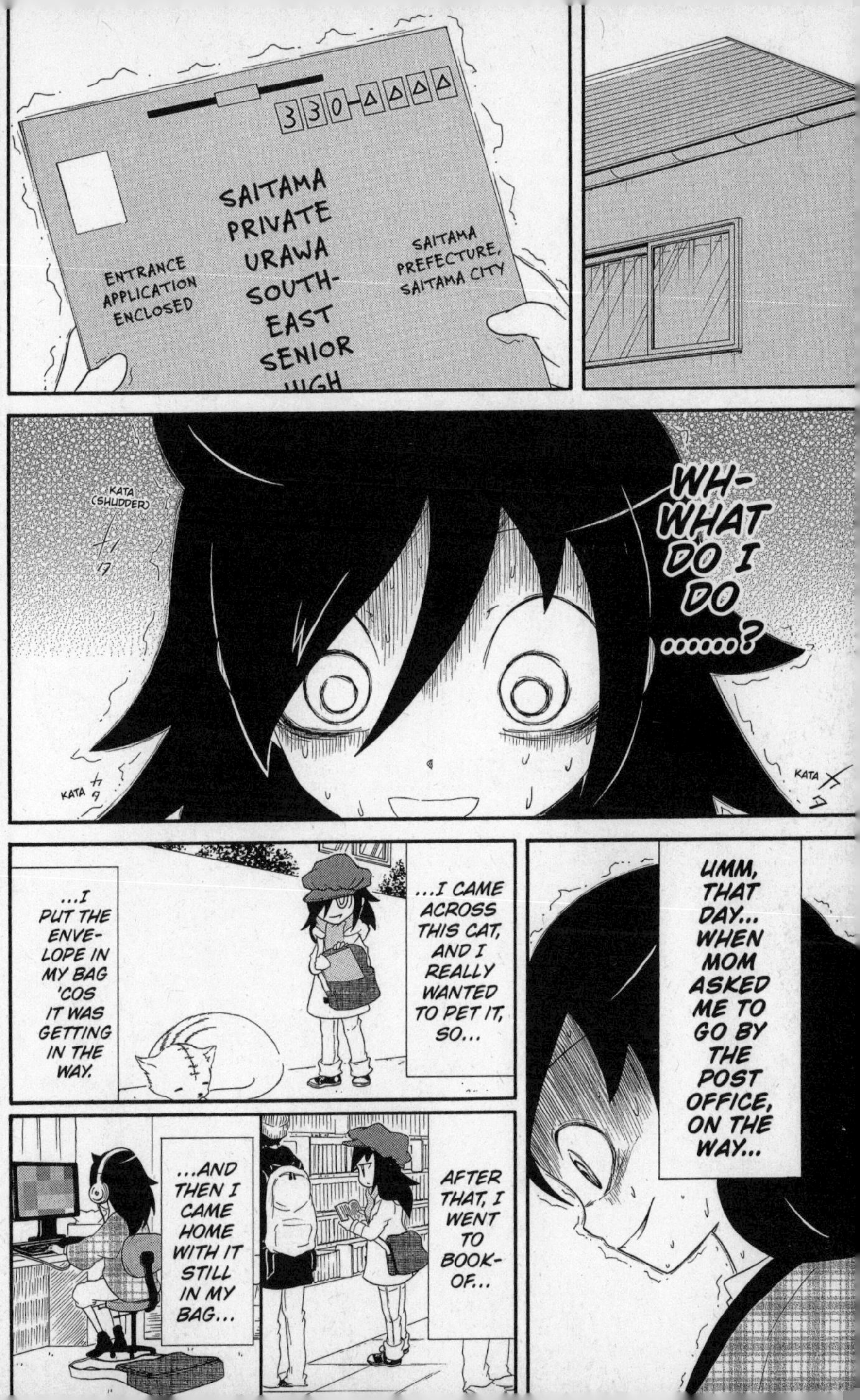

330-△△△△
SAITAMA PREFECTURE, SAITAMA CITY
SAITAMA PRIVATE URAWA SOUTH-EAST SENIOR
ENTRANCE APPLICATION ENCLOSED
KATA
WH-WHAT DO I DO ......?
KATA
KATA (SHUDDER)
UMM, THAT DAY... WHEN MOM ASKED ME TO GO BY THE POST OFFICE, ON THE WAY...
...I CAME ACROSS THIS CAT, AND I REALLY WANTED TO PET IT, SO...
...I PUT THE ENVE-LOPE IN MY BAG 'COS IT WAS GETTING IN THE WAY.
AFTER THAT, I WENT TO BOOK-OF...
...AND THEN I CAME HOME WITH IT STILL IN MY BAG...

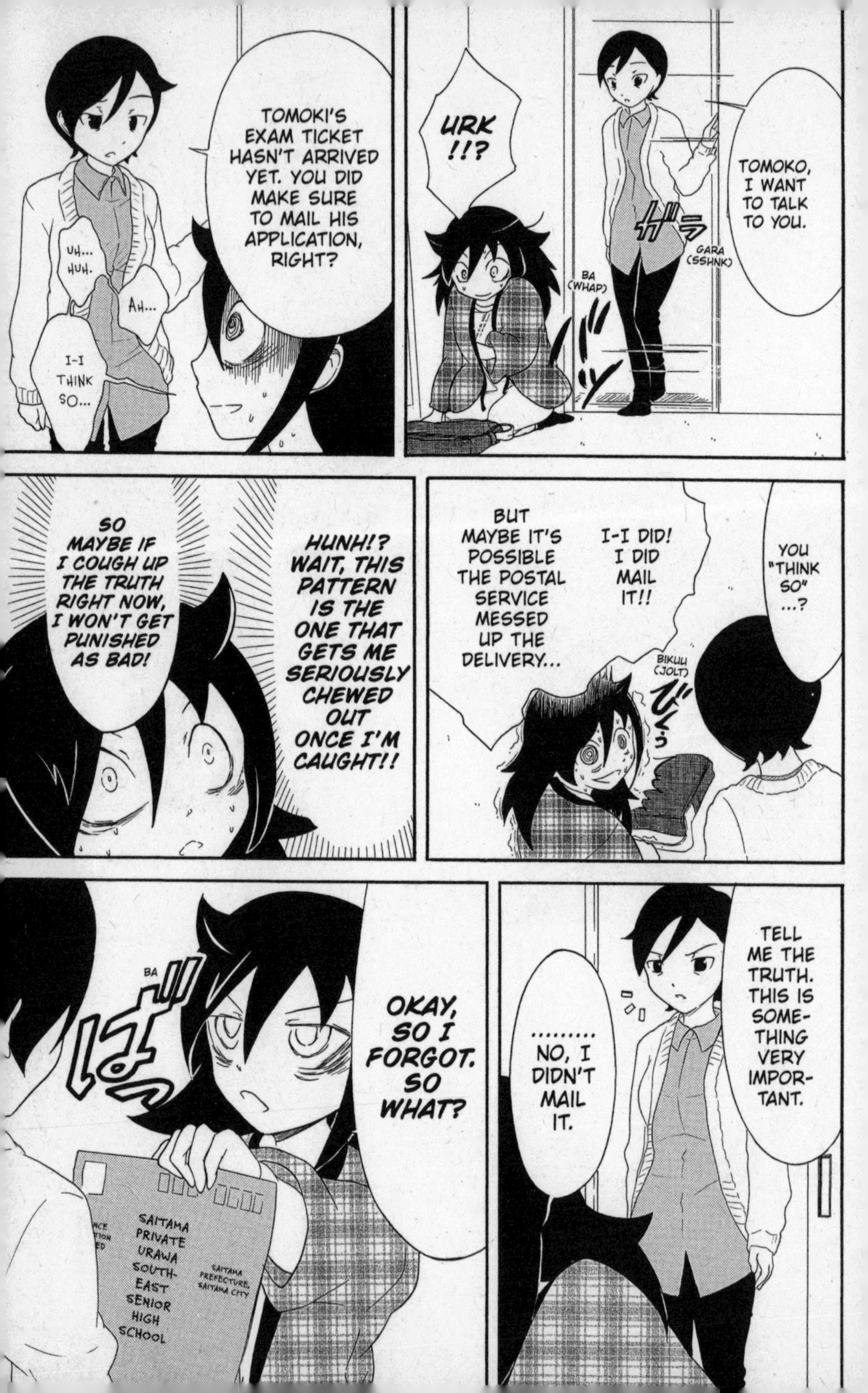
TOMOKO, I WANT TO TALK TO YOU.
GARA (SSHNK)
BA (WHAP)
URK!!?
TOMOKI'S EXAM TICKET HASN'T ARRIVED YET. YOU DID MAKE SURE TO MAIL HIS APPLICATION, RIGHT?
UH... HUH.
AH...
I-I THINK SO...
YOU "THINK SO" ...?
BIKUU (JOLT)
I-I DID! I DID MAIL IT!!
BUT MAYBE IT'S POSSIBLE THE POSTAL SERVICE MESSED UP THE DELIVERY...
HUNH!? WAIT, THIS PATTERN IS THE ONE THAT GETS ME SERIOUSLY CHEWED OUT ONCE I'M CAUGHT!!
SO MAYBE IF I COUGH UP THE TRUTH RIGHT NOW, I WON'T GET PUNISHED AS BAD!
TELL ME THE TRUTH. THIS IS SOMETHING VERY IMPORTANT.
.... NO, I DIDN'T MAIL IT.
OKAY, SO I FORGOT. SO WHAT?
BA
SAITAMA PRIVATE URAWA SOUTHEAST SENIOR HIGH SCHOOL
SAITAMA PREFECTURE, SAITAMA CITY

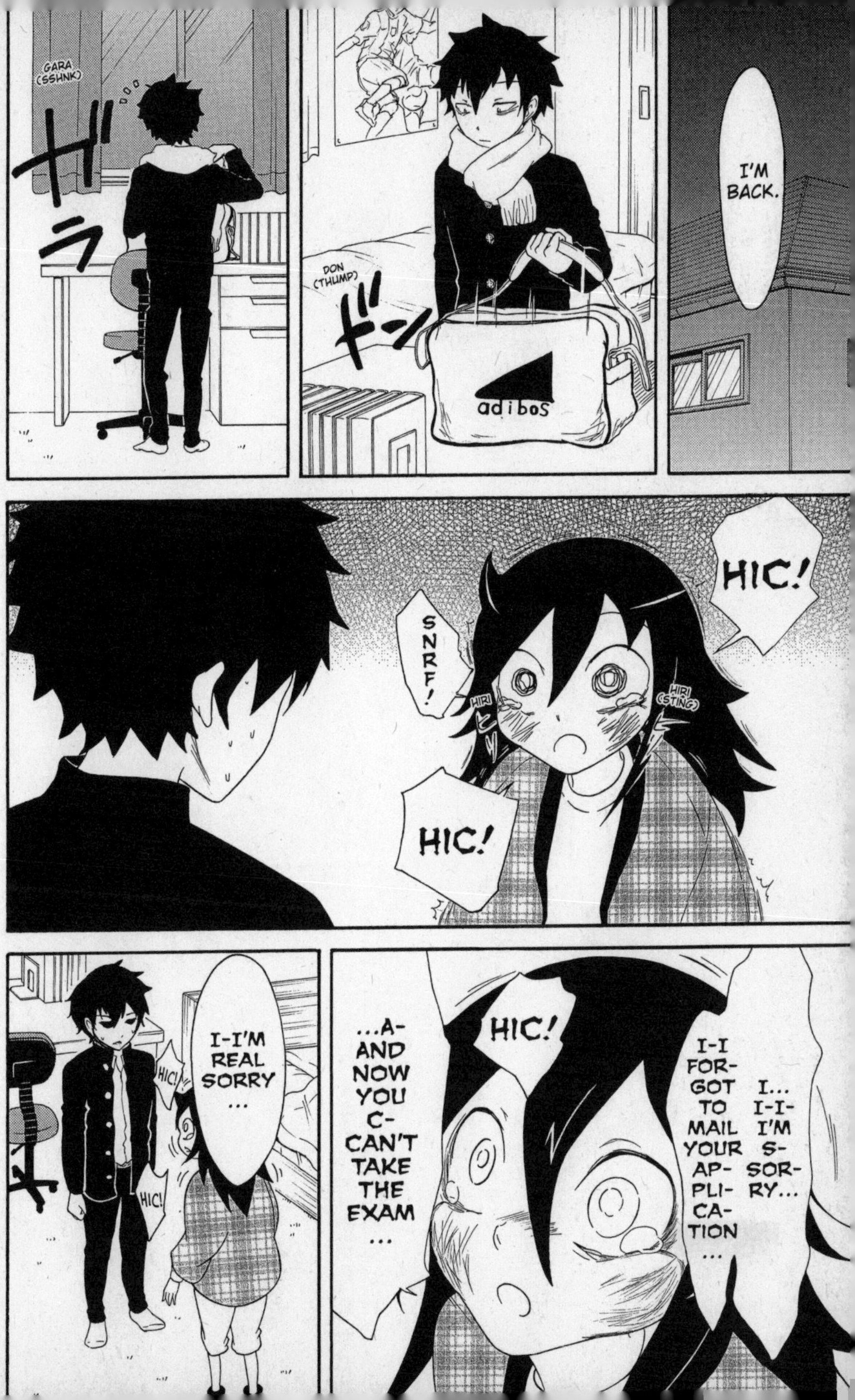
I'M BACK.
DON (THUMP)
GARA (SSHNK)
HIC!
SNRF!
HIRI (STING)
HIRI
HIC!
I... I-I-I'M S-SORRY...
I-I FORGOT TO MAIL YOUR APPLICATION...
HIC!
...A-AND NOW YOU C-CAN'T TAKE THE EXAM...
I-I'M REAL SORRY...
HIC!
HIC!

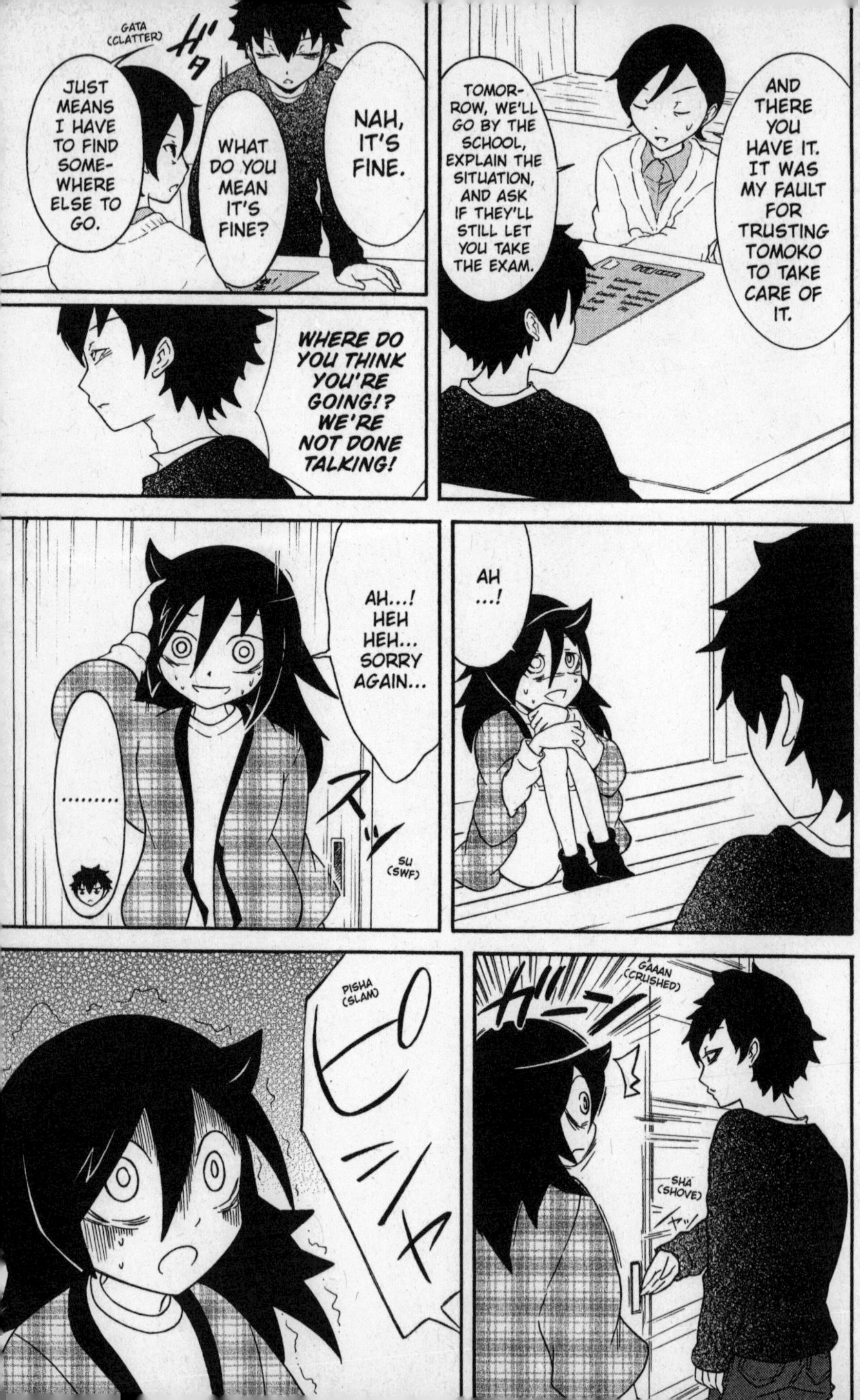
AND THERE YOU HAVE IT. IT WAS MY FAULT FOR TRUSTING TOMOKO TO TAKE CARE OF IT.
TOMORROW, WE'LL GO BY THE SCHOOL, EXPLAIN THE SITUATION, AND ASK IF THEY'LL STILL LET YOU TAKE THE EXAM.
GATA (CLATTER)
NAH, IT'S FINE.
WHAT DO YOU MEAN IT'S FINE?
JUST MEANS I HAVE TO FIND SOMEWHERE ELSE TO GO.
WHERE DO YOU THINK YOU'RE GOING!? WE'RE NOT DONE TALKING!
AH ...!
AH...! HEH HEH... SORRY AGAIN...
SU (SWF)
....
GAAAN (CRUSHED)
SHA (SHOVE)
PISHA (SLAM)

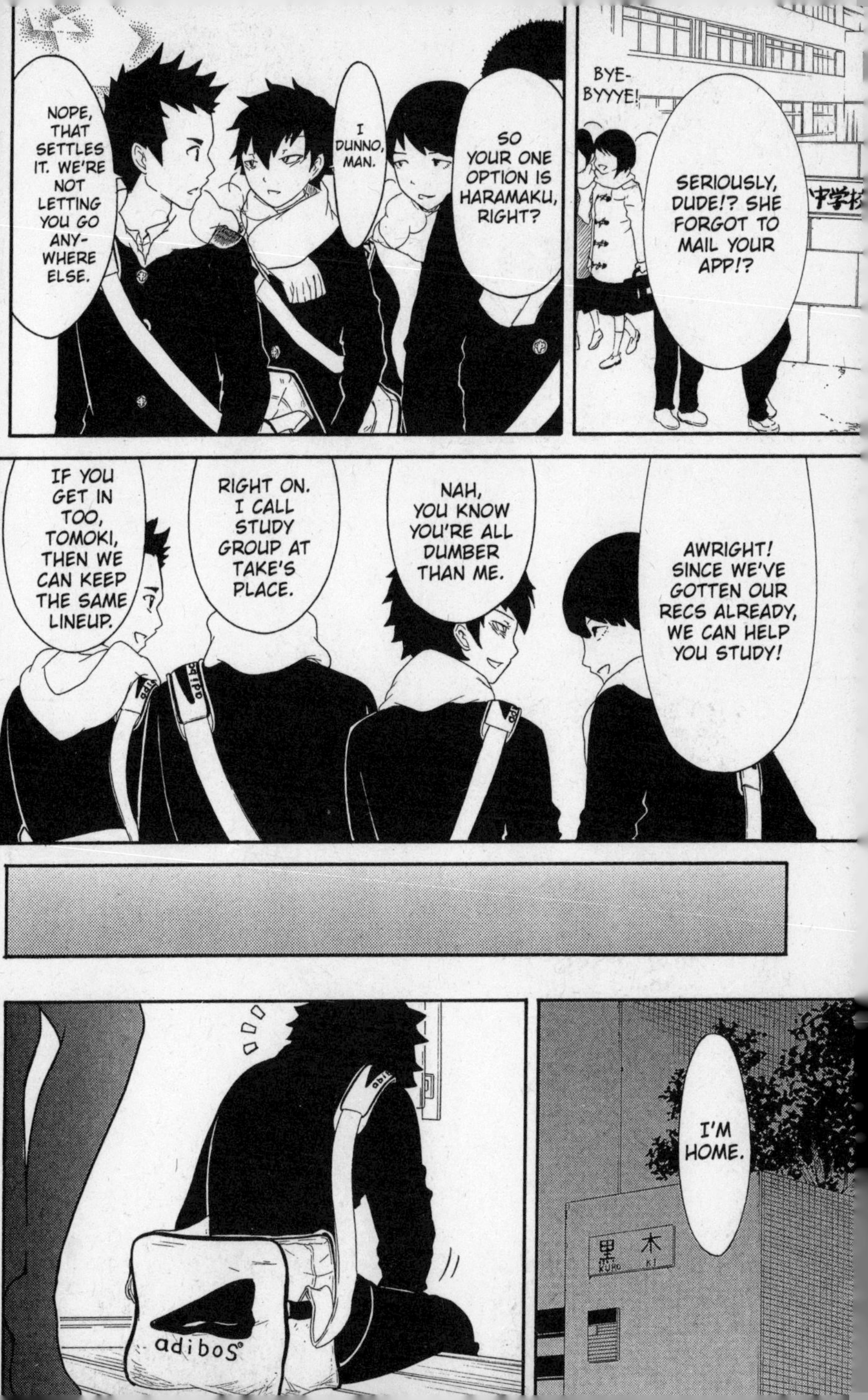
BYE-BYYYE!
中学校
SERIOUSLY, DUDE!? SHE FORGOT TO MAIL YOUR APP!?
SO YOUR ONE OPTION IS HARAMAKU, RIGHT?
I DUNNO, MAN.
NOPE, THAT SETTLES IT. WE'RE NOT LETTING YOU GO ANYWHERE ELSE.
AWRIGHT! SINCE WE'VE GOTTEN OUR RECS ALREADY, WE CAN HELP YOU STUDY!
NAH, YOU KNOW YOU'RE ALL DUMBER THAN ME.
RIGHT ON. I CALL STUDY GROUP AT TAKE'S PLACE.
IF YOU GET IN TOO, TOMOKI, THEN WE CAN KEEP THE SAME LINEUP.
I'M HOME.
黒 木
KURO KI
adiboS

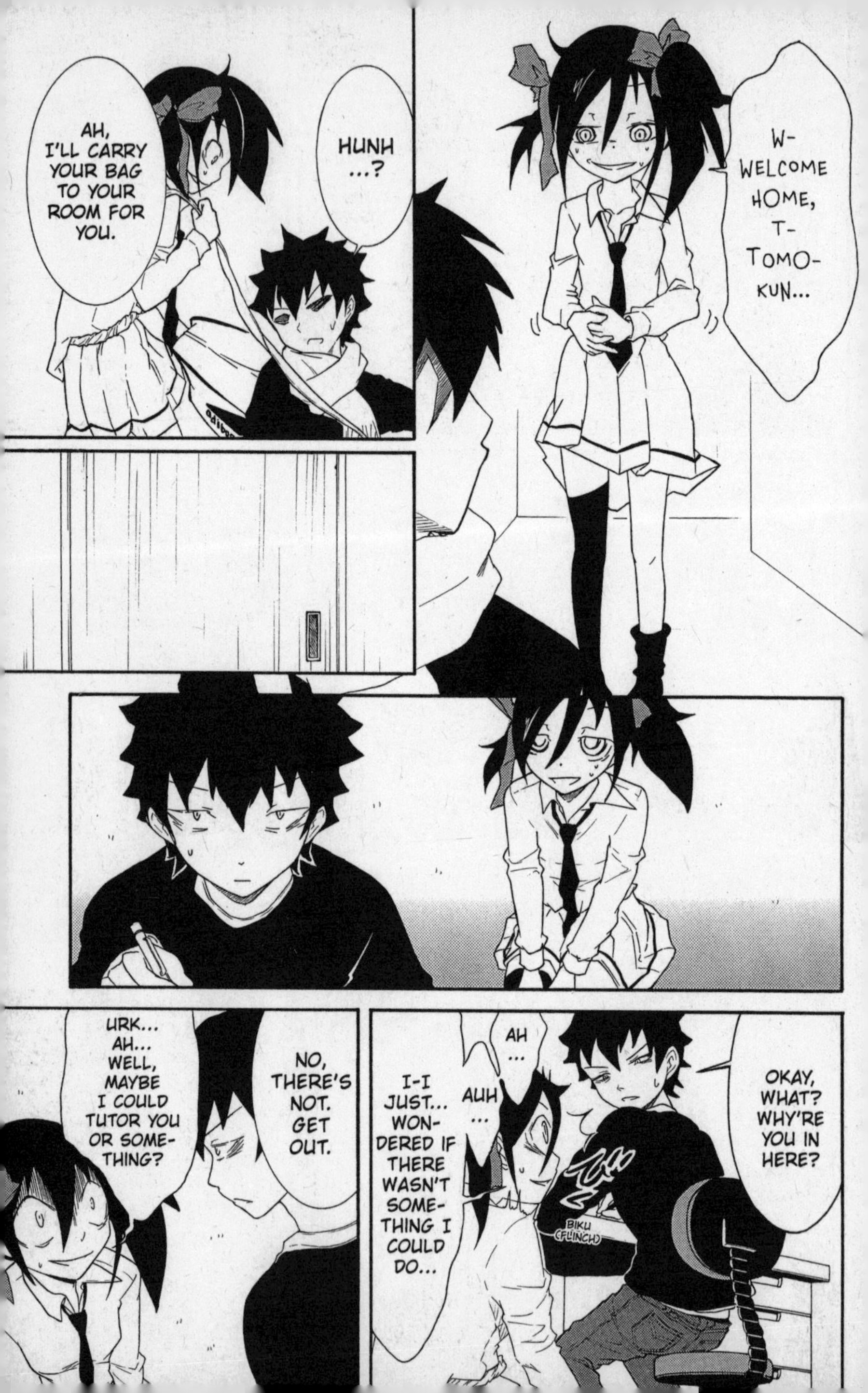
W-WELCOME HOME, T-TOMO-KUN...
HUNH ...?
AH, I'LL CARRY YOUR BAG TO YOUR ROOM FOR YOU.
OKAY, WHAT? WHY'RE YOU IN HERE?
BIKU (FLINCH)
AH ...
AUH ...
I-I JUST... WON-DERED IF THERE WASN'T SOME-THING I COULD DO...
NO, THERE'S NOT. GET OUT.
URK... AH... WELL, MAYBE I COULD TUTOR YOU OR SOME-THING?

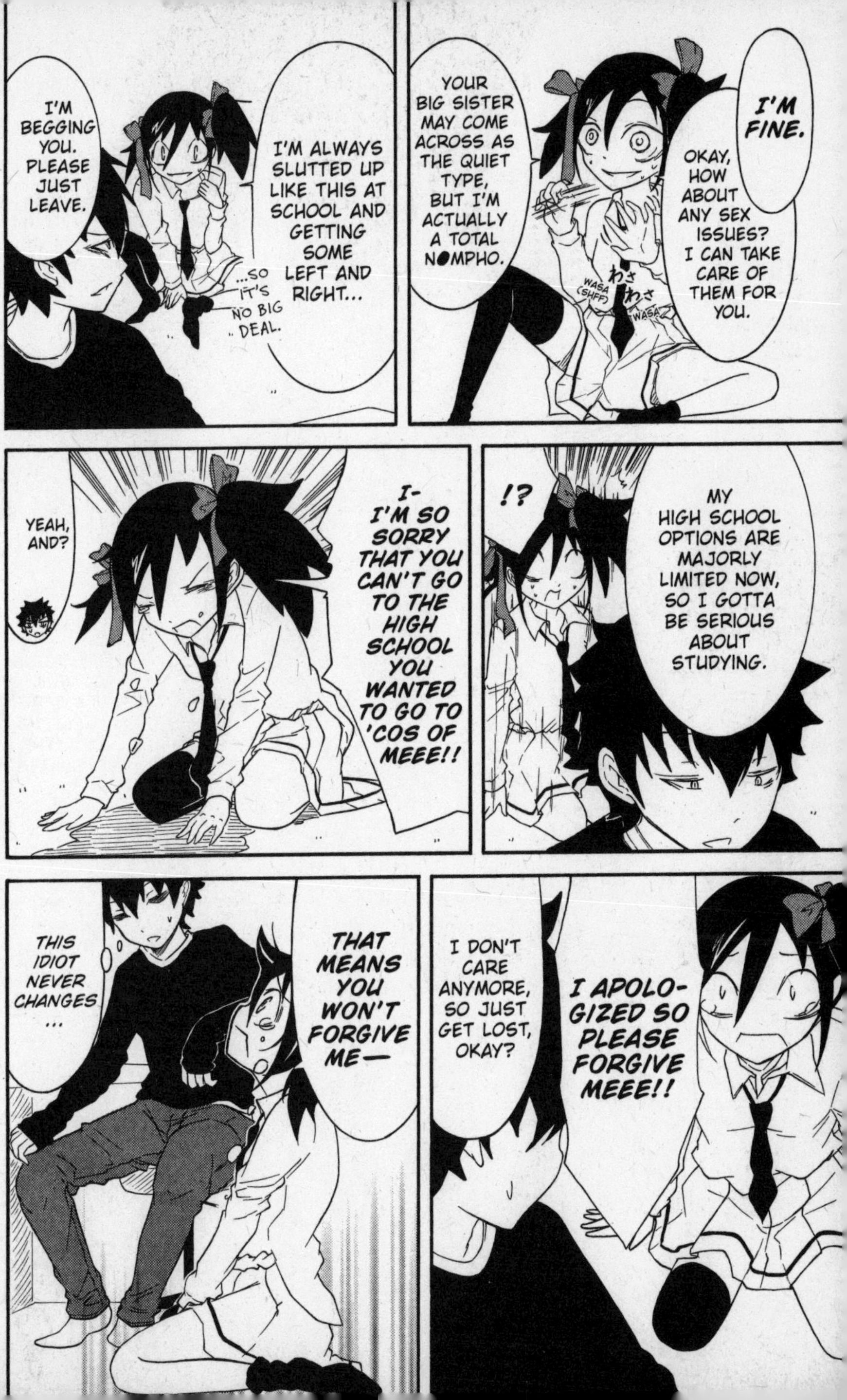
I'M FINE.
OKAY, HOW ABOUT ANY SEX ISSUES? I CAN TAKE CARE OF THEM FOR YOU.
WASA (SHFF)
わさ わさ
WASA
YOUR BIG SISTER MAY COME ACROSS AS THE QUIET TYPE, BUT I'M ACTUALLY A TOTAL N●MPHO.
I'M ALWAYS SLUTTED UP LIKE THIS AT SCHOOL AND GETTING SOME LEFT AND RIGHT...
...SO IT'S NO BIG DEAL.
I'M BEGGING YOU. PLEASE JUST LEAVE.
MY HIGH SCHOOL OPTIONS ARE MAJORLY LIMITED NOW, SO I GOTTA BE SERIOUS ABOUT STUDYING.
!?
I- I'M SO SORRY THAT YOU CAN'T GO TO THE HIGH SCHOOL YOU WANTED TO GO TO 'COS OF MEEE!!
YEAH, AND?
I APOLOGIZED SO PLEASE FORGIVE MEEE!!
I DON'T CARE ANYMORE, SO JUST GET LOST, OKAY?
THAT MEANS YOU WON'T FORGIVE ME—
THIS IDIOT NEVER CHANGES...

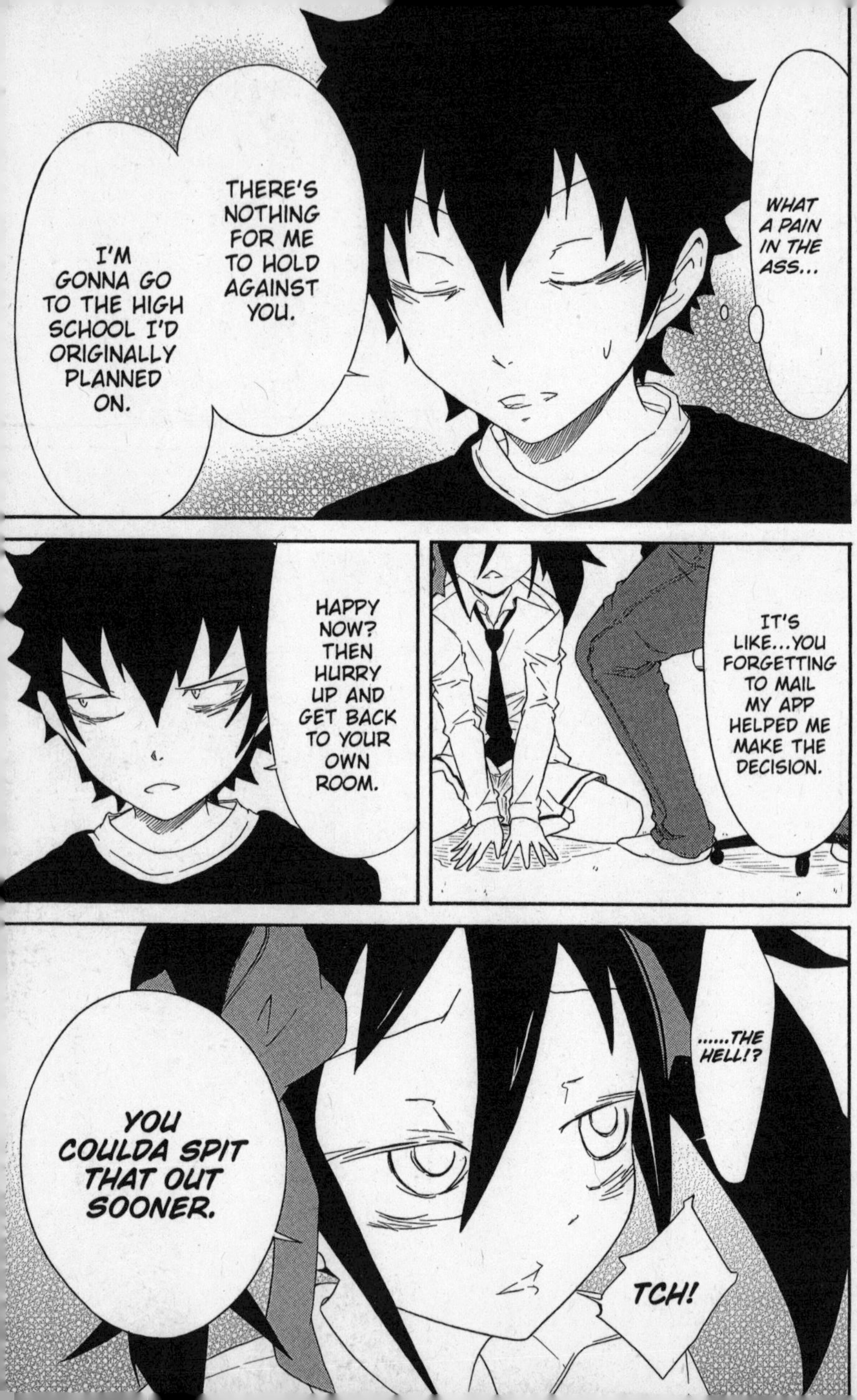
WHAT A PAIN IN THE ASS...
THERE'S NOTHING FOR ME TO HOLD AGAINST YOU.
I'M GONNA GO TO THE HIGH SCHOOL I'D ORIGINALLY PLANNED ON.
IT'S LIKE...YOU FORGETTING TO MAIL MY APP HELPED ME MAKE THE DECISION.
HAPPY NOW? THEN HURRY UP AND GET BACK TO YOUR OWN ROOM.
......THE HELL!?
YOU COULDA SPIT THAT OUT SOONER.
TCH!

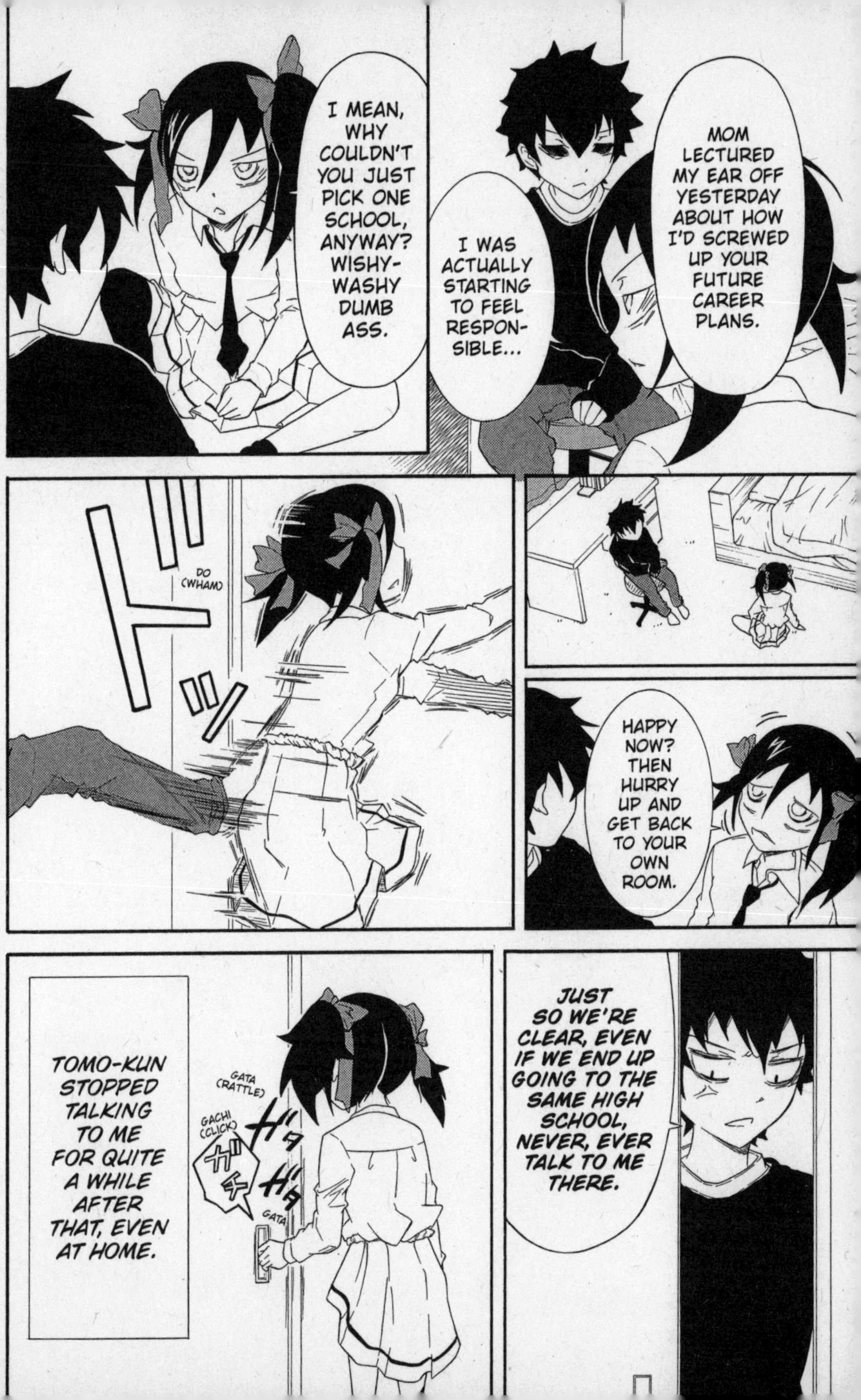
MOM LECTURED MY EAR OFF YESTERDAY ABOUT HOW I'D SCREWED UP YOUR FUTURE CAREER PLANS.
I WAS ACTUALLY STARTING TO FEEL RESPON-SIBLE...
I MEAN, WHY COULDN'T YOU JUST PICK ONE SCHOOL, ANYWAY? WISHY-WASHY DUMB ASS.
HAPPY NOW? THEN HURRY UP AND GET BACK TO YOUR OWN ROOM.
DO (WHAM)
JUST SO WE'RE CLEAR, EVEN IF WE END UP GOING TO THE SAME HIGH SCHOOL, NEVER, EVER TALK TO ME THERE.
TOMO-KUN STOPPED TALKING TO ME FOR QUITE A WHILE AFTER THAT, EVEN AT HOME.
GATA (RATTLE)
GACHI (CLICK)
GATA

No Matter How I Look at It, It's You Guys' Fault I'm Not Popular!

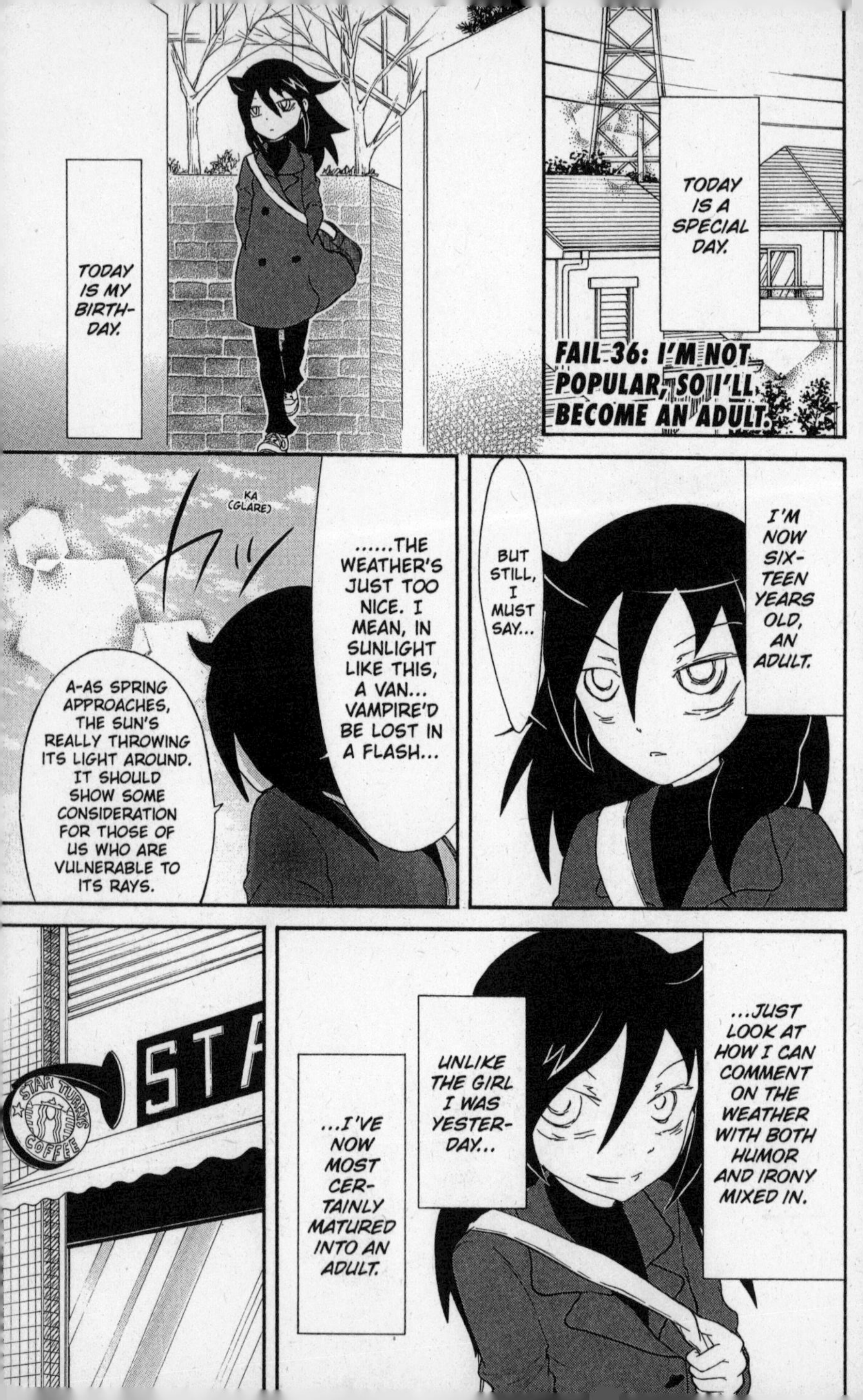
TODAY IS A SPECIAL DAY.
FAIL 36: I'M NOT POPULAR, SO I'LL BECOME AN ADULT.
TODAY IS MY BIRTHDAY.
I'M NOW SIXTEEN YEARS OLD, AN ADULT.
BUT STILL, I MUST SAY...
......THE WEATHER'S JUST TOO NICE. I MEAN, IN SUNLIGHT LIKE THIS, A VAN... VAMPIRE'D BE LOST IN A FLASH...
KA (GLARE)
A-AS SPRING APPROACHES, THE SUN'S REALLY THROWING ITS LIGHT AROUND. IT SHOULD SHOW SOME CONSIDERATION FOR THOSE OF US WHO ARE VULNERABLE TO ITS RAYS.
...JUST LOOK AT HOW I CAN COMMENT ON THE WEATHER WITH BOTH HUMOR AND IRONY MIXED IN.
UNLIKE THE GIRL I WAS YESTERDAY...
...I'VE NOW MOST CERTAINLY MATURED INTO AN ADULT.
STAR TURBY'S COFFEE
STA

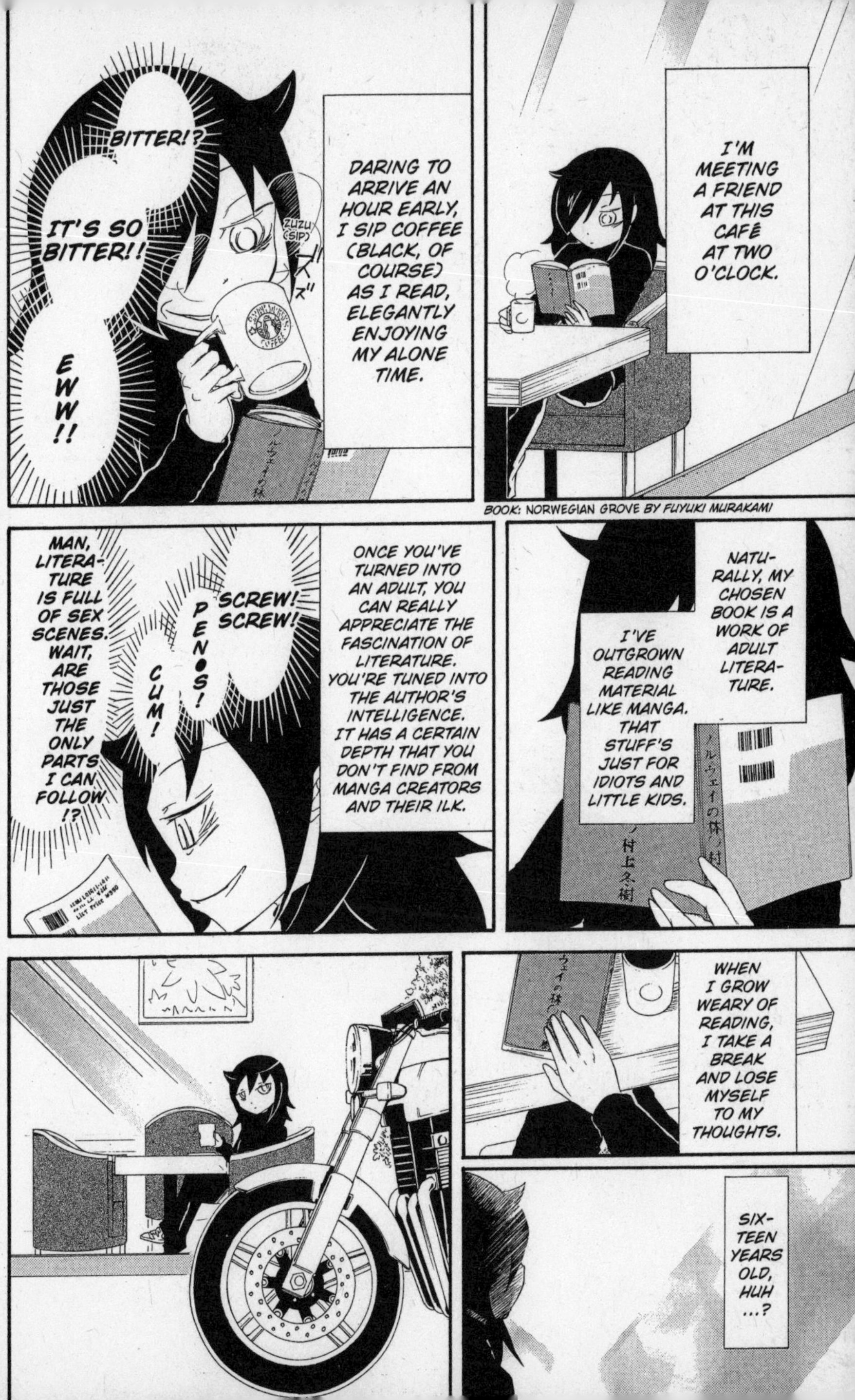
I'M MEETING A FRIEND AT THIS CAFÉ AT TWO O'CLOCK.
DARING TO ARRIVE AN HOUR EARLY, I SIP COFFEE (BLACK, OF COURSE) AS I READ, ELEGANTLY ENJOYING MY ALONE TIME.
ZUZU (SIP)
BITTER!?
IT'S SO BITTER!!
EWW!!
BOOK: NORWEGIAN GROVE BY FUYUKI MURAKAMI
NATURALLY, MY CHOSEN BOOK IS A WORK OF ADULT LITERATURE.
I'VE OUTGROWN READING MATERIAL LIKE MANGA. THAT STUFF'S JUST FOR IDIOTS AND LITTLE KIDS.
ONCE YOU'VE TURNED INTO AN ADULT, YOU CAN REALLY APPRECIATE THE FASCINATION OF LITERATURE. YOU'RE TUNED INTO THE AUTHOR'S INTELLIGENCE. IT HAS A CERTAIN DEPTH THAT YOU DON'T FIND FROM MANGA CREATORS AND THEIR ILK.
SCREW! SCREW!
PEN●S!
CUM!
MAN, LITERATURE IS FULL OF SEX SCENES. WAIT, ARE THOSE JUST THE ONLY PARTS I CAN FOLLOW!?
WHEN I GROW WEARY OF READING, I TAKE A BREAK AND LOSE MYSELF TO MY THOUGHTS.
SIXTEEN YEARS OLD, HUH...?

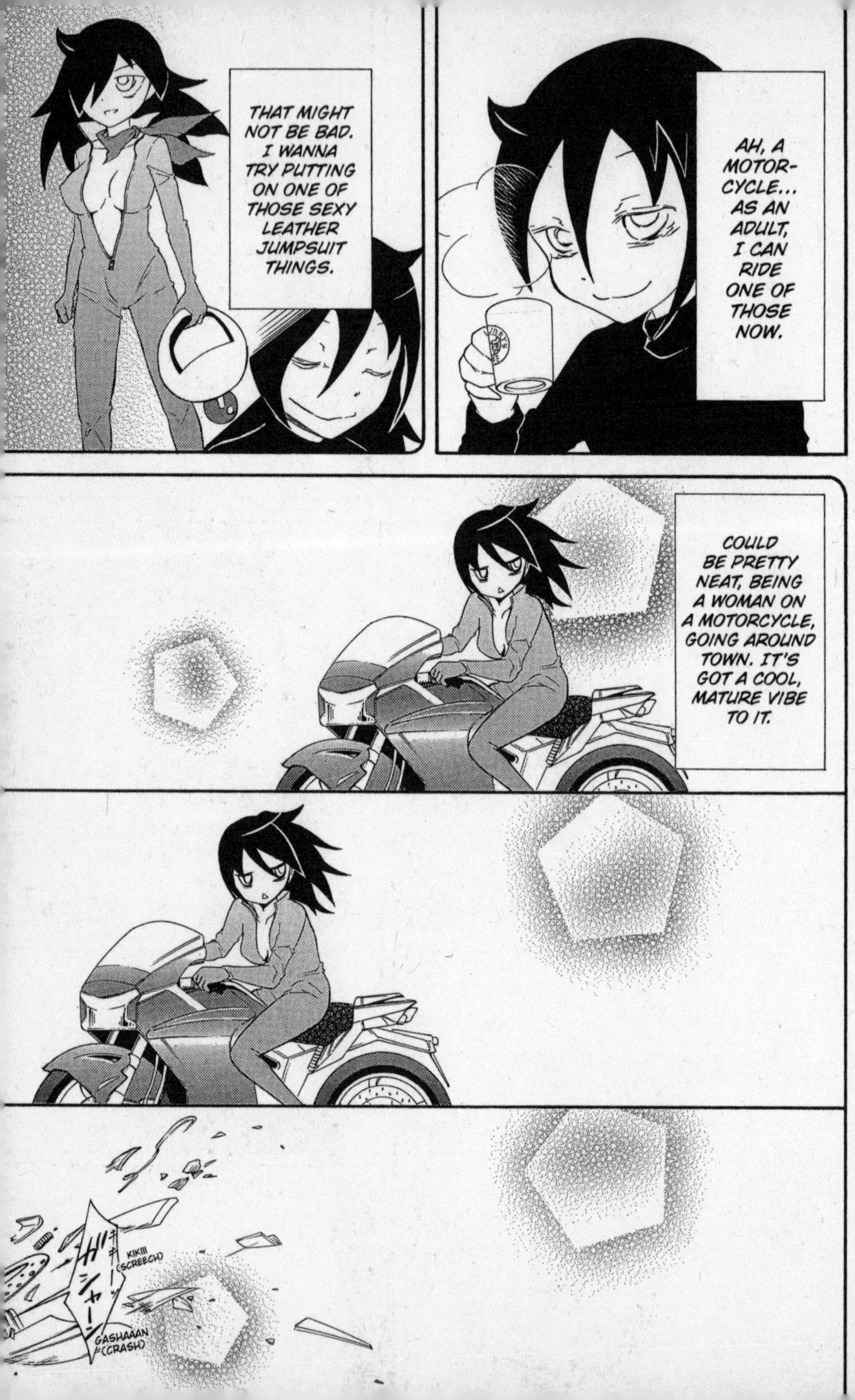
AH, A MOTOR-CYCLE... AS AN ADULT, I CAN RIDE ONE OF THOSE NOW.
THAT MIGHT NOT BE BAD. I WANNA TRY PUTTING ON ONE OF THOSE SEXY LEATHER JUMPSUIT THINGS.
COULD BE PRETTY NEAT, BEING A WOMAN ON A MOTORCYCLE, GOING AROUND TOWN. IT'S GOT A COOL, MATURE VIBE TO IT.
KIKIII (SCREECH)
GASHAAAN (CRASH)

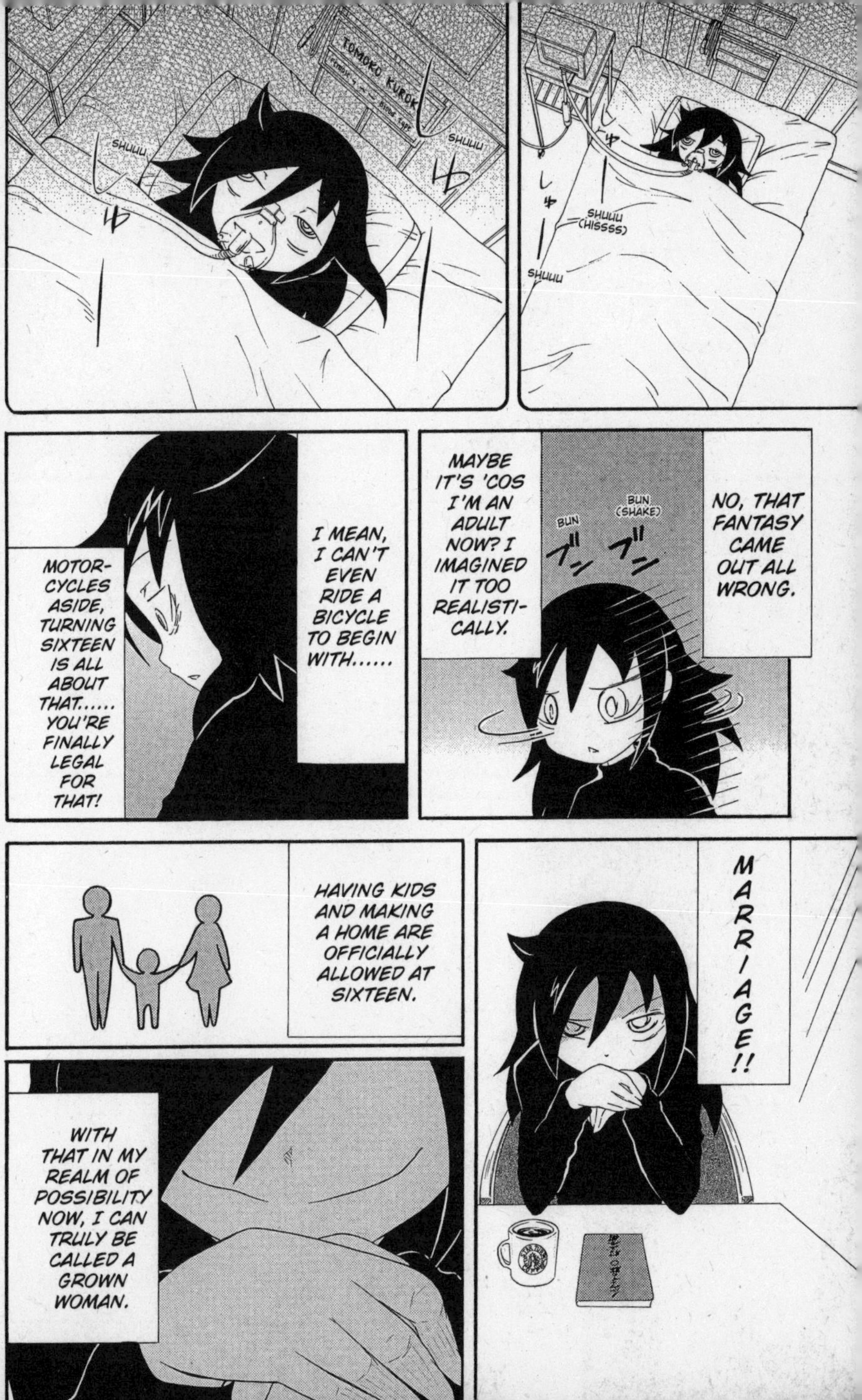
SHUUU (HISSSS)
SHUUU
TOMOKO KUROKI
SHUUU
SHUUU
NO, THAT FANTASY CAME OUT ALL WRONG.
MAYBE IT'S 'COS I'M AN ADULT NOW? I IMAGINED IT TOO REALISTICALLY.
BUN (SHAKE)
BUN
I MEAN, I CAN'T EVEN RIDE A BICYCLE TO BEGIN WITH......
MOTORCYCLES ASIDE, TURNING SIXTEEN IS ALL ABOUT THAT...... YOU'RE FINALLY LEGAL FOR THAT!
MARRIAGE!!
HAVING KIDS AND MAKING A HOME ARE OFFICIALLY ALLOWED AT SIXTEEN.
WITH THAT IN MY REALM OF POSSIBILITY NOW, I CAN TRULY BE CALLED A GROWN WOMAN.

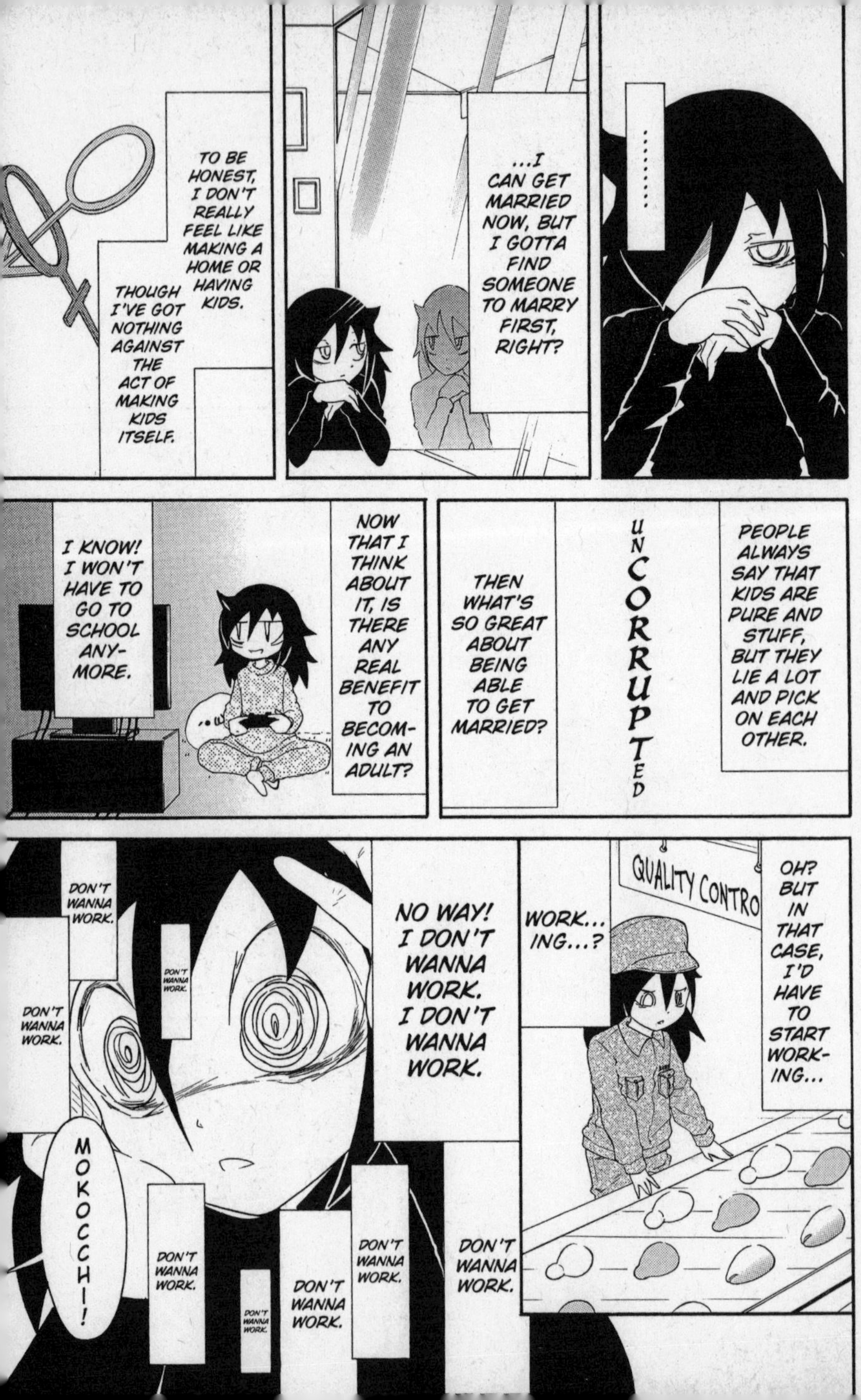
……
…I CAN GET MARRIED NOW, BUT I GOTTA FIND SOMEONE TO MARRY FIRST, RIGHT?
TO BE HONEST, I DON'T REALLY FEEL LIKE MAKING A HOME OR HAVING KIDS.
THOUGH I'VE GOT NOTHING AGAINST THE ACT OF MAKING KIDS ITSELF.
PEOPLE ALWAYS SAY THAT KIDS ARE PURE AND STUFF, BUT THEY LIE A LOT AND PICK ON EACH OTHER.
UNCORRUPTED
THEN WHAT'S SO GREAT ABOUT BEING ABLE TO GET MARRIED?
NOW THAT I THINK ABOUT IT, IS THERE ANY REAL BENEFIT TO BECOMING AN ADULT?
I KNOW! I WON'T HAVE TO GO TO SCHOOL ANYMORE.
OH? BUT IN THAT CASE, I'D HAVE TO START WORKING…
QUALITY CONTRO
WORK… ING…?
NO WAY! I DON'T WANNA WORK. I DON'T WANNA WORK.
DON'T WANNA WORK.
DON'T WANNA WORK.
DON'T WANNA WORK.
DON'T WANNA WORK.
DON'T WANNA WORK.
DON'T WANNA WORK.
DON'T WANNA WORK.
DON'T WANNA WORK.
MOKOCCHI!

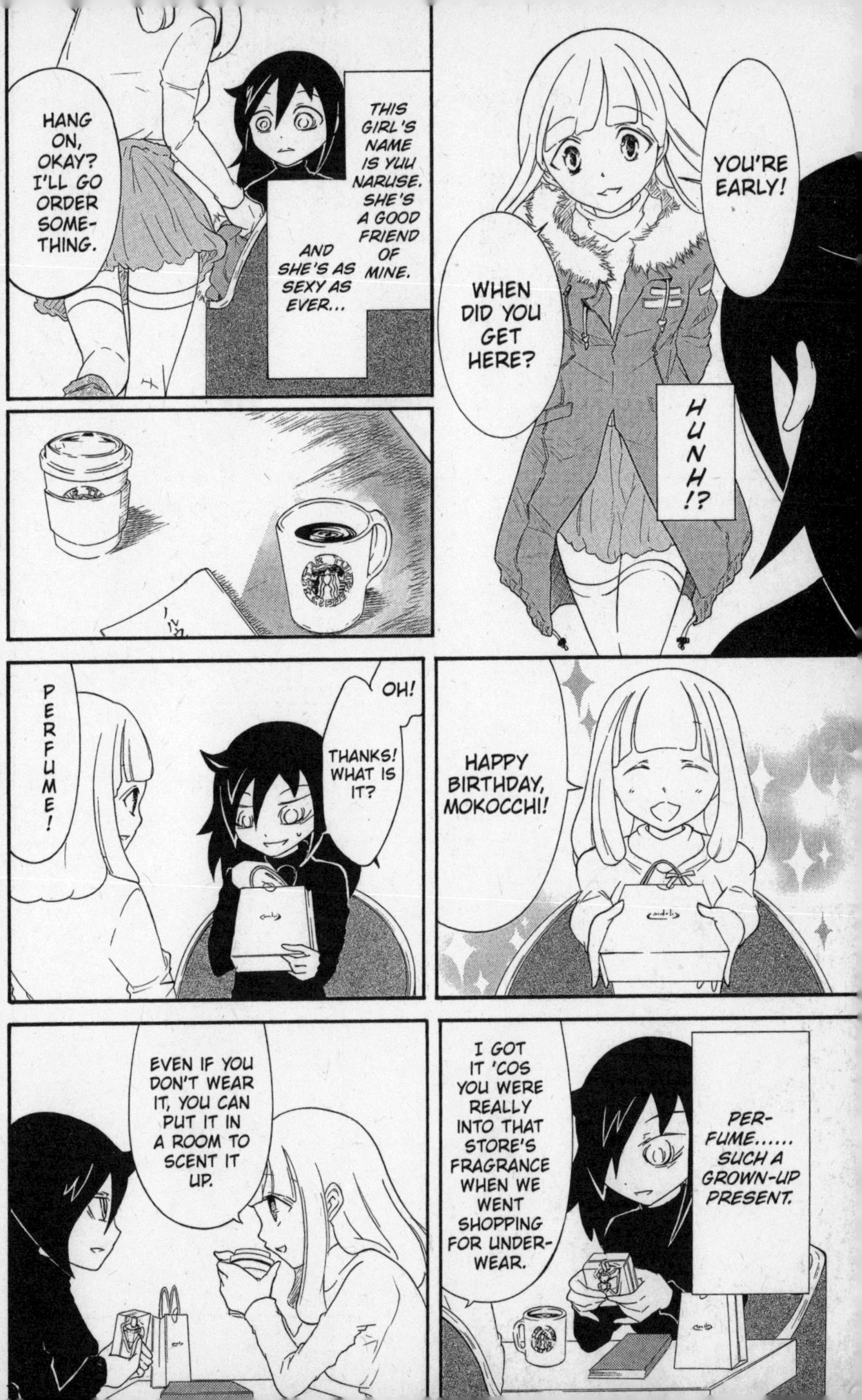
YOU'RE EARLY!
WHEN DID YOU GET HERE?
HUNH!?
THIS GIRL'S NAME IS YUU NARUSE. SHE'S A GOOD FRIEND OF MINE.
AND SHE'S AS SEXY AS EVER...
HANG ON, OKAY? I'LL GO ORDER SOMETHING.
HAPPY BIRTHDAY, MOKOCCHI!
OH!
THANKS! WHAT IS IT?
PERFUME!
PERFUME...... SUCH A GROWN-UP PRESENT.
I GOT IT 'COS YOU WERE REALLY INTO THAT STORE'S FRAGRANCE WHEN WE WENT SHOPPING FOR UNDERWEAR.
EVEN IF YOU DON'T WEAR IT, YOU CAN PUT IT IN A ROOM TO SCENT IT UP.

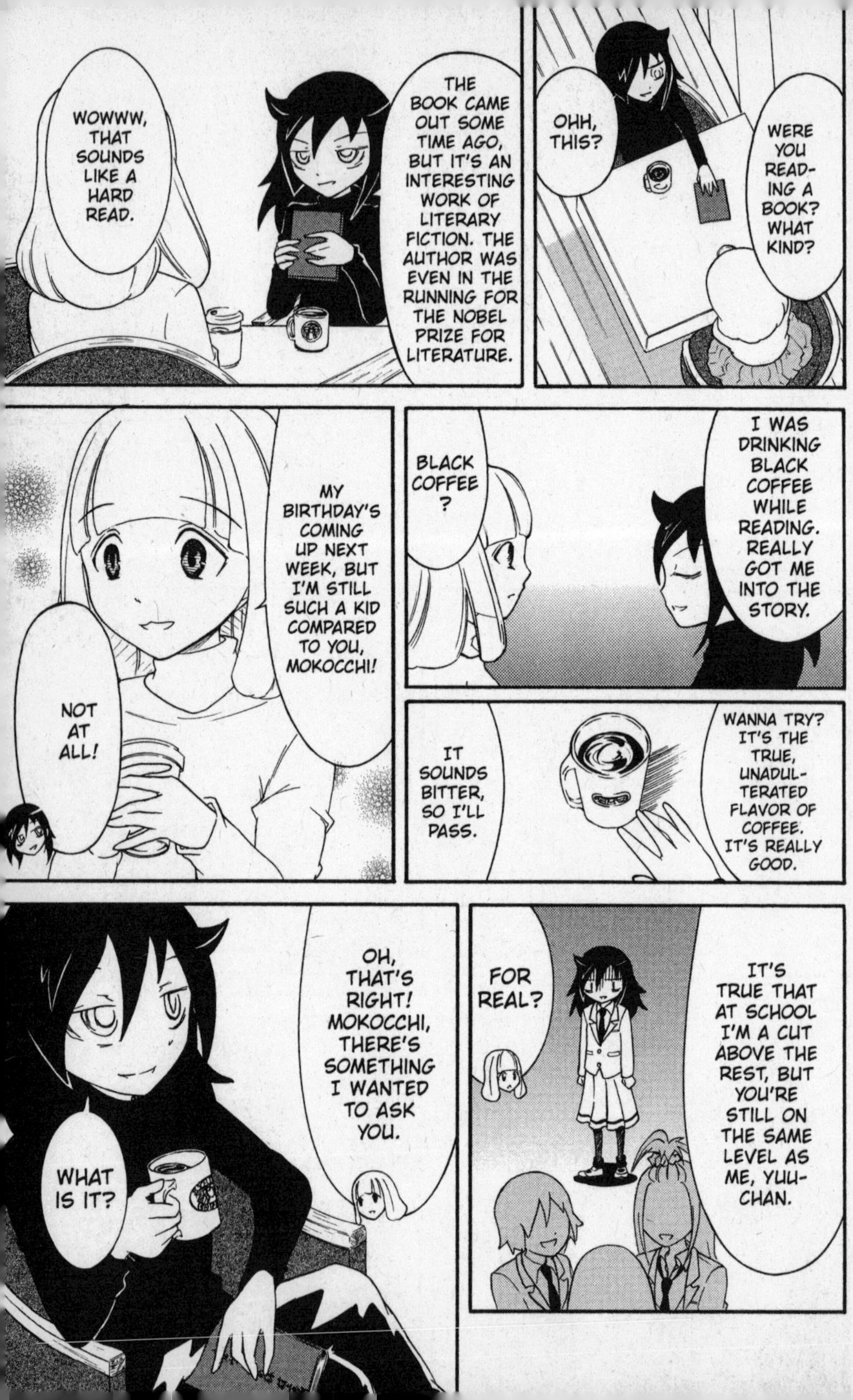
WERE YOU READING A BOOK? WHAT KIND?
OHH, THIS?
THE BOOK CAME OUT SOME TIME AGO, BUT IT'S AN INTERESTING WORK OF LITERARY FICTION. THE AUTHOR WAS EVEN IN THE RUNNING FOR THE NOBEL PRIZE FOR LITERATURE.
WOWWW, THAT SOUNDS LIKE A HARD READ.
I WAS DRINKING BLACK COFFEE WHILE READING. REALLY GOT ME INTO THE STORY.
BLACK COFFEE?
WANNA TRY? IT'S THE TRUE, UNADULTERATED FLAVOR OF COFFEE. IT'S REALLY GOOD.
IT SOUNDS BITTER, SO I'LL PASS.
MY BIRTHDAY'S COMING UP NEXT WEEK, BUT I'M STILL SUCH A KID COMPARED TO YOU, MOKOCCHI!
NOT AT ALL!
IT'S TRUE THAT AT SCHOOL I'M A CUT ABOVE THE REST, BUT YOU'RE STILL ON THE SAME LEVEL AS ME, YUU-CHAN.
FOR REAL?
OH, THAT'S RIGHT! MOKOCCHI, THERE'S SOMETHING I WANTED TO ASK YOU.
WHAT IS IT?

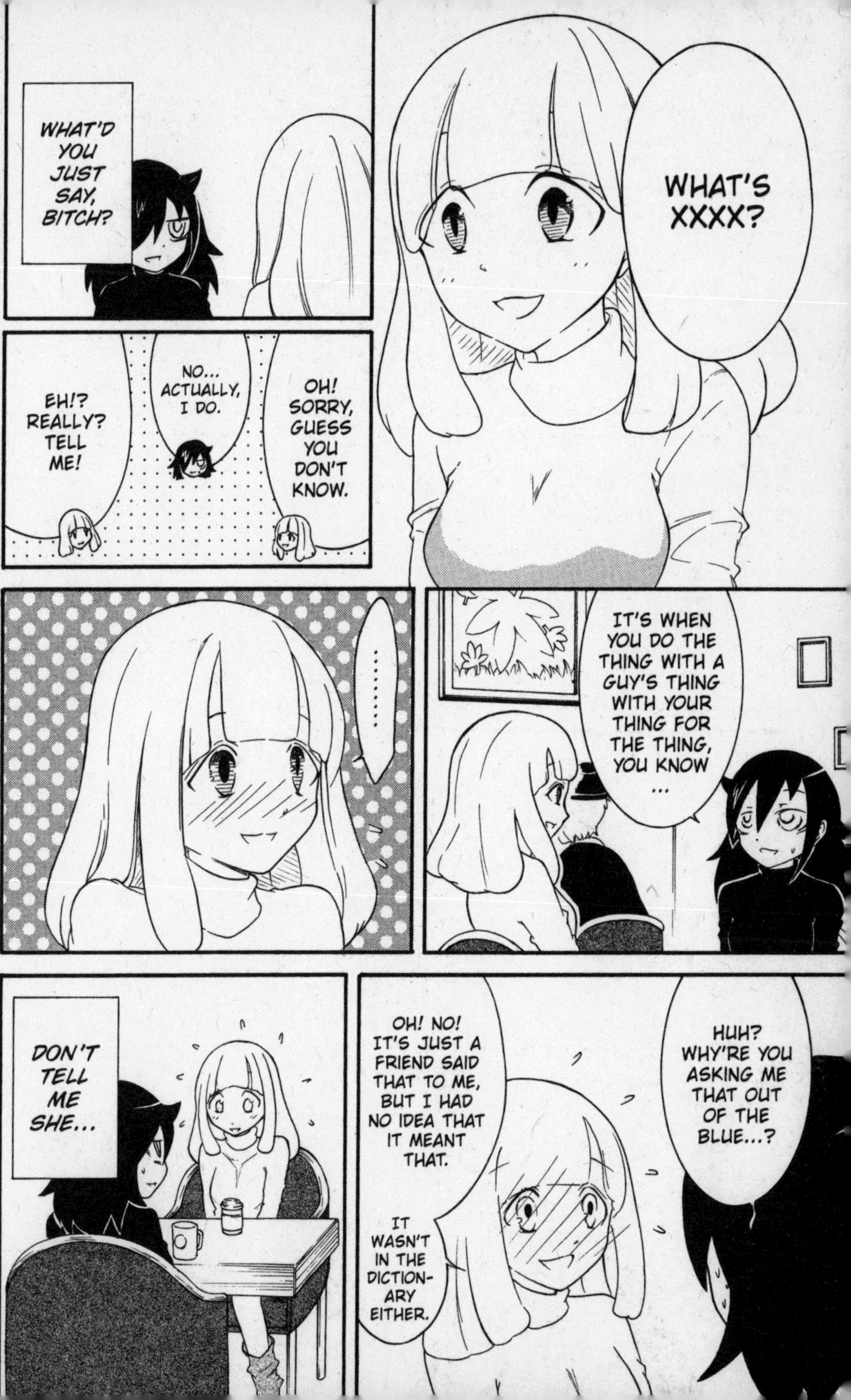
WHAT'S XXXX?
WHAT'D YOU JUST SAY, BITCH?
OH! SORRY, GUESS YOU DON'T KNOW.
NO... ACTUALLY, I DO.
EH!? REALLY? TELL ME!
IT'S WHEN YOU DO THE THING WITH A GUY'S THING WITH YOUR THING FOR THE THING, YOU KNOW...
......
HUH? WHY'RE YOU ASKING ME THAT OUT OF THE BLUE...?
OH! NO! IT'S JUST A FRIEND SAID THAT TO ME, BUT I HAD NO IDEA THAT IT MEANT THAT.
IT WASN'T IN THE DICTIONARY EITHER.
DON'T TELL ME SHE...

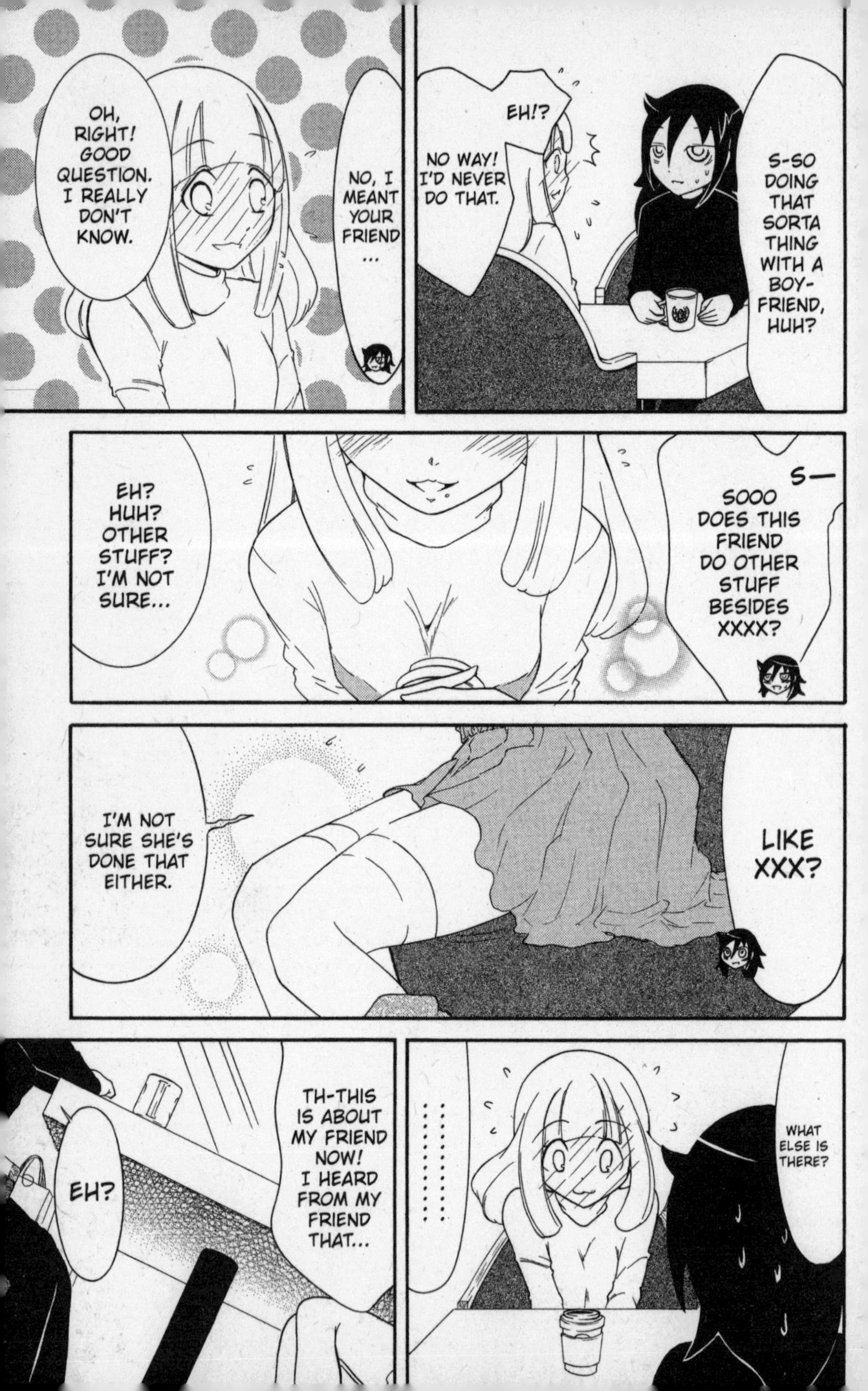
S-SO DOING THAT SORTA THING WITH A BOY-FRIEND, HUH?
EH!?
NO WAY! I'D NEVER DO THAT.
NO, I MEANT YOUR FRIEND ...
OH, RIGHT! GOOD QUESTION. I REALLY DON'T KNOW.
S—
SOOO DOES THIS FRIEND DO OTHER STUFF BESIDES XXXX?
EH? HUH? OTHER STUFF? I'M NOT SURE...
LIKE XXX?
I'M NOT SURE SHE'S DONE THAT EITHER.
WHAT ELSE IS THERE?
......
TH-THIS IS ABOUT MY FRIEND NOW! I HEARD FROM MY FRIEND THAT...
EH?

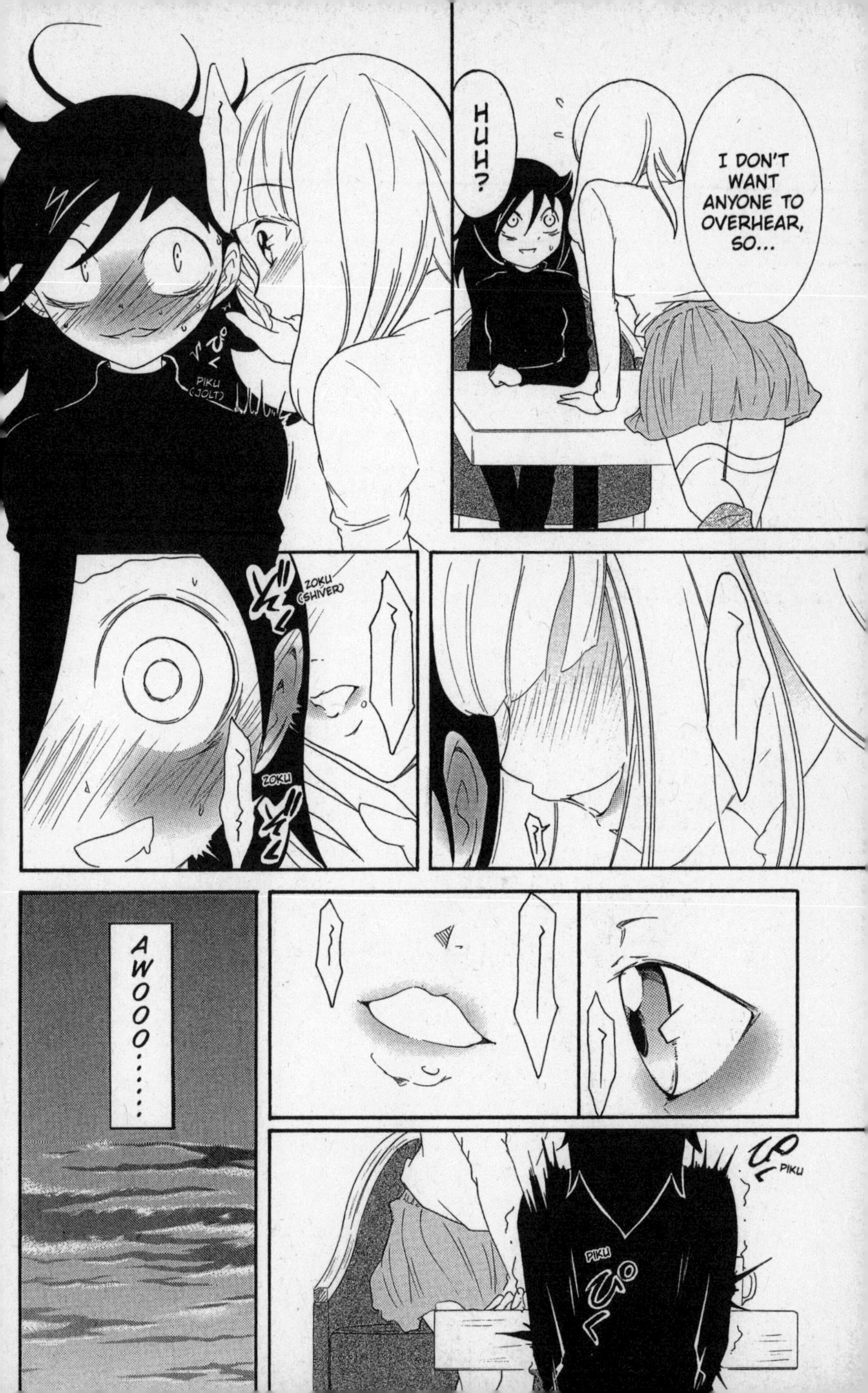
I DON'T WANT ANYONE TO OVERHEAR, SO...
HUH?
PIKU (JOLT)
ZOKU (SHIVER)
ZOKU
PIKU
PIKU
AWOOO......

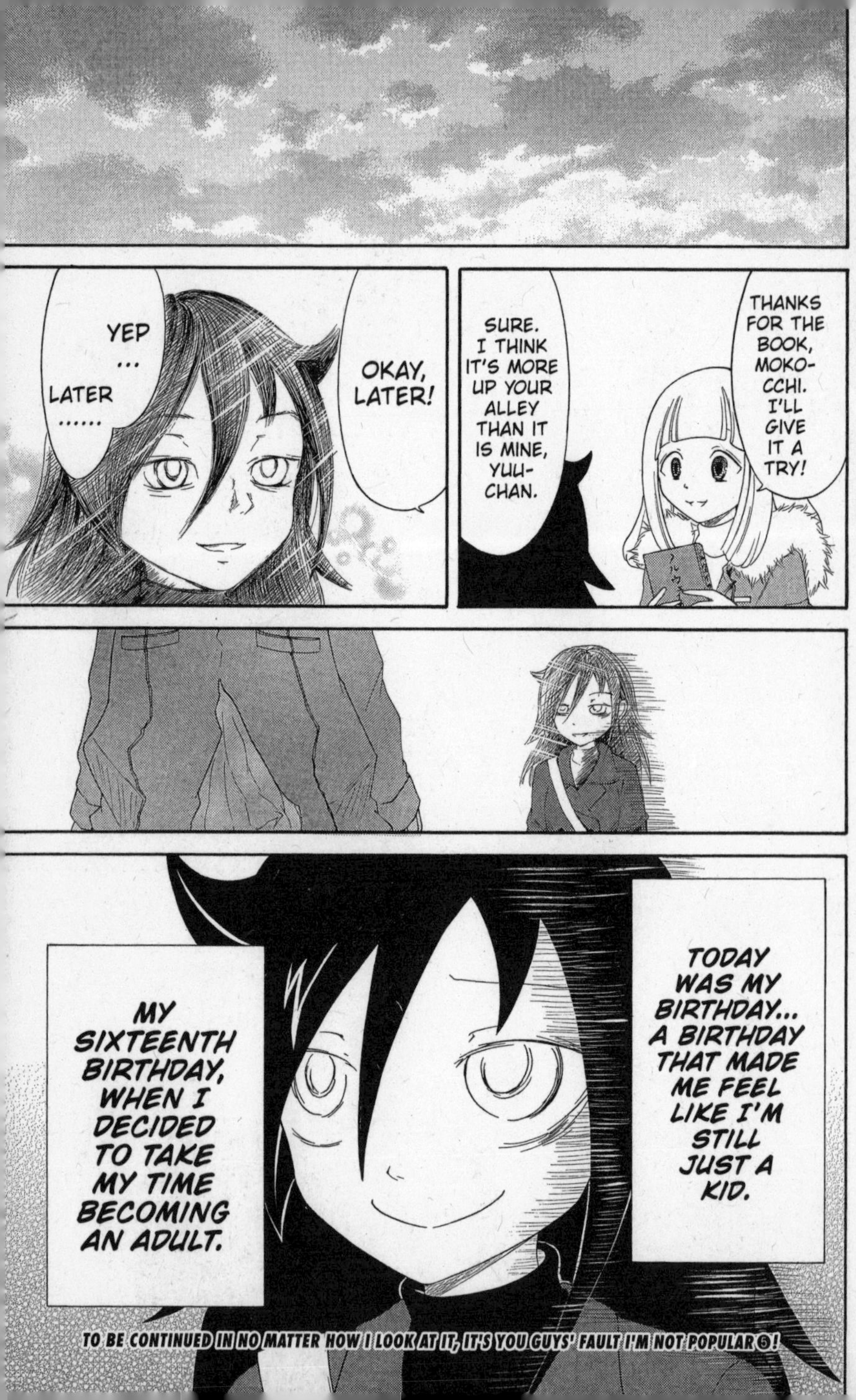
THANKS FOR THE BOOK, MOKO-CCHI. I'LL GIVE IT A TRY!
SURE. I THINK IT'S MORE UP YOUR ALLEY THAN IT IS MINE, YUU-CHAN.
OKAY, LATER!
YEP ... LATER ......
TODAY WAS MY BIRTHDAY... A BIRTHDAY THAT MADE ME FEEL LIKE I'M STILL JUST A KID.
MY SIXTEENTH BIRTHDAY, WHEN I DECIDED TO TAKE MY TIME BECOMING AN ADULT.
TO BE CONTINUED IN NO MATTER HOW I LOOK AT IT, IT'S YOU GUYS' FAULT I'M NOT POPULAR 5!

No Matter How I Look at It, It's You Guys' Fault I'm Not Popular!

AFTERWORD, ANIME STORIES, CURRENT STATUS, ET CETERA.

CHIBA-KUN CAME BY THE NEIGHBORHOOD YOKADO. I'VE NEVER HAD SO MUCH FUN.

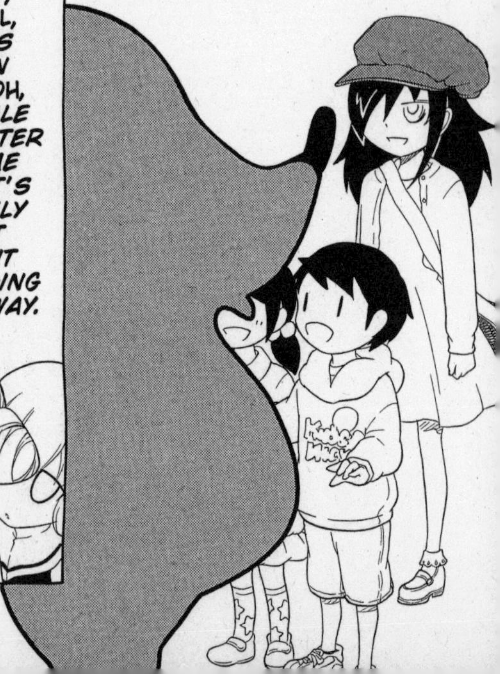

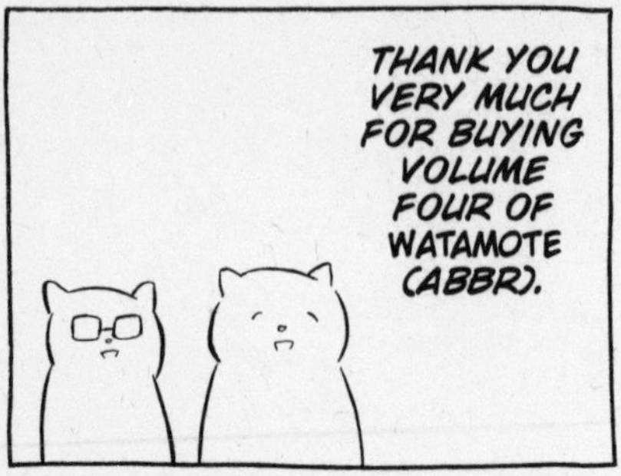
THANK YOU VERY MUCH FOR BUYING VOLUME FOUR OF WATAMOTE (ABBR).

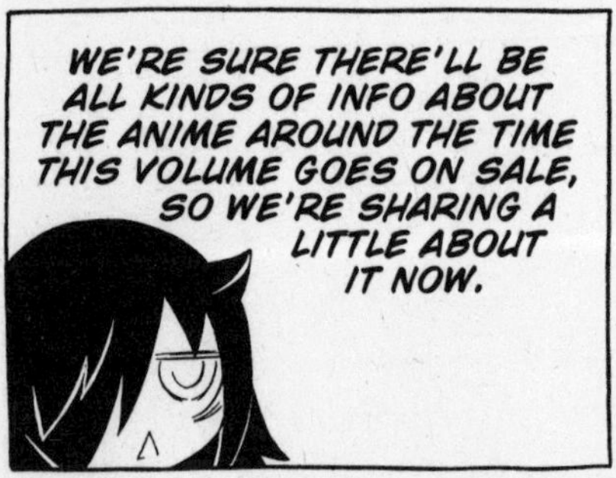
WE'RE SURE THERE'LL BE ALL KINDS OF INFO ABOUT THE ANIME AROUND THE TIME THIS VOLUME GOES ON SALE, SO WE'RE SHARING A LITTLE ABOUT IT NOW.

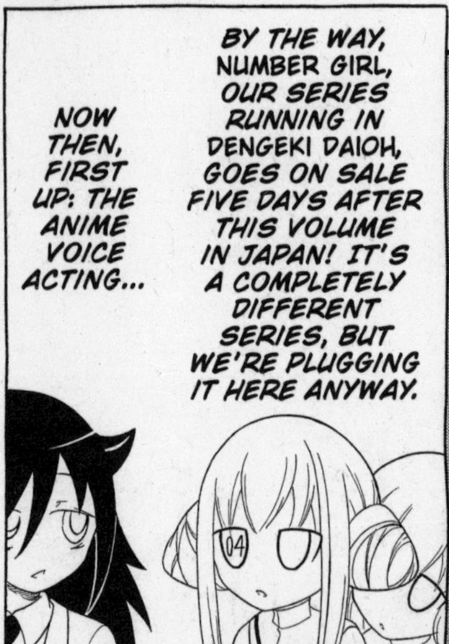
BY THE WAY, NUMBER GIRL, OUR SERIES RUNNING IN DENGEKI DAIOH, GOES ON SALE FIVE DAYS AFTER THIS VOLUME IN JAPAN! IT'S A COMPLETELY DIFFERENT SERIES, BUT WE'RE PLUGGING IT HERE ANYWAY.
NOW THEN, FIRST UP: THE ANIME VOICE ACTING...

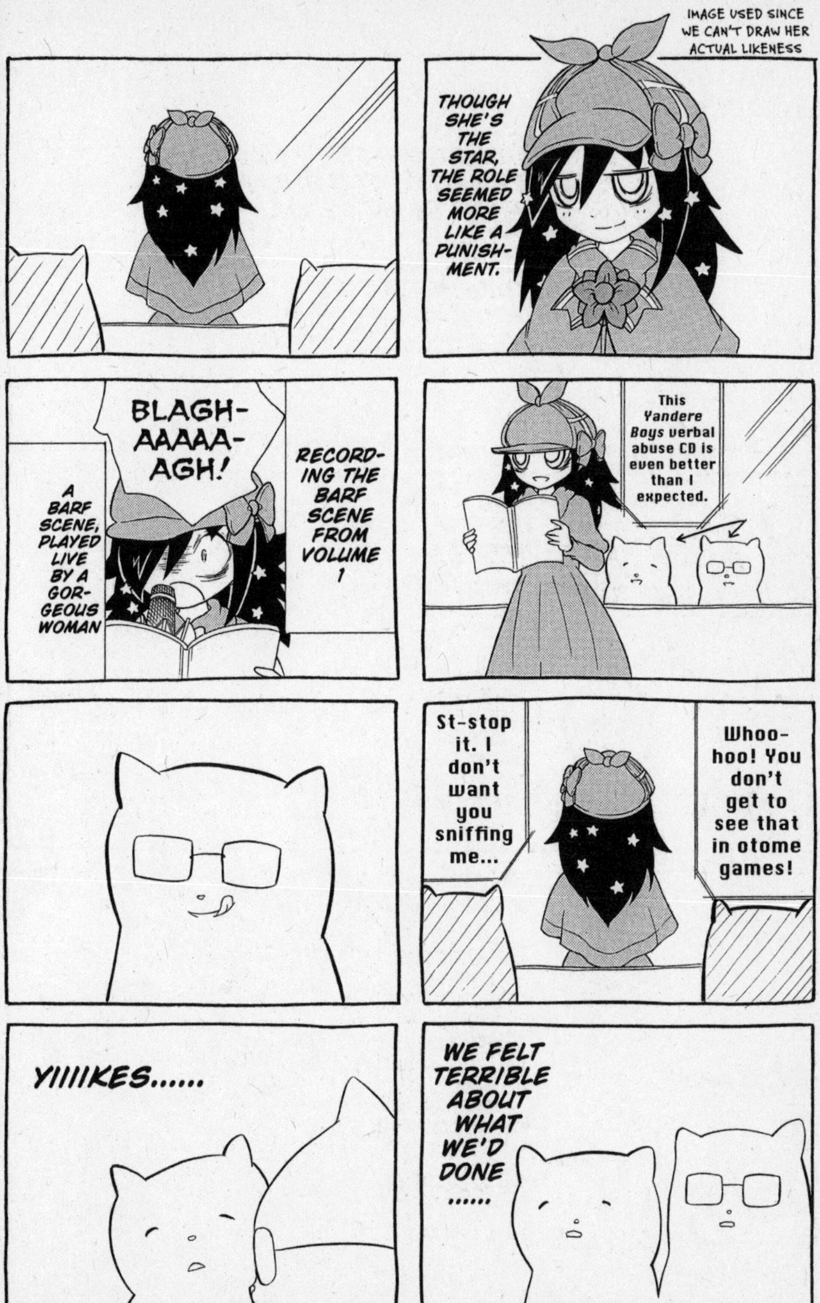
IMAGE USED SINCE WE CAN'T DRAW HER ACTUAL LIKENESS
THOUGH SHE'S THE STAR, THE ROLE SEEMED MORE LIKE A PUNISHMENT.
This *Yandere Boys* verbal abuse CD is even better than I expected.
RECORDING THE BARF SCENE FROM VOLUME 1
BLAGH-AAAAA-AGH!
A BARF SCENE, PLAYED LIVE BY A GORGEOUS WOMAN
Whoo-hoo! You don't get to see that in otome games!
St-stop it. I don't want you sniffing me...
WE FELT TERRIBLE ABOUT WHAT WE'D DONE ......
YIIIIKES......

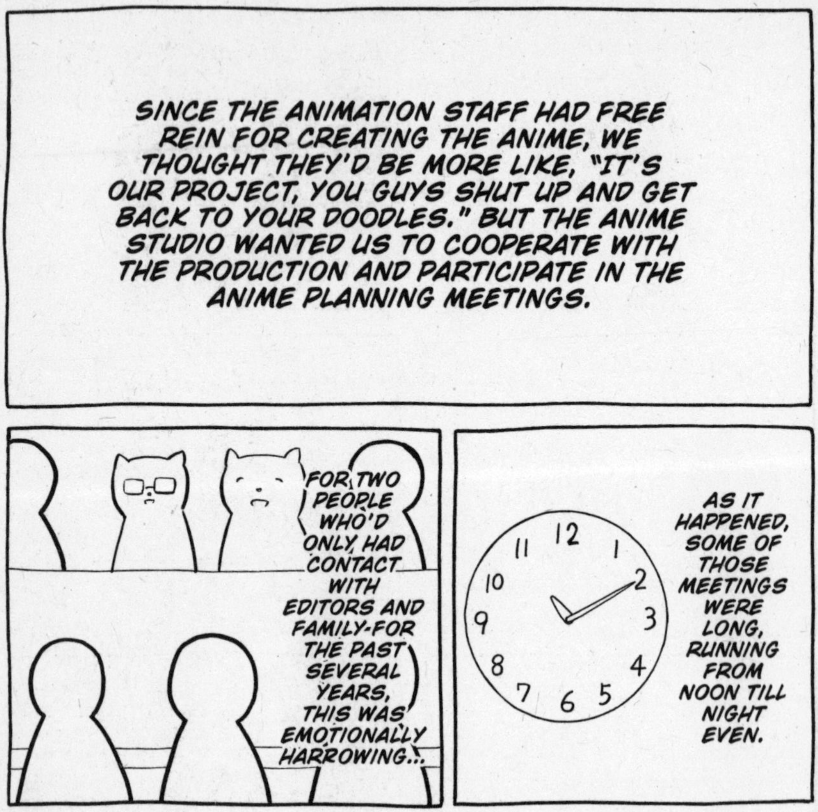
SINCE THE ANIMATION STAFF HAD FREE REIN FOR CREATING THE ANIME, WE THOUGHT THEY'D BE MORE LIKE, "IT'S OUR PROJECT, YOU GUYS SHUT UP AND GET BACK TO YOUR DOODLES." BUT THE ANIME STUDIO WANTED US TO COOPERATE WITH THE PRODUCTION AND PARTICIPATE IN THE ANIME PLANNING MEETINGS.
AS IT HAPPENED, SOME OF THOSE MEETINGS WERE LONG, RUNNING FROM NOON TILL NIGHT EVEN.
FOR TWO PEOPLE WHO'D ONLY HAD CONTACT WITH EDITORS AND FAMILY-FOR THE PAST SEVERAL YEARS, THIS WAS EMOTIONALLY HARROWING...
ARTIST
AFTER THE ARTIST'S EMOTIONAL STRESS BEGAN TAKING ITS TOLL ON HER MANGA WORK, SHE STOPPED COMING TO THE MEETINGS PARTWAY THROUGH PRODUCTION.

HELP BY ASSISTANT YUUJI ASAKURA-SAN

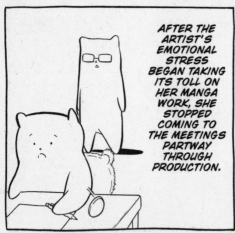

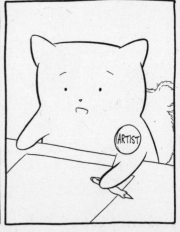

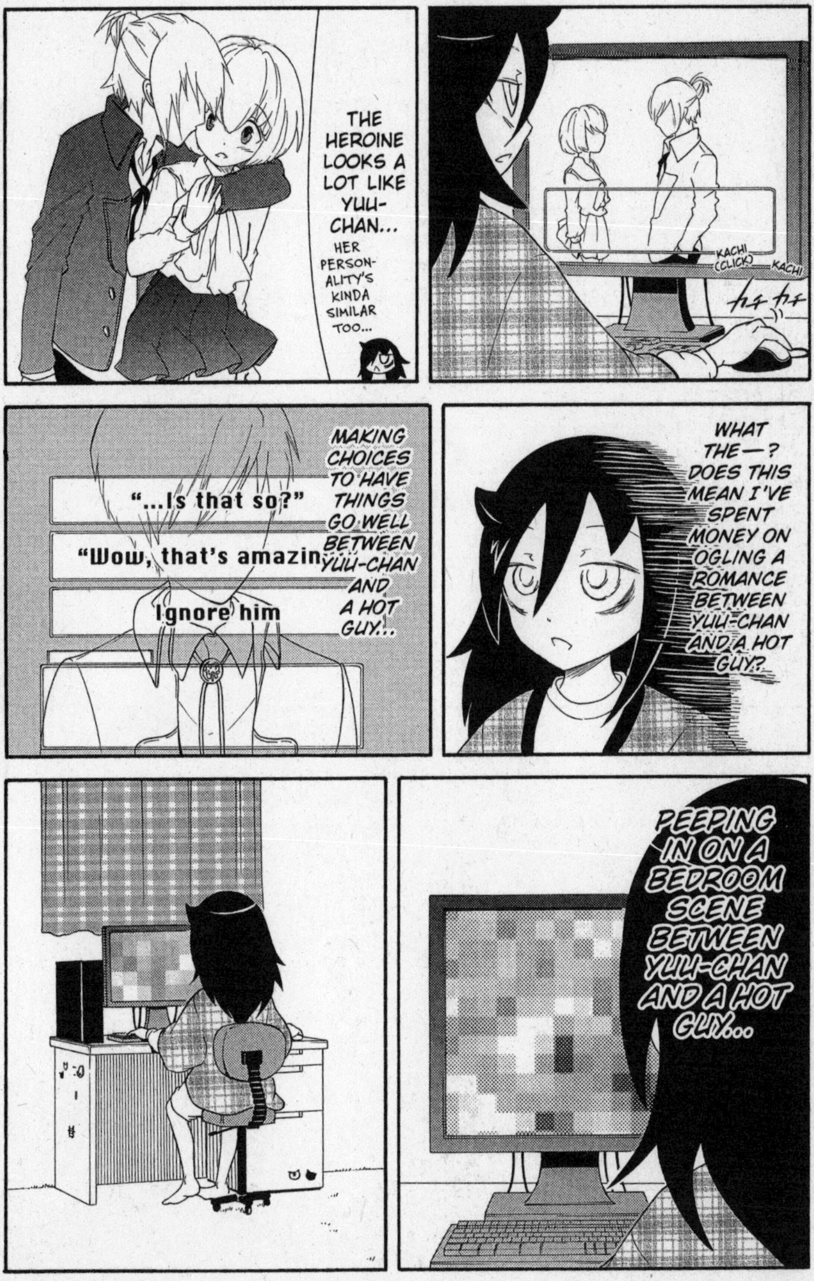
KACHI (CLICK) KACHI
カチ カチ
THE HEROINE LOOKS A LOT LIKE YUU-CHAN...
HER PERSONALITY'S KINDA SIMILAR TOO...
WHAT THE—? DOES THIS MEAN I'VE SPENT MONEY ON OGLING A ROMANCE BETWEEN YUU-CHAN AND A HOT GUY?
MAKING CHOICES TO HAVE THINGS GO WELL BETWEEN YUU-CHAN AND A HOT GUY...
"...Is that so?"
"Wow, that's amazin
Ignore him
PEEPING IN ON A BEDROOM SCENE BETWEEN YUU-CHAN AND A HOT GUY...

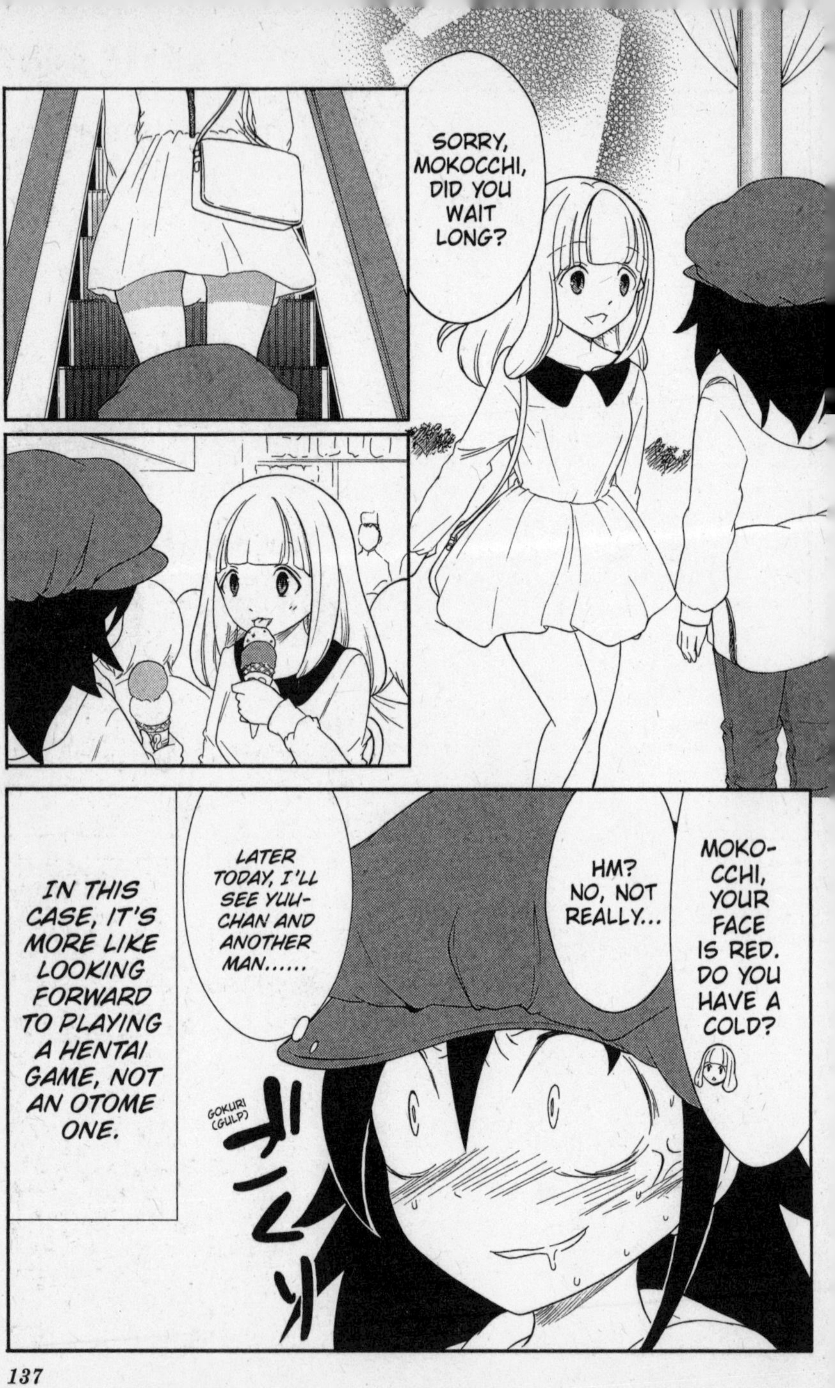
SORRY, MOKOCCHI, DID YOU WAIT LONG?
MOKOCCHI, YOUR FACE IS RED. DO YOU HAVE A COLD?
HM? NO, NOT REALLY...
LATER TODAY, I'LL SEE YUU-CHAN AND ANOTHER MAN......
IN THIS CASE, IT'S MORE LIKE LOOKING FORWARD TO PLAYING A HENTAI GAME, NOT AN OTOME ONE.
GOKURI (GULP)

TRANSLATION NOTES 1

PAGE 5
A **hostess** is a woman who works at a cabaret (or hostess) club and entertains male clients by talking to them, singing karaoke with them, preparing their drinks, and lighting their cigarettes.

PAGE 7
When Tomoko mentions the **white-haired kids from AK●RA**, she's referring to the Espers, kids with the appearance of old people due to government experimentation, in the classic anime film adaptation of the manga *AKIRA* by Katsuhiro Otomo.

PAGE 12
"No way there're gonna be any other rotten girls moonlighting at a hostess club in their first year of high school like me...Ah, I'll take that as a compliment," is Tomoko's variation of a long copy-pasta from the Japanese message board 2channel that became an Internet meme.

PAGE 13
Kabuki-chou is a neighborhood in Shinjuku, Tokyo near Shinjuku Station known for its nightlife.

PAGE 14
This **sign** at the entrance of First Avenue (Ichibangai) in Kabuki-chou actually exists. The businesses near the sign are mostly above board, but more adult establishments crop up the deeper in you go, especially down side streets. These include the health massage parlor and the soapland—a kind of brothel where women "bathe" men with their bodies—seen on the page, both of which are decidedly neither healthy nor squeaky-clean.

PAGE 16
In the original, this man refers to the **uncensored DVDs** as "unmosaiced DVDs." In Japan, it's illegal to show adult genitals, even in porn, so genitalia is obscured with mosaics.

PAGE 16
Police 24 Hours (*Keisatsu Nijuuyonji*) is a reality show that follows police officers on patrol and is broadcast in the evening on major networks in Japan. It is similar to the U.S. series, *Cops*, focusing mostly on attention-grabbing crimes related to sex, violence, and drugs.

PAGE 16
Robot Restaurant is a real cabaret club in Kabuki-chou, where the floor show features battles between robots with sexy female torsos like the ones shown here.

PAGE 23
Shiritori is a Japanese word game where each person takes turns saying a word that starts with the last syllable from the previous word, until they admit defeat or say a word that ends in "n," which is a syllable in Japanese that can never begin a word. The original exchange here was *sao* (slang for "penis") and *oppai* ("breasts").

PAGE 24
In the original, Tomoko uses the word *chichibukuro* (literally, "boob bags") for Yuu-chan's **"boobtacular"** dress. It can refer to big breasts or to a style of dress that impossibly accentuates a big bust.

PAGE 34
In Japan, the word **marathon** refers to long distance runs undertaken by schoolchildren, and the distance may vary from that of a standard marathon.

PAGE 35
The **Kazu Dance** is a reference to Japanese soccer player Kazuyoshi Miura's victory dance following his scoring of a goal. It involves waving one hand in the air while grabbing his crotch with the other.

PAGE 36
24 Hour Television is an annual Nippon TV telethon that includes a marathon run for charity.

PAGE 36
Yu●ker is short for Yunker Energy (Yunker Koutei Eki), a popular health tonic produced by Satou Pharmaceutical Co., Ltd. that contains caffeine and various Chinese herbal ingredients, including viper and civet tincture.

PAGE 42
"Think in the opposite way!" (*"Gyaku ni kangaerunda!"*) is a catchphrase from Part 1 of the manga series *JoJo's Bizarre Adventure* by Hirohiko Araki. Protagonist Jotaro Kujo learned the concept from his father and uses it to find a creative solution in a tough fight.

PAGE 47
"You sewage spewed from the shitter!" is Tomoko loosely quoting a villain's insult from latter Part 5 of *JoJo's Bizarre Adventure* (*"Benki ni hakidasareta tankasu-domo ga!!"*)

PAGE 48
The original narration for **"Guess I'll put the go in goal right here, right now"** is a near-exact quote from Misuzu in a poignant scene from the final episode of *Air*, the anime series based on a visual novel.

PAGE 51

The original chapter title of Fail 31 — **I'm Not Popular, So I'll Be Delusional** — is *Motenaishi, Chuunibyou Demo...* ("I'm Not Popular, But Even With *Chuunibyou...*"). *Chuunibyou*, literally "second-year middle school disease," is a Japanese term for the wild fantasies and delusions of grandeur that adolescents are often prone to and very embarrassed about once they outgrow them. Several recent light novels and anime have touched on this phenomenon, including one called *Chuunibyou Demo Koi ga Shitai!* to which the chapter title is referencing.

PAGE 52

Many high schools in Japan have students complete a **career path and curriculum survey** to choose between either literature or science as their focus starting their second year. This is one of the few choices of curriculum that students get since there is little time for electives.

PAGE 54

To●neko is a reference to Torneko, a popular weapon merchant character in the *Dragon Quest* video game series who has even gotten his own spin-off games.

PAGE 54

Tomoko uses **RPGs** to mean "Rocket-Propelled Grenades," but Yuu-chan thinks she means "Role-Playing Games."

PAGE 60

Kanto is the region of Japan comprising Tokyo and the immediate surrounding prefectures.

PAGE 60

Winter tends to be mild in the Kanto region, usually staying above freezing temperatures and with some snow, but not a lot, hence the weather report calling out **"snow even in the Kanto region."**

PAGE 62

The **major cleaning** Tomoko's mom is talking about is *oosouji*, the big household cleanup done on the final day(s) of the year, a tradition adopted from China.

PAGE 62

A *kotatsu* is a heated table, like the one Tomoko is drowsing under. Japanese homes tend not to have central heating, so a *kotatsu* is a very popular and cozy way to keep warm in the winter.

PAGE 64

It's a common trope for the male **protagonist in a light novel** to be domestic, breaking stereotypes in a stereotypical fashion. Another common trope is for the male protagonist to be dense and unable to pick up on a girl's interest in them.

PAGE 66

Kenshirou is the main character in the *Fist of the North Star* series created by Tetsuo Hara and Buronson. Part of the story involves Kenshirou fighting his three older "brothers" who were trained in the same martial art.

PAGE 66

"Untan!" is a reference to an ad-lib by the voice actress for Yui, a character in the anime series *K-ON!* about a school pop music club, from a scene where she plays the castanet.

PAGE 68

Shokot●n is a reference to Japanese female celebrity Shoko Nakagawa, aka. "Shokotan," who likes to wear cicada skins as a fashion statement.

PAGE 75

Kiyota is saying **"as long as it's not the 24th"** here because another of Japan's unique secular Christmas traditions is treating Christmas Eve as a big date night to spend with that special someone, much like New Year's Eve in the United States.

PAGE 76

Animal Double-Crossing is a parody of the Nintendo 3DS video game known as *Animal Crossing: New Leaf.* The original title here was *Chikushou no Mori.* Though *chikushou* can mean "beast," its main use is as a Japanese curse word.

PAGE 78

B3 is a parody of *Persona3*, or *P3*, the ultra-popular Japanese RPG for PS2. The character shown on the screen is Mitsuru Kirijou, the model for Tomoko's hairstyle in this chapter.

PAGE 78

NAKAMO WAX is a parody of a real product called NAKANO STYLING WAX.

PAGE 86

New Year's Day is a big family holiday in Japan (much like Christmas in the West), when children get **new year's gifts** (*otoshidama*) of one or more paper money bills sent or presented to them in nice envelopes. This is also another tradition with Chinese origins.

PAGE 87

"Start of Spring Excellent Luck" is a traditional phrase often used in New Year's decorations in Japan, since the year used to begin in early spring before the adoption of the western calendar.

TRANSLATION NOTES 3 ·······················

PAGE 87

New Year's cards (*nengajou*) are postcards that practically everyone in Japan sends to rarely seen friends and family to let them know how they're doing, much like Christmas cards in the West. They're timed to be delivered right on New Year's Day, making it a heavy workday for the postal service.

PAGE 89

Gorou I●ogashira is a reference to Gorou Inogashira, the protagonist of the manga and drama series *Kodoku no Gourmet* (*"The Solitary Gourmet"*). He looks like an ordinary businessman but had long years of martial arts training as a youth, which he readily uses on restaurant staff or customers with whom he takes issue.

PAGE 92

One New Year's Day tradition is the **shrine visit** (*hatsumode*) for the first time that year to make an offering and prayer for the new year.

PAGE 94

A person's **first dream of the year** is thought to be very significant.

PAGE 95

PAS● is a reference to *PASH!*, an *otome* magazine. Tomoko appears to be reading the December 2012 issue, which featured the main characters for the anime series *TIGER & BUNNY* on the cover.

PAGE 95

The **dice game** (*sugoroku*) that comes with the magazine is traditionally a children's board game played by rolling a die and advancing the rolled number of spaces. The **pinning game** (*fukuwarai*) is a game where a blindfolded person pins eyes, a nose, a mouth, et cetera, onto a face, similar to "Pin the Tail on the Donkey." Both are games commonly played on New Year's Day in Japan. The games in the magazine, however, feature *otome* game (*oto-ge*) themes.

PAGE 100

Am●-Talk is most likely a reference to *Ame-Tooku*, short for *Ameagari Kesshitai no Tooku Bangumi Ame-Tooku*, a variety talk show on TV Asahi.

PAGE 100

The **"quit paying attention to things that aren't there" treatment** as well as the girl with the eyepatch (Mei Misaki) as whom Tomoko is imagining herself are from the novel/anime/manga series *Another* by Yukito Ayatsuji.

PAGE 102

In the original, Tomoko puns on her last name, Kuroki, with *kuuki*, the word for "air," which is translated as **Low-Key**.

PAGE 102

T●rraformar is a reference to *Terra Formars*, a very popular sci-fi manga series where giant mutated humanoid cockroaches take over Mars. To fight them, Earth sends over humans who have undergone operations called the "BUGS Procedure" to give them powers held by a particular insect or animal.

PAGE 102

A **hyaluronic acid injection** is a procedure used mainly for cosmetic lip augmentation and wrinkle removal. The person-stats textbox style here matches that used to introduce the super-powered characters in *Terra Formars*.

PAGE 103

People wear a different pair of shoes inside Japanese schools than outside, partly out of tradition and partly to keep the floors clean. So Tomoko squishing a cockroach with her indoor shoe is even grosser than you'd think and is why the teacher suggests, **"Why don't you go clean off your shoe?"**

PAGE 107

Saitama is a prefecture located north of the Tokyo metropolis, as opposed to their current home prefecture Chiba, which is located southeast of Tokyo.

PAGE 109

Haramaku, the name of Tomoko's school, is a combined reference to a private school branch in Chiba Prefecture called Shibuya Pedagogical Academy - Makuhari Junior/Senior High School ("Shibumaku," for short) and another private school located right next door to it called Shouwa Institute - Shuuei Junior/Senior High School.

PAGE 110

There is no actual school by the name of **Saitama Urawa South-East**, but there is one for each of the standard four cardinal directions.

PAGE 116

In the original, Tomoko uses the word *yariman* for **nympho**, which is slang for a woman who engages in proactive sexual behavior with a large, unspecified number of men.

PAGE 122

Norwegian Grove by Fuyuki Murakami is a parody of *Norwegian Wood* by famous contemporary Japanese novelist Haruki Murakami.

PAGE 133

Chiba-kun is the mascot for Chiba Prefecture.

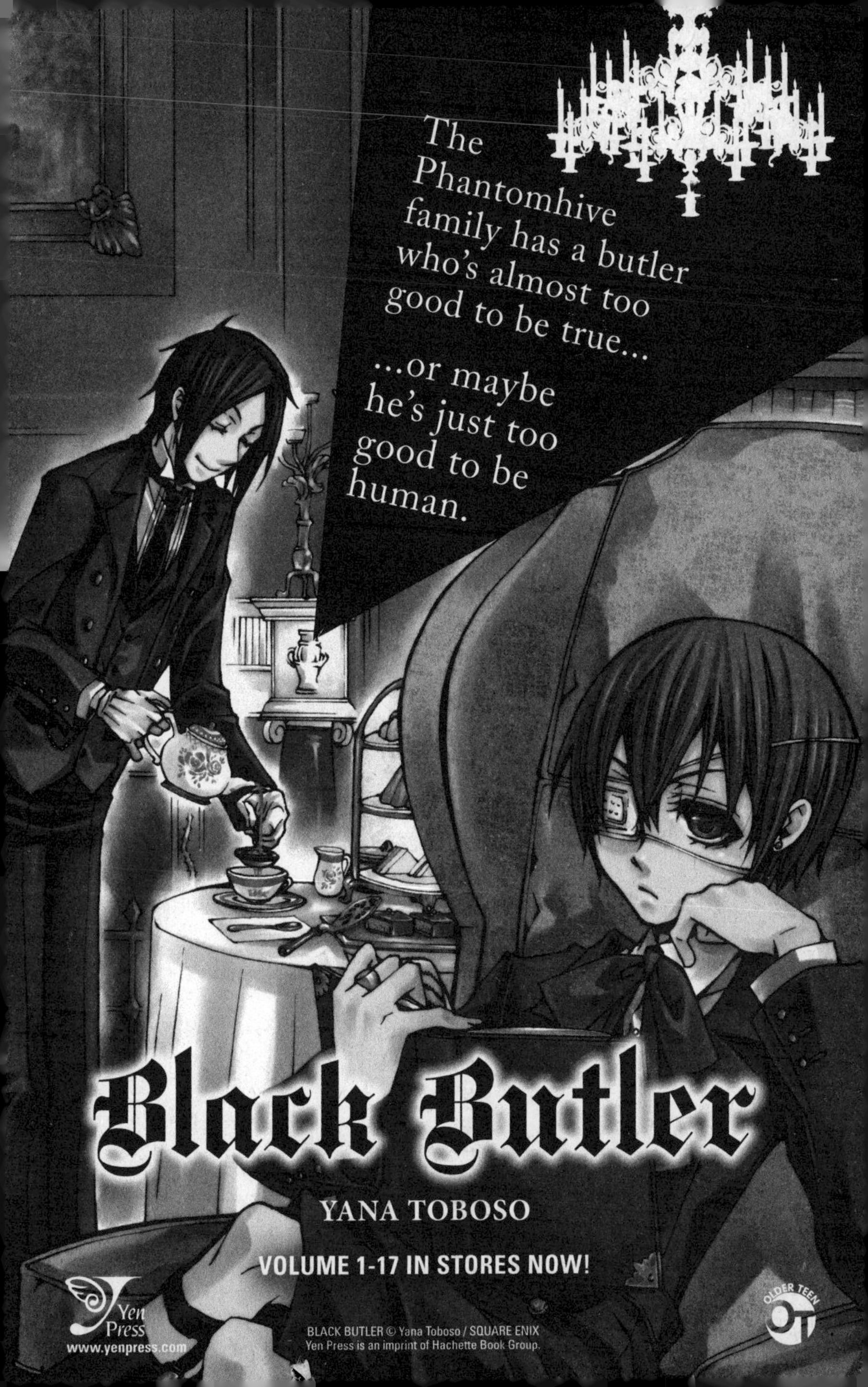
The Phantomhive family has a butler who's almost too good to be true...
...or maybe he's just too good to be human.
Black Butler
YANA TOBOSO
VOLUME 1-17 IN STORES NOW!
Yen Press
www.yenpress.com
BLACK BUTLER © Yana Toboso / SQUARE ENIX
Yen Press is an imprint of Hachette Book Group.
OLDER TEEN
OT

WELCOME TO IKEBUKURO, WHERE TOKYO'S WILDEST CHARACTERS GATHER!!

AS THEIR PATHS CROSS, THIS ECCENTRIC CAST WEAVES A TWISTED, CRACKED LOVE STORY...

AVAILABLE NOW!!

NO MATTER HOW I LOOK AT IT, IT'S YOU GUYS' FAULT I'M NOT POPULAR! ④

NICO TANIGAWA

Translation/Adaptation: Krista Shipley, Karie Shipley
Lettering: Lys Blakeslee

WATASHI GA MOTENAI NOWA DOU KANGAETEMO OMAERA GA WARUI! Volume 4 © 2013 Nico Tanigawa / SQUARE ENIX CO., LTD. First published in Japan in 2013 by SQUARE ENIX CO., LTD. English translation rights arranged with SQUARE ENIX CO., LTD. and Hachette Book Group through Tuttle-Mori Agency, Inc.

Translation © 2014 by SQUARE ENIX CO., LTD.

Yen Press
Hachette Book Group
237 Park Avenue, New York, NY 10017

www.HachetteBookGroup.com
www.YenPress.com

Yen Press is an imprint of Hachette Book Group, Inc. The Yen Press name and logo are trademarks of Hachette Book Group, Inc.

First Yen Press Edition: July 2014

ISBN: 978-0-316-37674-7

10 9 8 7 6 5 4 3 2 1

BVG

Printed in the United States of America